The Politics of Congress

FIFTH EDITION

David J. Vogler

Wheaton College

Allyn and Bacon, Inc.

Boston • London • Sydney • Toronto

Copyright © 1988, 1983, 1980, 1977, 1974 by
Allyn and Bacon, Inc.
A Division of Simon & Schuster
7 Wells Avenue
Newton, MA 02159

Library of Congress Cataloging-in-Publication Data

Vogler, David J.
  The politics of Congress.

  Includes index.
  1. United States. Congress. I. Title.
JK1061.V63 1988 328.73 87–11426
ISBN 0–205–10621–8

Series Editorial Assistant: Alicia Reilly
Production Coordinator: Helyn Pultz
Editorial-Production Service: Woodstock Publishers' Services
Cover Administrator: Linda Dickinson
Cover Designer: Christy Rosso

Printed in the United States of America

10 9 8 7 6 5 4 3 2 1   92 91 90 89 88 87

To all the Voglers and the
Marshalls and to Alice who
is both.

Contents

8 ☆ Policies and Budgets   247

9 ☆ Representation and Lawmaking: Interests and Presidents   281

Preface

Congressional change has been a topic of debate and a matter of concern for as long as the United States government has existed. The framers of the Constitution looked to biennial elections as a way of linking the House of Representatives to changes in society. They also feared that the regular infusion of new members, frequent changes in structure, and constant revision of policies would have an unsettling effect on Congress and the national government. James Madison expressed concern about "the mischievous effects of a mutable government" in *Federalist 62*: "A continual change even of good measures is inconsistent with every rule of prudence and every prospect of success." That was one of the arguments he used for having six-year terms for senators, and it is one of the reasons why the same constitutional structure that has permitted great congressional change has also provided a high degree of continuity.

The fifth edition of this book reflects the changes in Congress since the preceding editions as well as the continuities in the politics of Congress. New chapters have been added and major sections of the book have been rewritten to reflect those changes. A new chapter on congressional elections and one on support systems have been added to the book. Reorganization of the book's structure is also reflected in the separate chapters on political parties, committees, and policies and budgets. The framework of analysis used in earlier editions, however, remains the same. The tension between lawmaking and representation continues to structure the politics of Congress, and an analytical framework based on those competing demands still serves as one of the best ways to get a handle on congressional behavior.

In writing all five editions of *The Politics of Congress*, I have been guided by two central questions: How do we evaluate Congress? And, So what? By providing some different perspectives for judging congressional performance and by relating these to reform proposals, I have sought to show that a person's judgment of Congress and his or her support of, or opposition to, specific reform proposals depend on a broad evaluation of the entire political system and not just on short-term legislative goals such as efficiency or standing up to the president. Judging Congress requires some information about the way things are, and I have attempted to provide this information without imposing my own interpretations of the way things ought to be. Furthermore, unless these facts about Congress are viewed within a framework of alternative ways in which the system might operate, they can do little toward expanding our critical understanding of the politics of Congress. For that reason the first chapter, in particular, focuses on alternative views of the way things ought to be as well as on the way things are.

Even if one understands the legislative process, one might ask, So what? Politics, after all, determines who gets what, and detailed explanations about congressional rules or the structure of the subcommittee system might not seem important when compared to the issues of nuclear war or the state of the economy. I have sought to provide some answers to the question of So what? by showing how the policies of government are shaped by the politics of Congress.

Many people helped me with this book over the years. Earlier editions contained an extensive listing of those who helped with each edition, and I thank them all again. Professors Henry Kenski of the University of Arizona and Philip Brenner of American University have been most generous with their suggestions and ideas for changes in the book over the years. Professor Sandy Maisel of Colby College offered a number of excellent suggestions for the fifth edition, and I have attempted to follow them all. In reorganizing the book's structure, I have also adopted most of the recommendations of Professor Candy Nelson of the American Political Science Association Congressional Fellows Program. That program and the Washington Semester Program at American University provided me with an opportunity to get to know the real world of Capitol Hill. My former boss and present congressman, Gerry Studds, continues to teach me and all of his constituents about Congress and U.S. politics. Between editions of this book, I learned a great deal from Professor Sidney Waldman of Haverford College by writing a book with him about Congress and democracy. A number of Wheaton students, Ellen Conlin, Jessica Graf, Anne-Marie Lasowski, Diane Michaels, Helen Morgan, and Suzanne Murphy helped by gathering information and assisting with tables and figures. Emily Pearce and Nancy Shepardson of Wheaton College helped immeasurably by typing the previous edition onto floppy disks. I also want to thank Alicia Reilly and Annette Joseph of Allyn and Bacon and Barbara Gracia of Woodstock Publishers' Services for their assistance in producing the book.

The Lawmaking Process

This chart shows the most typical way in which proposed legislation is enacted into law. There are more complicated as well as simpler, routes, and most bills fall by the wayside and never become law. The process is illustrated with two hypothetical bills—House bill No. 1 (HR 1) and Senate bill No. 2 (S 2). Each bill must be passed by both houses of Congress in identical form before it can become law. The path of HR 1 is traced by a solid line, that of S 2 by a broken line. However, in practice most legislation begins as similar proposals in both houses.

A bill is first introduced in each house and then goes to a full committee first and then usually to a specialized subcommittee for study, hearings, revisions, and approval. The bill returns to the full committee where more hearings and revision may occur. The full committee may approve the bill and recommend its chamber pass the proposal. Committees rarely give a bill an unfavorable report; rather, no action is taken, thereby killing it.

In the House, many bills go before the Rules Committee for a "rule" expediting floor action, setting conditions for debate and amendments on the floor. Some bills are "privileged" and go directly to the floor. Other procedures exist for noncontroversial or routine bills. In the Senate, special "rules" are not used; the leadership normally schedules action through unanimous consent agreements.

When the bill reaches the floor of each chamber, it is debated, usually amended, passed or defeated. If passed, it goes to the other chamber to follow the same route through committee and floor stages. (If the other chamber has already passed a related bill, both versions go straight to a conference committee.) Once both chambers have passed related bills, a conference committee of members from both houses is formed to work out differences. When a compromise has been reached this version of the bill is sent back to each house for approval. If the conference committee bill is passed in both houses, it is then sent to the President who can either sign it into law or veto it and return it to Congress. Congress may override a veto by a two-thirds majority vote in both houses; the bill then becomes law without the President's signature.

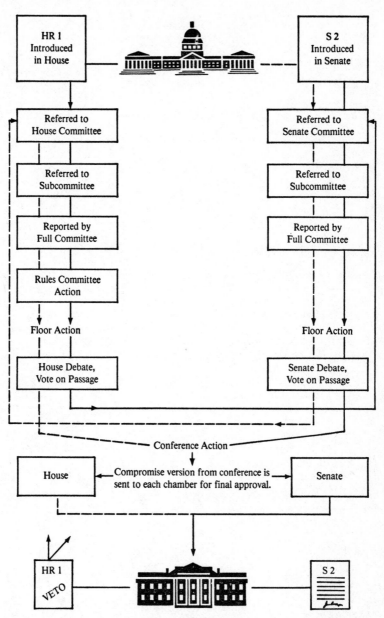

HR 1
Introduced
in House

S 2
Introduced
in Senate

Referred to
House Committee

Referred to
Senate Committee

Referred to
Subcommittee

Referred to
Subcommittee

Reported by
Full Committee

Reported by
Full Committee

Rules Committee
Action

Floor Action

Floor Action

House Debate,
Vote on Passage

Senate Debate,
Vote on Passage

Conference Action

House

Compromise version from conference is
sent to each chamber for final approval.

Senate

HR 1
VETO

S 2

Compromise version approved by both houses is sent to President who can either sign it into law or veto it and return it to Congress. Congress may override veto by a two-thirds majority vote in both houses; bill then becomes law without President's signature.

Adapted from: *Congressional Quarterly Guide to Current American Government* (Washington, D.C.: Congressional Quarterly, Inc., 1982), p. 145.

1

Judging Congress

The United States government will have a balanced budget by 1991. That statement is not a campaign promise, it is the law. At least it was the law as passed by Congress in 1985 before the U.S. Supreme Court declared sections of the law unconstitutional in 1986. The Balanced Budget and Emergency Deficit Control Act of 1985 established limits on the size of federal budget deficits for the six fiscal years, 1986–1991. The deficit ceiling for 1985, the first year affected by the act, was approximately $172 billion; by the final year, 1991, the maximum deficit permitted under the law would be zero. Congress passed the deficit reduction act just three months after the proposal had been introduced in the Senate by two freshmen Republicans, Phil Gramm of Texas and Warren Rudman of New Hampshire, and a senior Democrat, Ernest Hollings of South Carolina. As the measure advanced through Congress and gained public recognition, headline writers and newscasters developed an abbreviated term for the deficit reduction bill—"Gramm-Rudman-Hollings"—and sometimes just "Gramm-Rudman."

Congress did not follow normal legislative procedures in passing Gramm-Rudman. For example, the important stage of committee hearings and analysis was effectively skipped as Congress rushed to act on the deficit bill. Despite the unusual aspects of congressional action on Gramm-Rudman, what Congress did in this case teaches us a great deal about the role of Congress in U.S. politics and raises important questions for judging that performance.

The Gramm-Rudman Act completely revised congressional budgeting procedures. It mandated steadily declining deficits until a balanced budget was achieved in 1991, and established an accelerated budget process with new deadlines for Congress to complete all appropriations and budget actions. The deadline for House action on all regular appropriations bills, for example, was moved from September to June. In August, the Congressional Budget Office (CBO) and the executive branch Office of Management and Budget (OMB) would review these congressional budget decisions and determine whether the projected deficit will fall within the limits imposed for that fiscal year (FY). If the budget produced by Congress did not meet the deficit goals for that year, a procedure for making "automatic" cuts would then be initiated.

These automatic cuts represented the heart of Gramm-Rudman, a means of enforcing that year's deficit limits. On or before August 20 of each year, the Congressional Budget Office and the Office of Management and Budget would report to the General Accounting Office (GAO) the estimated deficit for that year and indicate what level of across-the-board cuts would be necessary to keep that deficit within the Gramm-Rudman limit. The law required that these cuts be equally divided between defense programs and domestic programs, and it exempted certain domestic programs such as Social Security and several anti-poverty and veterans' programs from those cuts. The GAO has five days to review the report and forward it to the president. On or before September 1, the president would issue a "sequester" order implementing the GAO report and reducing federal spending by a uniform percentage.

In passing Gramm-Rudman, Congress also provided for a suspension of automatic cuts in a recession or war and established a "fallback" procedure requiring congressional approval of the automatic cuts in the event that the procedure outlined above was invalidated by the courts.

The deficit reduction law, which was approved by wide margins in both chambers (61–31 in the Senate and 271–154 in the House), was a dramatic response to the dominant political issue of the 1980s. The deficit limits established by the act provide some clear-cut standards for judging congressional performance on the budget:

FY	Deficit Limit (billions)
1986	$171.9
1987	$144
1988	$108
1989	$72
1990	$36
1991	$0

A comparison of the actual or projected deficit for any of these fiscal years with that stated in Gramm-Rudman can provide a rough indication of how realistic Congress was when it passed the deficit reduction law and how well that law is working to reduce the federal deficit. Any thorough evaluation, of course, would include the effects of those cuts on government programs and people's lives. An important aspect of the Gramm-Rudman Act was that it provided a relatively clear yardstick for gauging congressional performance over a six-year period.

Many senators and representatives registered strong opinions on Gramm-Rudman even before the first cuts were made in fiscal 1986. New Mexico Republican and Senate Budget Committee head, Pete Domenici, described the legislation as "the most ambitious and well-crafted attempt to achieve a balanced budget in all the years I've been here." On the other hand, Sen. J. Bennett Johnston, a conservative Democrat from Louisiana, depicted Gramm-Rudman as "legislative Armageddon," and called it "the most damaging to the constitutional process, the most extreme piece of legislation I have seen in the Senate in 12 years." The defense cuts mandated by the law led New York Sen. Patrick Moynihan to warn his colleagues: "Gramm-Rudman is a suicide pact." Rep. Lynn Martin, an Illinois Republican who sits on the House Budget Committee, smiled and said: "I have great faith in Gramm-Rudman. And I still leave cookies for Santa Claus." Even one of the chief architects of the bill, New Hampshire Sen. Warren Rudman, called it "a bad idea whose time has come."[1]

As these reactions make clear, Gramm-Rudman was something more than just a reform in the congressional budget process. By serving to insulate budget-cutting decisions from electoral politics, what some people referred to as governing by automatic pilot, the legislation was a clear acknowledgment of past congressional failure to balance the budget. What was wrong with Congress that made it necessary to remove from its hands the final say over budget cuts? Were they saying to the executive branch, "Stop me before I spend again"? In passing Gramm-Rudman, Congress was also passing judgment on itself, on what it saw as wrong with the institution, its past actions, and its fiscal policies.

A court case arising out of Gramm-Rudman provides another perspective on Congress. Critics of the bill had questioned its constitutionality as the proposal moved through both chambers. President Reagan expressed similar reservations when he signed the bill into law. A section of the Gramm-Rudman act provided a means for quickly getting a court ruling on these constitutional issues by giving members of Congress authority to bring suits challenging the law's constitutionality and by providing for an accelerated process of Supreme Court review. Taking advantage of those provisions, twelve members of Congress filed suit in the federal district court in Washington on the same day that President Reagan signed the bill into law.

The author of that lawsuit was thirty-five-year-old Rep. Mike Synar, a fourth-term member from Oklahoma. In developing the case, Synar regularly consulted with one of the country's foremost constitutional scholars, Harvard Law School Professor Lawrence H. Tribe. Just nine years earlier, Synar himself had been a student in a constitutional law course at the University of Oklahoma where he earned a grade of B− for the semester. Synar joked that if he won the case he would appeal his grade and described his leadership position in the Gramm-Rudman court challenge as a "freak accident." The congressman had received none of the committee assignments he wanted in his freshman year and wound up serving on two committees that no one else wanted—Judiciary and Government Operations. Being on those committees and developing a reputation as a good negotiator led to Synar's being named to the House-Senate conference on Gramm-Rudman and being given the responsibility for evaluating the bill from a legal standpoint. The rise of this junior member in less than ten years from a B− constitutional law student to the leader of a constitutional challenge to a major act of Congress is a reflection of the decentralized and accessible structure of the national legislature. Having won a great deal of media attention and visibility as a result of this case, Representative Synar made no secret of the fact that he was contemplating either a Senate race or a campaign for leader of the House Democratic Caucus in the near future—a fact that suggests a need to consider the motivations behind lawmakers' actions.

The court challenge to Gramm-Rudman was based on two constitutional issues. One issue was that the provision in Gramm-Rudman gave the head of the General Accounting Office and the director of the Congressional Budget Office, both of whom are part of the legislative branch of government, the power to determine budget cuts. This action violated the constitutional principle of separation of powers because those officers shared that power with the executive branch's director of the Office of Management and Budget. The separation of powers argument was also levied against that part of the law giving the head of the General Accounting Office, a congressional agency, the power to direct the president to make budget cuts.

The second constitutional challenge to the deficit reduction law was based on the opening words of Article I of the Constitution: "All legislative powers herein granted shall be vested in a Congress of the United States." Critics of Gramm-Rudman argued that the law, in essence, gave legislative powers to three unelected officials. Again, the focus was on the role of the CBO, OMB, and GAO officials in making cuts if Congress failed to produce a balanced budget. While the law's proponents argued that those officials were carrying out the will of Congress, critics contended that such cuts had the effect of cancelling earlier spending decisions made by Congress, something that could only be done by a new law. Under Article I, said the challengers of the law, only Congress has that lawmaking power. Critics regarded this delegation of legislative responsibility with particular alarm because it concerned the power of the purse, which is generally considered to be the most important of Congress's constitutional powers.

Representative Synar captured the essence of this argument when he said: "I'm not an opponent of the concept of a balanced budget. But I think Gramm-Rudman is an outright abdication of our constitutional powers set forth by the Founding Fathers. They wanted us to make the tough decisions, because we were elected officials. If you turn that decision over to unelected bureaucrats, you basically shrink from your responsibilities."[2]

In July 1986, the U.S. Supreme Court ruled the central provision of Gramm-Rudman was unconstitutional because it gave executive powers to the comptroller general, who as head of the General Accounting Office is under the control of Congress. The Court declared the grant of executive powers to a legislative officer was a violation of the separation of powers doctrine of the Constitution. The fallback provisions of Gramm-Rudman required that Congress itself make uniform budget cuts to meet the deficit limits of the law, and those provisions became effective after the Supreme Court's decision. Congressional action on the fiscal 1987 budget, however, suggested to many that taking the automatic cuts provision out of Gramm-Rudman, in effect, removed the teeth from the deficit reduction law. Congress approved initial cuts of almost $12 billion in fiscal 1987 spending, but it missed every one of the Gramm-Rudman deadlines for the year and the deficit target of $144 billion. As Congress began work on the fiscal 1988 budget, which under Gramm-Rudman must bring the deficit down to $108 billion, the actual deficit figure for the previous year was estimated to be more than $30 billion above the $144 billion limit. That, in turn, meant Congress would have to find ways to cut more than $60 billion from the deficit in fiscal 1988.

The deficit reduction law and the court challenge to it illustrate two opposing tendencies that are perhaps the most fundamental determinants of the structure of Congress and the behavior of its members. The chief responsibility of Congress is that of lawmaking—of passing laws and budgets to support them. But the authority of Congress to do that rests on its being a representative body. The problem that Representative Synar and others had with Gramm-Rudman was a belief that this extraordinary attempt to meet lawmaking responsibilities had the effect of undercutting Congress's representational authority. In particular, Synar and his colleagues argued that the procedure for automatic cuts effectively gave lawmaking power to the unelected directors of CBO, OMB, and GAO. Because those officers were appointed rather than elected, they did not have the representative authority that Congress and its members have gained through elections in fixed geographical districts.

The structure of Congress and the behavior of its members is largely determined by these primary, and often conflicting, goals of lawmaking and representation. Public judgments about both the institution of Congress and individual members also reflect the tension between these goals. Congressional reforms generally seek to improve either the lawmaking or representational capabilities of Congress, but an improvement in one often comes at some cost in the other. New members of Congress may find that they can best come to understand the institution and its policy decisions by analyzing the conflicts growing out of this dual responsibility for both lawmaking and representation. As was seen in the case of Gramm-Rudman, a strong effort to improve lawmaking may have effects that weaken representation. On the other hand, one could argue that it was the representational nature of Congress—the support for programs favored by constituents—that produced budget deficits and the perceived need for Gramm-Rudman in the first place. By considering only the representational or the lawmaking function of Congress, one would get a limited or distorted picture of the institution. A recognition that the national legislature is charged with both lawmaking and representation and that those are often opposing goals provides a valuable framework for learning about Congress and its members.[3]

Congress and Public Opinion

Members of Congress quickly learn that there is a public image of Congress that they can use to their advantage. An Oklahoma senator knows that he can draw a laugh from a homestate audience with this opening line: "I'm going to give you some good news: Congress is out of session."[4] Another senator talked about the heady experience of coming to Washington as an upset winner and becoming an instant celebrity sought out for talk shows and parties. When a waiter at a fashionable dinner party ignored the senator's request for more butter, the lawmaker said, "Maybe you don't know who I am." The waiter listened as the senator identified himself and then replied: "Maybe you don't know who I am." The senator said that he didn't, and the waiter dramatically informed him: "I'm the guy in charge of the butter." A similar theme appeared in a representative's account of a meeting with constituents where the lawmaker made it clear that he was not to blame for city problems such as potholes in streets or inadequate garbage pickup. Even so, a constituent came up after the meeting to complain about trash collections. When the congressman advised the constituent to talk to the mayor or to the commissioner of sanitation, she replied: "Well, I didn't want to start that high."[5]

Senators and representatives, of course, are not alone in using the public image of Congress as a way to get laughs. Satire and humor directed at the national legislature are a long-standing tradition, from the days of Mark Twain and Will Rogers to contemporary Washington humorists James Boren and Mark Russell. Boren carried the theme to another art form in his metal sculpture entitled "The Congress." The sculpture, said Boren, portrayed the spirit of the place, including "the posturing flag wavers, the shuffling clowns, the itchy palms, the back scratchers, the loophole artists, the yoyos and the clanging sounds of the ever-present dingalings."[6]

Congress is a topic that humorists can use for harmless laughter as they do with subjects like spouses or mail delivery. Similar behavior by incumbent senators and representatives, however, has more profound consequences for the institution and for U.S. politics. The humor that incumbents direct at Congress is part of a more general pattern in which individual members of Congress run for reelection by running against the institution. We would expect challengers for congressional seats to run on a platform of correcting what is wrong with Congress. What incumbents have to gain by doing this is not quite as evident. It begins to make sense only when we look at public attitudes toward both Congress as a whole and toward individual members of the institution.

Figure 1–1 provides a broad picture of public opinion of Congress as it is reflected in: (1) national surveys that ask people to rate the job done by Congress, (2) surveys that ask people to rate the job done by the member of Congress from that district, and (3) the reelection rate for incumbent representatives and senators.

What do we learn about Congress and public opinion from Figure 1–1? First, it shows that the public's rating of the institution of Congress changes a great deal from year to year, while the rating of individual members has been more constant. Second, incumbent representatives seeking reelection have been returned at a consistently high rate, but the reelection rate for senators has varied a great deal over the years. Third, public opinion polls have consistently found that people give higher job ratings to the member from their own district than they give to Congress as a whole.

The general patterns seen in Figure 1–1—the wide fluctuations in how the public rates Congress, the strong approval that

FIGURE 1-1 Public Views of Congress and Its Members

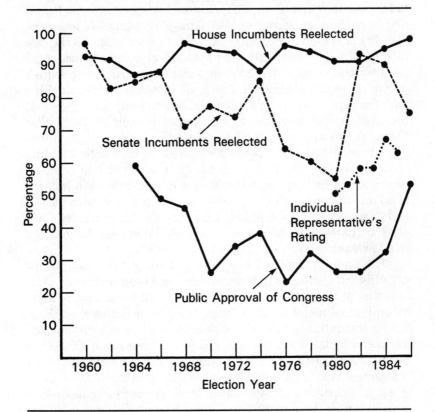

Source: Adapted by author from Gallup Polls, Harris Polls, and *Congressional Quarterly Weekly Report* data.

people give to their own representatives, and the return of nine out of ten incumbents seeking reelection—raise the question of why people approve of their own representatives even when they do not think much of Congress as a whole. If only 20 percent of the public approves of the job being done by Congress in 1976 and 1980, why is it that more than 90 percent of the incumbents running for reelection in those years are returned to office? There is a certain illogic in voters sending back to Washington essentially the same cast of characters who were involved in the bad performance of the previous year.

Professor Glenn R. Parker has analyzed the fluctuations in

congressional popularity over a thirty-five-year period. In his article, "Some Themes in Congressional Unpopularity," Parker discusses how negative public ratings of Congress are most closely connected to declining economic conditions, the absence of international crises, and the election of activist presidents.[7] Another congressional scholar has demonstrated that the high points of positive public opinion of Congress have coincided with the high points of congressional productivity. In Figure 1–1, the highest approval rating of Congress is seen in 1965, after Congress had approved the Great Society programs of the Johnson administration. Similarly, the increase in the public standing of Congress in 1981 and 1985 has been attributed to congressional action on taxes and the budget in particular. While there is no one-to-one relationship between the number of bills passed and these polls, public judgments about the institution of Congress are based to some extent on how well it appears to be doing as a lawmaking body.[8]

The findings reflected in Figure 1–1 suggest that people apply different standards in judging their own representatives. During most of this period, the public ratings of the job being done by individual members of Congress were much higher than those for the institution. At times, the proportion of people giving their own representatives a positive rating was twice that giving the institution a positive rating. Constituents did not hold their own representatives responsible for the poor performance of Congress. This pattern is most clear in a number of independent polls taken in the late 1970s. A 1978 New York Times poll, for example, found that 31 percent of those polled approved of the job Congress had been doing while 62 percent approved of the work being done by their own representative. The U.S. House Commission on Administrative Review commissioned another national poll during this period with similar results—the positive ratings for individual members outnumbered those for the institution by a two-to-one margin.[9]

The survey conducted for the House Commission also showed that people seemed to be using different standards in judging Congress as an institution and evaluating the performance of their own representatives. The reasons given for both negative and positive evaluations of the institution of Congress emphasized the legislative function. To determine how well the institution of Congress is doing, people look at its legislative track record; to judge how well an individual member is doing, they consider that member's performance in advancing the interests of the district.

We can see this difference when we look at some of the specific reasons given for respondents' evaluations of Congress. Both positive and negative evaluations of the institution generally included references to the legislative function—"they are doing their work, passed a lot of bills"; "passed many good bills that were later vetoed"; "they passed increases in Social Security, helped the economy"; "can't see that anything has changed, no signs of improvement, they have not done anything"; "haven't done anything about inflation, prices, the economy"; "haven't done all they could, lots of problems they did not deal with, e.g., energy, crime, etc."

A quite different focus is found in the reasons given for both positive and negative evaluations of the performance of individual members. These had more to do with the representation of district interests than they did with lawmaking—"represents his district well, works hard for the district"; "his contact, listens to you, is available, cares about his constituents and what they think"; "keeps you well informed, sends newsletters, bulletins"; "haven't heard about him"; "all he did was vote the party line, played party politics"; "doesn't keep in touch, doesn't keep us informed."[10]

The explanations people give for their judgments about Congress and about individual representatives gives additional meaning to Figure 1–1. The contrast between the high individual ratings and low institutional ratings, a difference that at first seemed inconsistent, reflects the presence of different standards of judgment. There is a recognition, once again, that Congress is both a lawmaking and a representational body. The standard used to evaluate the performance of Congress as a whole is based on lawmaking, whereas the standard to evaluate individual members is based on representation.

Other Views of Congress

Twenty years of service in the House of Representatives led former Rep. Barber Conable of New York to conclude: "Congress lives by four horrid aphorisms: Never adopt a political philosophy that won't fit on a bumper sticker. If you have to explain something, you're already in trouble. When you're drowning in a sea of economic illiteracy, don't drink the water. . . . Swim prettily. Any rooster who sticks his head above the tall grass will get hit by a rock."[11] An opinion written by U.S. Supreme Court Justice Lewis F. Powell, Jr., in a major federalism case pointed to a different problem with Congress: "Federal legislation is drafted primarily by the staffs of congressional committees. In view of the hundreds of bills introduced at each session of Congress and the complexity of many of them, it is virtually impossible for even the most conscientious legislators to be truly familiar with many of the statutes enacted." As a result, Powell said, members of the national legislature are much less likely than are state and local officials to know about and adapt policy to local concerns.[12]

Senators have expressed equally critical views of Congress. Despite his success on the deficit reduction bill, for example, New Hampshire Sen. Warren Rudman had talked openly of quitting the Senate in 1986. Rudman's frustration with the Senate was summed up this way by a friend and colleague: "He has a low tolerance for empty rhetoric and sloganeering."[13] Iowa's John Culver, who left the Senate in the same year Rudman entered it, had criticized the institution in much the same terms. "It's hard," he said, "to put up with a lot of the baloney around here—the posturing. A lot of guys up here are robots. They just go around making speeches and shaking hands and voting politically."[14] Another senator, one who retired after serving six years, was asked while still in office if he had any regrets about leaving Congress. With the cameras rolling in the radio-television gallery of the Senate, he replied: "I can't wait to get out of this chickenshit outfit."[15]

A number of state officeholders expressed a similar view of Congress when asked why they had decided against running for the House or Senate. "I've been there, I know what happens," said the attorney general of North Carolina, who had ten years of staff experience on Capitol Hill. "When I go up to Washington now I see all those people scurrying about making all this noise about this piece of legislation or that piece, which will probably never see the light of day." A New York Suffolk County executive, in saying why he would not be a candidate for the House, commented: "I can make a decision, order it implemented and in six months see if it has worked or not. But in Congress, it is like elephants making love. It takes two years before you can see whether what you've done has had any results."[16]

Not all senators, of course, share the view expressed by Arizona Sen. Barry Goldwater, who retired in 1986: "If this is the world's greatest deliberative body, I'd hate to see the world's worst." A fellow conservative Republican, Sen. Strom Thurmond of South Carolina, for example, called Congress "one of the greatest institutions devised by man." Kansas Republican Robert Dole also disagreed with Goldwater's assessment. "The Senate is known as the world's greatest deliberative body, and with good reason," said Dole, for "the Senate is democracy in action. It is an institution where legislative compromises are actually hammered out. Though it sometimes takes a while, and we may go through some contortions to get there, the Senate is an institution that ultimately reflects all the strengths and the weaknesses, the past and the future, the hopes and aspirations, of the American people we know we serve." Louisiana Sen. Russell Long, who retired with Goldwater, had this to say about the institution where he served for nearly forty years: "I love the Senate. I love it as an institution, even with all its defects—and it has plenty. It's doing what the founding fathers expected of it, that is to allow all ideas to enter, but hopefully only let the good ones to emerge. Every now and then we permit a horrible idea to emerge, but by and large the Senate does a good job."[17]

Representatives also can be found expressing judgments about the institution that are less harsh than the one offered by Barber Conable earlier. Rep. Tony Coelho (D-CA), for example, described Congress as "the most dynamic institution in our government—forever changing, forever responding to the will of the people." Massachusetts Rep. Barney Frank had this to say: "Nobody in the House of Representatives is anybody's boss. And what that means is that efficiency will always be much less than in a more hierarchically organized or in a financially organized place. When you take that into account and you take into account the complex issues we deal with, I think the institution functions reasonably well." Rep. Don Bonker (D-WA) agreed: "Given the complexity of today's issues, the intense regional, economic and even partisan interests that come to bear on legislation, the overall record is not all that bad."[18]

Evaluations of particular sessions of Congress follow the same pattern seen in evaluations of the institution in general: There is much disagreement about congressional performance. At the end of the first session of the Ninety-ninth Congress in December 1985, for example, Senate minority leader Robert C. Byrd concluded: "From the standpoint of productive, progressive legislation, this session has been, I think, the worst I have seen since I've been here." Byrd, who had represented West Virginia in the Senate for more than twenty-five years, described the previous session as one in which, "We haven't done much, and what we have done, we've done under the pressure of final deadlines that came up after we had missed all the others."[19] When others looked at what Congress had done in 1985, however, they came to conclusions directly opposite to Byrd's. A summary article on the same session in the highly regarded *Congressional Quarterly Weekly Report*, for example, concluded: "Congress seized the legislative initiative from the White House in 1985 and dominated the Capitol Hill agenda to a degree unmatched since President Reagan took office almost five years ago." Congressional scholar Norman Ornstein agreed: "This year came as close to congressional government as we've had in a long time."[20]

Whenever members of Congress, scholars, and the general public judge Congress and its members they do so in reference to some basic notions about what Congress and those members should be doing. It is also clear that individual voters may at the same time have almost directly opposing views about the performance of Congress as a whole and that of their own representatives. These differences emerge because Congress and its members are expected to perform a number of functions in the political system.

A short introductory book on Congress is expected to cover the more important facts about congressional behavior. In the following pages, I will present some of the findings of political scientists who have studied Congress. But a clear understanding of this empirical information must be built upon an awareness of the different frameworks within which such facts may be interpreted. The purpose of any political science course is to develop a critical faculty for interpreting and evaluating information, not simply to memorize facts. Laying out some intricate scheme of how members of Congress are chosen to serve on particular committees might help give teachers a basis for exam questions and students a focus of study for such exams, but it does little to bring either party closer to an answer to the underlying question, So what? That question can only be answered by first looking at the divergent views of what Congress is supposed to be doing in the U.S. political system and then evaluating the information about actual congressional behavior within these normative frameworks.

"What is" takes on life only when we compare it with different notions of "what should be." Throughout this book I will include discussions of reform proposals, whether successful or not, because of their tendency to bring to the surface the major issues of congressional politics. Recurring issues and actions of congressional reform provide one ground for bringing underlying values and empirical information face to face.

In this chapter, I outline some of the different ideas people have about what Congress is supposed to do. By presenting various notions about what Congress is and should be, I hope to provide not only a framework for evaluating the various reforms and proposed changes in the system but also a means for interpreting the facts about how the present system operates.

The Functions of Congress

Everyone will agree that there are certain functions that Congress should perform for the political system as a whole. Voters have expectations of what their representatives and senators should be doing for them. Politicians, political scientists, and the general public all have standards for evaluating the performance of Congress. Reformers seek to change certain parts of the system to make it more able to perform some functions. We all agree that Congress should be the representative branch and that a member of Congress should perform many activities as the representative of his or her district. There is a similar understanding of the need for Congress to arrive at decisions and pass legislation. In addition to representation and lawmaking, Congress and its members are expected to engage in overseeing the administration of programs, educating the general public about public policy issues, and assisting individuals who are having problems with the government. The relative importance that members and observers of Congress give to these different activities can lead to quite different ideas about proper congressional behavior and widely varying judgments about the performance of Congress and its individual members.

REPRESENTATION

Congress is sometimes described as a forum where the interests and demands of all groups in society are expressed. A member of Congress is expected to act as a spokesperson for the ethnic, economic, racial, religious, political, and professional groups within his or her geographic district. That is how Congress becomes, in James Madison's words, "a substitute for a meeting of citizens in person."[21] The idea of Congress as a slow-moving, deliberative body is also associated with representation in this sense. Political scientists have suggested that the representation accorded by Congress contributes to political stability, that it provides a safety valve by permitting potentially disruptive groups to voice their grievances and demands. Similarly, the agonizingly slow movement toward decision on issues such as tax reform and civil rights is regarded by some observers as important because the consensus produced by such deliberation means that the decision, when it comes, will be regarded as legitimate by almost all groups in society.

Much of the debate over the role of Congress has to do with expectations stemming from this conception of representation. If a landslide presidential election is regarded as a mandate for certain policies, how can the citizen who disagrees with such policies have his or her views expressed? If one out of every five persons in a congressional district is black or Hispanic, should a congressional representative devote all of his or her efforts to implementing the white majority position on a civil rights measure or should the representative also articulate the demands of his or her nonwhite constituents? If certain groups and interests in a district or state support the losing House or Senate candidate does that mean that they are denied representation for that term?

These questions suggest that members of Congress are responsible not only for implementing majority decisions through their voting behavior but also for expressing the interests of electoral minorities in congressional debate and representing those interests in constituent casework. For Congress to be representative in this sense, it must be decentralized and provide easy access to all groups and interests, not just those who are part of the district majority. The representation of local interests in debates over national policy, which often brings members into conflict with presidential or national party positions, is another manifestation of representation through interest articulation.

LAWMAKING

Representation is a continuous process, a series of actions without clear-cut endings. The very characteristics that help to make Congress a representative institution (decentralization, open access, attention to local interests) make it difficult for Congress to call an end to representation and pass laws. Members of Congress themselves know this to be a recurring problem with the institution. When a shortfall of funds threatened to bankrupt the Social Security system in the early 1980s, a representative on the committee responsible for that program had this to say: "Don't expect leadership from us. Congress isn't equipped to lead. It's a representative institution, with all that means for stalemate."[22] A major justification for Gramm-Rudman's procedure of automatic cuts in spending was that it forced a conclusion. "Without an automatic spending cut, you don't guarantee an outcome," suggested Rep. Richard Gephardt (D-MO). Senate Budget Committee Chairman Pete Domenici (R-NM) agreed: "The process will force something to happen so if we don't do our job our job will be done for us."[23]

Clearly, Congress is expected to do more than represent the many interests in society. At some point it must end the talk and act. The word *congress* itself derives from the Latin for "a coming together," a clearer indication of action, of legislating than the European term, *parliament*, which comes from the French verb, *parler*, "to talk." Representation often takes the form of talking, of debate. Lawmaking requires an end to debate and "a coming together" to pass or defeat legislation.

Members of Congress are both representatives and legislators. Being a representative, however, produces a different set of expectations than those of being a legislator. For example, on one hand, representation through interest articulation includes the representation of a broad array of minority interests. A member of Congress is expected to introduce into legislative deliberations not just the positions of an electoral majority in the state or district but also the positions of significant minorities. It is the constituency's policy debate, and not just its final decision, that is brought into the legislative process.

On the other hand, when it comes time for a legislator to vote, expectations change. A legislator's vote is expected to be in accordance with an electoral majority. The reference point might be the primary or general election vote in the district, the most recent presidential election, or a policy mandate associated with a national political party. A member of congress from a district that is 20 percent nonwhite might feel that he or she should represent all constituents in policy debates on civil rights legislation but follow the electoral majority's position in voting on the matter.

The institutional requirements for effective lawmaking are

also different from those of representation. Instead of the decentralization that favors representation, effective lawmaking requires the coordination of effort and forcing of action that is more likely to be found in a centralized institution. The many points of access in a decentralized and representative structure can also serve as points of delay or defeat of the collective action needed to legislate. The representation of local and regional interests can also work against reaching agreement and producing a bill to address a national problem. An example of the latter was the representation of western farmers' interests in hiring temporary foreign workers and those of geographically concentrated Hispanic interests in preventing employment discrimination, both of which worked against passage of an immigration reform bill in 1986. What helps Congress to be a representative institution, in short, often makes lawmaking more difficult.

ADMINISTRATIVE OVERSIGHT

The explosion that destroyed the space shuttle *Challenger* and killed all seven crew members in January 1986, was a tragedy that will stay forever with those who saw the live coverage or films of the disaster on national television. The immediate question on everyone's mind became: Why did this happen? In seeking answers as to why the booster rocket exploded, government leaders and the public asked questions about the management of the National Aeronautics and Space Administration (NASA) and its running of the shuttle program. Although the leaders of key committees and subcommittees said that they would put off a full investigation of the accident and of NASA until a special presidential commission charged with that task had completed its work, a Senate Commerce subcommittee did hold a hearing three weeks after the *Challenger* explosion in order to review that commission's investigation. In addition, congressional timetables for making spending decisions required House and Senate panels to make decisions about NASA's budget before the commission's study was completed. At a hearing to deal with that budget, Representative Edward Boland (D-MA), chairman of an appropriations subcommittee, told NASA Administrator James Fletcher that the management of his agency had to be improved before additional funds would be voted, and that "until we feel NASA's house is in order, this subcommittee can withhold funds for new programs."[24]

The Senate subcommittee's review, Representative Boland's warning, and the full congressional investigation of the space program in the following months had an immediate aim of correcting the errors that led to the January explosion. But in a broader sense, they represented an attempt by Congress to see that its policies regarding the space program would be followed and that the administration of the program would be both efficient and effective. This congressional oversight of program administration is clearly linked to lawmaking. For it would do little good for Congress to pass laws that were not being implemented or were being administered in ways that did not produce the intended effects. Representation is also a part of the oversight process because that process provides a number of forums for the representation of a wide range of constituent, agency, client, and interest group positions.

The congressional oversight growing out of the *Challenger* disaster was unusual both as to its cause and in the high level of press coverage and public awareness. Oversight itself, however, is a regular part of the congressional routine. The laws passed by Congress are implemented through administrative regulations and executive programs, and it is up to Congress to make sure that those regulations and programs accomplish what Congress intended. In addition, congressional oversight can indicate areas where additional legislation is needed, provide opportunities for judging the efficiency of administrative agencies, and serve as a means for holding administrators accountable for their actions.

Although other terms—scrutiny, inspection, control, supervision, review—are sometimes used to describe this activity, the Legislative Reorganization Act of 1946 formalized oversight by requiring each standing committee to "exercise continuous watchfulness of the execution by the administration agencies concerned of any laws" falling within that committee's jurisdiction.[25] Subsequent reorganizations and committee reforms in the 1970s required committees to issue biennial oversight reports, created oversight subcommittees on many committees, expanded the powers and resources of the General Accounting Office, and increased the size of committee staffs. This surge in oversight activities led House leaders to officially designate the last Congress of that decade, the Ninety-sixth Congress (1979–1981), the "Oversight Congress."

Congress has available to it a number of instruments for overseeing administrative agencies. As we saw in the case of NASA, congressional hearings and control over appropriations are two important vehicles of congressional oversight. Other direct and formal techniques of administrative oversight include General Accounting Office (GAO) audits of executive agencies and programs, the inclusion of periodic reporting requirements in some legislation, and program evaluations conducted by the GAO, the Congressional Research Service (CRS), the Congressional Budget Office (CBO), and the Office of Technology Assessment (OTA). Another important form of administrative oversight prior to its being declared unconstitutional by the U.S. Supreme Court in its 1983 *Chadha* decision was the legislative veto, based on provisions found in over 200 statutes giving Congress the right to approve or disapprove certain executive actions. Congressional oversight of administration also takes place in less formal ways. These ways include the routine consultation and discussion among legislators, congressional staff, and executive officials about legislative intent and program operations, and the endless servicing of constituent needs through casework that exposes legislators and their staff to the effects of program administration.

EDUCATION

A group of senators, staffers, musicians, and hundreds of spectators got together in a Senate hearing room in September 1985, to watch rock videos. Frank Zappa was there. Twisted Sister appeared on screen and Dee Snider was there in person. John Denver explained to the group what "Rocky Mountain High" meant to him. Not everyone enjoyed the videos. South Carolina Sen. Ernest Hollings said, "It is outrageous filth and we must do something about it." Sen. Paula Hawkins of Florida showed two videos and a number of posters that she considered obscene. After watching videos, hearing witnesses, and discussing ways to control lyrics without violating the First Amendment, the members of the Senate Commerce, Science, and Transportation Committee adjourned without taking any legislative action. Committee Chairman John Danforth (R-MO) had these words for people disappointed by this lack of action: "The be-all and end-all of everything is not congressional legislation. The purpose of the hearing is to provide a forum."[26]

The congressional role of raising issues and providing forums for educating the public is considered by many to be one of the most important activities of Congress. Woodrow Wilson, for example, had this to say in his 1885 book, *Congressional Government*: "Quite as important as legislation is vigilant oversight of administration; and even more important than legislation is the instruction and guidance in political affairs which the people might receive from a body which kept all national concerns suffused in a broad daylight of discussion."[27] The comments of former Rep. Bob Eckhardt (D-TX) suggest that education was considered to be just as important nearly a hundred years later:

> The function of education makes of Congress a sounding board, a lectern, and a stump and is extremely important. It is one that most of the members elected from New York tend to use extensively. I have sometimes said, maybe a little harshly, that they have been elected to the New York Times rather than the U.S. Congress, and they have used the Congress merely as a place from which to express views that may change the course of the country.[28]

Much of Congress's gathering and dissemination of information is a by-product of its other functions. Public hearings can be convenient forums for articulation of interests, gathering of information useful to lawmaking, and performance of administrative oversight. But sometimes a legislator or group of legislators will seek to raise issues and disseminate information even when that activity is not directly related to these other functions.

Both chambers have select committees that are charged with studying and investigating a particular area rather than writing legislation. Examples in the Ninety-ninth Congress (1985–1986) included the Senate Select Committee on Ethics and its Special Aging Committee, and the House Select Committees on Aging, on Children, Youth and Families, and on Narcotics Abuse and Control. House and Senate rules stated that these committees were responsible for conducting studies and reporting their findings to the parent chamber but that they could report legislation.

There are many good reasons why a member of Congress might put a great deal of effort into these educational activities. A representative or senator might hope that publicizing the extent of problems in one area will generate constituent demands that eventually will lead to new legislation. Even if the legislator were to write off the chance of government solutions to a problem, however, he or she might feel that a democratic government has a responsibility to educate and inform citizens. Or, a representative or senator might believe that educating the public about the conditions under which some people live can be an important way of developing public tolerance of minorities and a shared sense of community. Congressional hearings and other forms of education also bring attention to those doing the educating, and this is an obvious benefit to legislators who must win elections.

CONSTITUENT SERVICE

Who do people call if their Social Security check is late, if the Veterans Administration denies eligibility for treatment, if a relative's application for entry into this country has been rejected by the Immigration and Naturalization Service, if a student loan has been drastically cut or eliminated because of new federal guidelines? Their representative or senator, of course. Some people will contact a member of Congress only after losing a battle with the bureaucracy. Others start with the congressional office. Members recognize, accept, and even encourage this representation to the federal bureaucracy of constituents with problems as a part of their job. But constituent service is not limited to serving as a constituent advocate in dealings with federal agencies. College interns with term paper assignments have known this for some time, and it is a lesson that more and more students seem to be learning earlier in their school careers. "A whole elementary school class wrote in asking for information on all 50 states," reported one legislative assistant. "Their letters said, 'I am doing a paper on Nebraska and cannot get to the school library; please send me all the information you can.' We figure the teacher wrote the letter on the board and told the students to copy it."[29] The legislator's staff called on the services of the Congressional Research Service and these children of voters were supplied with the requested information.

Here is how a former representative, Luther Patrick, described a modern member of the House:

> [A] Congressman has become an expanded messenger boy, an employment agency, getter-out of the Navy, Army, and Marines, a wardheeler, a wound healer, trouble shooter, law explainer, bill finder, issue translator, resolution interpreter, controversy-oil-pourer, glad hand extender, business promoter, veterans affairs adjuster, ex-servicemen's champion, watchdog

for the underdog, sympathizer for the upperdog, kisser of babies, recoverer of lost baggage, soberer of delegates, adjuster for traffic violations and voters straying into the toils of the law, binderup of broken hearts, financial wet nurse, a good samaritan, contributor of good causes, cornerstone layer, public building and bridge dedicator and ship christener.[30]

The most common cases brought to congressional offices are inquiries about the status of an agency's handling of a particular problem, requests for services and information, or appeals for favorable or preferential treatment. Cases are more likely to be initiated by individual constituents than by organized groups. Some are "offensive" cases that call for government action; others are "defensive" cases in which a constituent is seeking relief or a reversal of action already taken. Although the variety and range of programs and issues that can generate cases is unlimited, a recent study by John Johannes found the casework agenda of congressional offices to be dominated by five agencies. These were, in order of frequency, Social Security (including Medicare), the Veterans Administration, the military services, the Justice Department (especially the Immigration and Naturalization Service, the Bureau of Prisons, and the Law Enforcement Assistance Administration), and the Department of Labor (most often the Occupational Safety and Health Administration, the Office of Workers' Compensation Programs, and the Black Lung and unemployment divisions).[31]

The term "ombudsman," which comes from some European governments that have independent, nonpartisan officials called "ombudsmen" who handle citizens' complaints and grievances, is often applied to the constituent service role of United States senators and representatives. Not everyone is satisfied with "the manner in which Congress has changed from legislators to ombudsmen", as one member made clear at a hearing of the House Commission on Administrative Review:

Rightly or wrongly, we have become the link between the frustrated citizen and the very involved Federal Government in the citizens' lives. Because the Federal Government is so often hard for them to deal with, they end up writing letters, getting letters back from computers, after a while throwing up their hands, and the last stop is the congressional office. So we become the ombudsmen.

I am not sure that it is a proper role for us to play, but we are in it. We do not have much choice. We continually use more and more of our staff time to handle citizen's complaints, constituents' problems.

I do not know how you get out of this, since it becomes apparent to most people that if you want to be reelected it is more important how you handle your constituents in their relationships and problems with the Government than it is how you vote. I think it is one of the reasons that at the same time that Congress is going down, down, down, in the overall opinion of the American public, the rate of incumbents being reelected is going up, up, up. I think that has nothing to do with how we vote, but I think it has a lot to do with the fact that we have a staff which spends an incredible amount of time handling constituent problems.[32]

Serving constituents in this way can help members to carry on the tasks of lawmaking and administrative oversight. Casework is an important form of intelligence gathering; it tells members and their staffs which programs need to be corrected through legislation and which agencies need closer scrutiny. Members know this, but they also know that there are trade-offs involved in allocating staff resources. The representative who appeared before the House Commission was not alone in drawing the conclusions he did. A survey of 153 House members and their staffs reflected this awareness of the electoral importance of the constituency service function and the feeling that it is a role forced upon House members rather than one freely chosen. When House members were asked which roles the House of Representatives *should* play, 82 percent mentioned the legislative role and 27 percent mentioned the ombudsman role. When they were asked which roles the public *expected* them to play, 87 percent mentioned the legislative role and 79 percent mentioned the ombudsman role.[33]

Conflicting Functions

The tension between lawmaking and constituency service is not limited to those two functions of Congress. An example discussed earlier is how making it easier for Congress to pass laws often requires limiting representation. These fundamental conflicts and tensions between the tasks of Congress led Nicholas Longworth, Speaker of the House from 1925 to 1931, to conclude that the only way for a member to be happy "is to realize that he has no chance."

> Suppose we pass a lot of laws. Do we get praised? Certainly not. We then get denounced by everybody for being a "Meddlesome Congress" and for being a "Busybody Congress."
>
> But suppose we take warning from that experience. Suppose that in our succeeding session we pass only a few laws. Are we any better off? Certainly not. Then everybody, instead of denouncing us for being a "Meddlesome Congress" and a "Busybody Congress" denounces us for being an "Incompetent Congress" and a "Do-Nothing Congress."
>
> Suppose, for instance, that we follow the President. Suppose we obey him. Suppose we heed his vetoes. What do we get called? We get called a "flock of sheep." We get called "echoes of the master's voice," a "machine."
>
> Suppose, then, we turn around and get very brave, and defy the President and override his vetoes. What, then do we get called? We get called "factionists." We get called "disloyalists." We get called "disrupters of the party." We get called "demagogues."[34]

Recognizing that Congress and its members are expected to make laws, represent interests, oversee executive agencies, educate the public about political issues, and resolve constituents' problems with the federal bureaucracy is a first step in understanding Congress and making judgments about the institution. But it is the conflicts that grow out of those functions that provide opportunities for gaining a fuller understanding of Congress. Speaker Longworth's portrait of members being "damned if you do and damned if you don't" makes life more difficult for the members but easier for those who study the institution.

Consider the five congressional functions discussed so far and some of the potential conflicts between them. Table 1–1 summarizes the differences between representation and lawmaking. The conflicts that develop from these two conceptions of the primary function of Congress have the greatest impact on the institution and what we think of it. Representation and lawmaking are not mutually exclusive, but increasing the potential for achieving one goal decreases the chances of satisfying the other.

TABLE 1–1 Differing Views on the Primary Function of Congress

Representation	Lawmaking
1. Congress is a forum for articulating group interests.	1. Congress is a decision maker that translates popular mandates into law.
2. Emphasis is put on representation of minorities.	2. Emphasis is put on majority rule.
3. Decentralized legislative structure is favored.	3. Centralized legislative system under party presidential leadership is favored.
4. Legislative coalitions are formed after elections—likely to be shifting pattern of dissimilar groups brought together through logrolling.	4. Legislative coalitions are formed at elections. Members of Congress are expected to follow party and presidential mandates reflected in elections.
5. *Public interest* is defined as the sum of the many constituency interests.	5. *Public interest* is defined in national terms as being more than just the sum of constituency interests.
6. Constituency casework is considered an important part of an individual legislator's role.	6. Casework is relegated largely to staff so as to free the legislator for important work.
7. Administrative oversight is regarded as a process for advancing ideas and information and for representing interests of constituent groups.	7. Administrative oversight is regarded as a process of insuring that mandates of earlier legislation are being carried out.
8. Chief criterion for evaluating legislative performance is the number of groups and interests considered in the legislative process.	8. Chief criterion for evaluating legislative performance is the efficiency with which electoral mandates are translated into policies.

On the individual legislator decision-making level, this conflict is reflected in the demand that a congressional member devote considerable time to the study and reflection needed for responsible lawmaking and at the same time be ready to respond to the unending flow of small favors sought by constituents. "I thought I was going to be Daniel Webster," remarked one congressman, "but I found that most of my work consisted of personal work for constituents." Said another: "The least appealing aspect of my job is the service we have to perform for constituents.... Too much of our time and energy is diverted in that direction with the result that the opportunity for creative thinking in a legislative way is greatly lessened."[35]

The conflict between representation and lawmaking is even more pronounced at the institutional level, both in general evaluations of Congress and in proposals reform. If a Congress maximizes the lawmaking functions of efficiently passing legislation, some will denounce it as a "rubber stamp" or "me too" Congress. If it maximizes representation and delays legislation so that all interests can have a say, it runs the risk of being tagged a "do nothing" Congress. Specific reform proposals also highlight the inherent conflict between representation and lawmaking. Debate over reform often produces one side seeking to improve the efficiency with which Congress performs its lawmaking function, and the other side contending that inefficiency is the price the legislature must pay if it is to maximize its representational potential.

In the Senate, this conflict is most evident in reform proposals for limiting debate and for giving the majority stricter controls over the long speeches known as filibusters, which individual senators employ to delay or block legislation. Senate leaders were particularly concerned about the Senate's image when it began televising its proceedings in June 1986. They felt that those who watched would be shocked and disappointed by the seeming lack of direction and delays in the way the Senate conducted its business. In an effort to correct some of these problems, Senate party leaders Robert Dole (R-KS) and Robert Byrd (D-WV) proposed a number of rules changes in early 1986. The reforms proposed by the two senators sought to prevent filibusters against motions to consider legislation and to make it more difficult to continue a filibuster after a cloture vote, a vote to limit debate and end a filibuster. Those who supported reform, such as Republican Sen. Daniel Evans of Washington, drew on the lawmaking values indicated in Table 1–1: "Ultimately, the majority in any body has to have the right to conduct its affairs." Opponents of the rules change drew more on the values of representation. Changing the filibuster rule, said Sen. Jesse Helms (R-NC), would be a "tragic mistake." "This is the only legislature in the world where a minority of one can get up and oppose a proposal as long as his stamina permits."[36]

The debate surrounding two major changes in Senate rules governing debate made in the 1970s also centered on the conflict between representation and lawmaking. A rules change in 1975 reduced the number of senators needed to invoke cloture. A rules change in 1979 established an absolute one-hundred-hour limit on debate time after a cloture vote, an attempt to end the practice of postcloture filibustering that had developed after the 1975 rules change. Prior to the earlier reform, the support of two-thirds of those present and voting (sixty-seven if all one hundred senators were present) was needed to invoke cloture and cut off a filibuster. The 1975 reform changed the number of senators needed to invoke cloture to three-fifths (sixty senators) of the total membership.

Senate debate on the filibuster rule raised the most fundamental issues about the representational and lawmaking functions of Congress. Those senators who emphasized the representational function of the Senate opposed any attempts to reduce the number of senators needed to involve cloture. Former Sen. William Fulbright suggested that the debate over changing the cloture rule raised the larger question of whether the Senate would "remain an element in the American constitutional process." Stressing the importance of representation over lawmaking, he went on to say:

> Some issues, such as civil rights and war-making power, arise in our kind of governmental community that need delay and consideration so that a compromise can be worked out. A simple majority—and that's what it would be if this rule is changed—should not have the right to impose a decision on a significant minority.[37]

Those who wanted no change in the existing cloture system felt that it represented the most important contribution of the United States Senate to the political process for it allowed full expression of the widest possible array of views.

On the other side of the debate, those supporting the rules change stressed the lawmaking responsibilities of Congress. "Eventually, the right of the Senate to vote will win out over the right of the Senate to debate," declared one senator early in the debate over the rules change.[38] After the successful passage of the reform of Rule 22 (the Senate rule governing cloture) in 1975, another senator predicted that the reform "will make the Senate more efficient, more democratic and more effective. With the reform of Rule 22 the Senate will be able to deal with the pressing problems of America in 1975."[39]

That those expectations were too high became clear the following year, however, when Sen. James Allen of Alabama was able to filibuster an antitrust bill even after a cloture vote. He did this by introducing scores of amendments to the bill and demanding time-consuming quorum calls and roll call votes. He was able to do this because the time spent on debating amendments, taking roll call votes, and quorum calls did not count against the one-hour time limit on debate imposed on each senator by the cloture vote. In 1977, two liberal senators used the same postcloture filibuster tactics to tie up debate on a natural gas pricing bill for nine days after the Senate had voted cloture. Widespread use of the postcloture filibuster in the Ninety-fifth Congress (1977–1978) led Senate majority leader Robert Byrd to complain that the problem "is not so much in getting cloture. The problem is what happens after cloture is invoked."[40]

At Byrd's strong urging, the Senate adopted a resolution in February 1979, that provided an absolute one-hundred-hour limit on the time allowed for debate, roll call votes, and quorum calls and that time limited the number of amendments that any senator could propose to a bill after cloture. Like the earlier reform, the 1979 Senate rules change highlighted the tension between lawmaking and representation. "We have to expedite the legislative process," argued Senator Byrd, "we don't live in the leisurely world of 75 years ago."[41] And once again we find opponents of the reform charging that Byrd was "more interested in the passage of legislation than in the content of legislation" and saying that the leadership "should not be permitted to operate the Senate like an automated data processor spewing forth law with machine-like precision."[42]

Debate on reforms in the House of Representatives has centered on the same issues of representation and lawmaking that had been debated by senators. The Legislative Reorganization Act of 1970 planted the seeds of reform in two important provisions: The first made it easier for members to call for recorded teller votes; the second produced an electronic voting system, which greatly facilitated the voting process. Some background on House voting procedures is helpful for understanding the importance of these two reforms.

Most of the business on the House floor since the first Congress in 1790 has been conducted under a procedure known as the Committee of the Whole House. This procedure is intended to maximize the lawmaking function of Congress. Instead of needing a majority (218 members) of the total membership to conduct business, the Committee of the Whole requires a quorum of only 100 members. Before the 1970 reform, there were only three ways of taking votes in the Committee of the Whole, and all votes were nonrecorded (that is, no record was made of how each member voted on the measure). The three procedures for voting were: (1) a voice vote, in which members yelled out ayes or nays; (2) a division vote, in which members stood to be counted; and (3) a teller vote, in which members filed past tellers (clerks) who counted those favoring and those opposing a measure. Roll call votes were not permitted under the Committee of the Whole procedure; they were subject to the larger quorum limitation of 218 members, a majority of the entire House membership. By acting on measures by voice, division, or teller votes, the Committee of the Whole is able to dispose of legislative measures rapidly and efficiently. A teller vote, the longest of the Committee of the Whole procedures, would take about ten minutes to complete as compared with the thirty minutes necessary for each roll call vote under the system before the electronic voting changes.

Because they allowed quick decision making, the fast voting procedures under the Committee of the Whole were seen as an efficient way for the House to meet its lawmaking responsibilities. But because the nonrecorded voting prevented accountability, critics suggested it was an obstacle to the House's effective fulfillment of its representational functions. Two basic patterns of behavior led to objections from those seeking accountability in House voting.

The first pattern was that only a fraction of the total House membership reported to the floor for the nonrecorded voting. Therefore, major policy issues were, in effect, being decided by a small number of representatives. The record showed only a voice vote, division vote, or teller vote passage, allowing no way for interested constituents to see how or if their representatives voted. The second was that the Committee of the Whole voting procedures permitted members, in effect, to vote on both sides of an issue. On roll call votes, when their position on a measure would be known to interested constituents, representatives could vote one way. Then they could gut the bill they had supported in roll call by anonymously voting for measures that undercut it in any of the nonrecorded voting procedures.

The conflicting demands of lawmaking and representation are clearly evident in these voting procedures. To be an effective lawmaking institution, the House must have a way to facilitate voting and to reduce the amount of time spent on passing bills. The various methods of voting under the Committee of the Whole procedure contributed to this goal. But to meet the demands of representation, constituents had to have some way to know how their representative voted on a measure. If the House used a series of time-consuming roll call votes, it would cripple itself as a major policymaker. The 1970 Reorganization Act contained a two-step solution to this dilemma: (1) a procedure for making recorded teller votes easier to come by and (2) an electronic voting system that greatly reduced the time spent on roll call voting.

The Legislative Reorganization Act provided that one-fifth of a quorum of the Committee of the Whole (twenty members) could call for a recorded teller vote. (In 1979, the number of members required to call for a recorded teller vote was changed to twenty-five.) Members would still march down the aisles and hand their cards to tellers, but now the cards would contain the representatives' names as well as how they voted. The effect was one that, in essence, brought roll call voting into the previously anonymous pattern of voting under the Committee of the Whole procedure. No longer could major amendments to bills be tacked on in the Committee of the Whole by a small group of representatives whose votes would not be known. The improved accountability of recorded votes and a much higher rate of members' participation in voting after the reform made this procedure more representative, but the time required for such roll calls worked against the Committee of the Whole's purpose of quickly and efficiently dispatching business before the House.

The second provision of the Reorganization Act sought to correct that problem. It states that "the names of members voting or present may be recorded through the use of electronic equipment." The electronic voting system went into effect in January 1973. On the floor of the House there are forty-four voting stations. When an electronic recorded vote is in progress, each member on the floor approaches one of these stations and pushes in a coded identification card, voting aye, nay, or present by pushing the appropriate button. At each end of the chamber a clock ticks down the remaining seconds of the fifteen minutes allowed for each vote, while a display panel above the Speaker's chair shows a running compilation of how each member voted. Individual consoles, which can provide regional, party, and other breakdowns of the vote, are provided for party leaders to assist them as they try to influence the outcome during the limited voting period.

Because they improve both accountability and efficiency, these provisions of the 1970 Act might be seen as advancing equally the representation and lawmaking functions of Congress. But the edge goes to representation. This is the case primarily because of the great increase in the number of recorded votes that took place after the 1973 change, going from a yearly average of 220 in the decade before 1973 to one of nearly 600 in the decade that followed.[43] Reforms that made it easier to call for recorded votes and that reduced the amount of time needed for such votes inevitably led to an increase in floor votes on many issues that would have been resolved in committee under the old system. Even when there are not direct scheduling conflicts, time spent on floor voting is time away from committee work, and it is committees that remain the primary workshops of legislation in the House. Even though there is an obvious overlap between the two spheres of action (committees and the House floor) and the two functions (representation and lawmaking), the tension between them remains.

Washington journalist Louis Kohlmeier, Jr., has suggested that "Congress is the least efficient, and most democratic, of the three branches."[44] Arizona Sen. Dennis DeConcini expressed a similar idea in Senate hearings on a proposal to limit the terms of members of Congress:

> What is sought here, then, is greater responsiveness and greater representativeness. By shortening terms I feel that legislative accountability will be enhanced and the forces which nurture it will be strengthened. This may be another way of saying that I have come to prefer democracy over efficiency.[45]

The measure of democracy in these cases is the representativeness of Congress, especially when compared to the executive and judicial branches. There are limits, however, on how far one can go in the direction of increasing representation without undermining the lawmaking ability of Congress. For as Theodore Lowi has pointed out, "a *perfectly representative* government would be virtually incapable of making a decision."[46]

John Stuart Mill and James Madison, whose political theories have greatly influenced U.S. political thought, described good legislatures as schools that teach members how to govern. In a recent study of the California legislature, William Muir more fully developed and applied this analogy of the legislature as a school. Muir discovered that legislators learned the most about any policy area when they were presented with contradictory information or with competing principles: "A legislator's realization that there were polar opposites to the theoretical principles he was learning in Sacramento was intellectually invigorating. He began to see that the dialectic between legislature and district could be counted on to generate useful pairs of principle and counterprinciple." As a result, Muir found that "legislators became wary of unopposed general principles." Legislators learned best when they sought to resolve conflicting information and competing principles.[47]

The values of lawmaking and representation and the conflicts between them discussed in this chapter provide students of Congress with the same opportunity for learning about the national legislature. As we have seen, this is most evident in debates over congressional reform. The final report of the House Commission on Administrative Review contains one of the most direct and comprehensive statements on the polar nature of those two values. The report describes the many characteristics of Congress that enhance representation, but then points out:

> A counter-pressure arises from legislative or policy responsibility, which emphasizes decisionmaking and policy output. Changes in House and caucus rules and procedures in recent years reflect this dichotomy: some reforms (the Speaker's responsibility to nominate Democratic members of the Rules Committee, the role of the Steering and Policy Committee, changes in the number required for various floor procedures) have been designed to effect more efficient decisionmaking; others (recorded teller votes, various committee procedures) have enhanced the representative function.
>
> The representative nature of the institution, which emphasizes consensus-building and a deliberative decisionmaking process, argues against an overriding emphasis on efficiency. An important function of the House is to represent citizen concerns, and

*to achieve policy outputs which can be accepted by all. An
emphasis on efficient decisionmaking resulting in rapid passage of numerous statutes, for example, may in fact not allow
enough time for needed consensus-building. Similarly, some
duplication of office operations, although perhaps not as efficient as a central service, may be more effective as a means of
carrying out representative and even legislative and oversight
responsibilities.*[48]

Both chambers of the national legislature are expected to
serve both functions, lawmaking and representation. Differences
over the value of particular legislative practices, of proposed reforms, and even of some policies can be, in effect, differences
over the relative importance given to lawmaking and representation. What one thinks Congress should be doing in these cases
will depend on judgments about the broader values of representation and efficient lawmaking.

Endnotes

1. Senator Domenici, quoted in Adam Pertman, "Congress OKs
Balanced Budget Bill," *Boston Globe*, December 12, 1985, p. 24; Senator
Johnston, quoted in Jonathan Fuerbringer, "Plan to Balance U.S. Budget
By '91 Delayed in Senate," *New York Times*, October 5, 1985, p. 1;
Senator Moynihan, quoted in Pertman, ibid.; Representative Martin,
quoted in Elizabeth Wehr, "Congress Begins to Feel Pinch of Gramm-
Rudman-Hollings," *Congressional Quarterly Weekly Report*, December
21, 1985, p. 2712; and Senator Rudman, quoted in Wehr, "Congress
Enacts Far-Reaching Budget Measure," *Congressional Quarterly Weekly
Report*, December 14, 1985, p. 2604.

2. Representative Mike Synar, quoted in Steven V. Roberts, "From
the Annals of Chutzpah and Jurisprudence," *New York Times*, January
3, 1986, p. A10.

3. William K. Muir, Jr., has discussed how paired contradictions
or "polarities" can serve as valuable frameworks for learning about leg-
islatures, policies, and other political behavior. See his discussion in
Legislature: California's School for Politics (Chicago: The University of
Chicago Press, 1985), pp. 52–55, and *Police: Streetcorner Politicians*
(Chicago: The University of Chicago Press, 1977), pp. 283–89.

4. Senator Don Nickles (R-OK), quoted in Steven V. Roberts, "Oklahoma Senator's Woes Reflect G.O.P. Concerns," *New York Times*,
January 5, 1986, p. A8.

5. Marjorie Hunter, "Capital Humor," *New York Times*, February
25, 1985, p. 12.

6. James F. Clarity and Warren Weaver, Jr., "Briefing," *New York Times,* September 24, 1985, p. A26.

7. Glenn R. Parker, "Some Themes in Congressional Unpopularity," *American Journal of Political Science,* vol. 21, no. 1 (February, 1977), pp. 93–109.

8. Randall B. Ripley, *Congress: Process and Policy* (New York: W. W. Norton, 1983), pp. 426–30, and *The Harris Survey,* 1985, #46, June 10, 1985 (Orlando, Fla.: *Tribune Media Services,* 1985), p. 2.

9. "Approval of Carter Drops to 46% in Poll," *New York Times,* April 14, 1978, p. 10, and Thomas E. Cavanagh, "The Two Arenas of Congress: Electoral and Institutional Incentives for Performance," a paper prepared for delivery at the 1978 annual meeting of the American Political Science Association, New York, N.Y., August 31 to September 3, 1978, p. 25.

10. Cavanagh, ibid., Appendix, Tables 5 and 6. Roger H. Davidson provides a good analysis of these surveys in "Why Do Americans Love Their Congressmen So Much More Than Their Congress?", *Legislative Studies Quarterly,* vol. 4, no. 1 (February, 1979), pp. 53–61.

11. Representative Conable, quoted in Paul Light, *Artful Work: The Politics of Social Security Reform* (New York: Random House, 1985), p. 13.

12. Justice Lewis F. Powell, Jr., dissenting opinion, *Garcia v. San Antonio Metropolitan Transit Authority,* 469 U.S. (1985).

13. Sen. William S. Cohen (R-ME), quoted in Diane Granat, "Senator Rudman: Taking the Deficit Personally," *Congressional Quarterly Weekly Report,* October 5, 1985, p. 1976.

14. Former Senator Culver, quoted in Elizabeth Drew, *Senator* (New York: Simon & Schuster, 1979), p. 56.

15. Quoted in Mary Russell and Robert G. Kaiser, "The Marathon: Nonstop 34 Hours of Waltzing, Stumbling, Struggling," *Washington Post,* October 16, 1978, p. A6.

16. "The Non-Candidates: Why Didn't They Run?" *Congressional Quarterly Weekly Report,* April 15, 1978, p. 892.

17. Sen. Barry Goldwater quoted in Alan Ehrenhalt, "Influence on the Hill: Having It and Using It," *Congressional Quarterly Weekly Report,* January 3, 1987, p. 4; Sen. Strom Thurmond, correspondence to author, June 26, 1986; Sen. Robert Dole, correspondence to author, May 19, 1986; Sen. Russell Long quoted in Pamela Fessler, "Russell Long: Tax Master and Senate Mentor," *Congressional Quarterly Weekly Report,* April 12, 1986, p. 801.

18. Rep. Tony Coelho, correspondence to author, July 7, 1986; Rep. Barney Frank quoted in "Flaws of Congress: Freshmen's Size-Up," *U.S. News and World Report,* October 5, 1981, p. 47.; Rep. Don Bonker quoted in "What Congress Really Thinks of Itself," *U.S. News and World Report,* January 14, 1980, p. 39.

19. Senator Byrd, quoted in Steven V. Roberts, "Many in Congress

Says Session of '85 Was Unproductive," *New York Times*, December 22, 1985, p.1.

20. Diane Granat, "On Balance, A Year of Taking the Initiative," *Congressional Quarterly Weekly Report*, December 28, 1985, pp. 2727–47. Norman Ornstein quoted on p. 2727.

21. James Madison, "Federalist 52," in Alexander Hamilton, John Jay, James Madison, *The Federalist* (1788: reprint, New York: Modern Library, n.d.), p. 343.

22. Unidentified Ways and Means Committee member, quoted in Paul Light, *Artful Work: The Politics of Social Security Reform* (New York: Random House, 1985), p. 21.

23. Representative Gephardt, quoted in Jonathan Fuerbringer, "Balanced Budget Bill: Conferees to Assess Its Impact," *New York Times*, October 16, 1985, p. A22.

24. Representative Boland, quoted in Steve Blakely, "Panel Votes $526 Million for NASA," *Congressional Quarterly Weekly Report*, May 17, 1986, p. 1134.

25. Morris S. Ogul, *Congress Oversees the Bureaucracy* (Pittsburgh: University of Pittsburgh Press, 1976), p. 5.

26. Irvin Molotsky, "Rock Hearing," *New York Times*, September 20, 1985, p. C8.

27. Woodrow Wilson, *Congressional Government* (New York: World Publishing Company, 1967), p. 195.

28. Former Representative Bob Eckhardt, in Norman J. Ornstein, ed., *The Role of the Legislature in Western Democracies* (Washington, D.C.: American Enterprise Institute, 1981), p. 97.

29. Bill Aseltyne, legislative assistant to Rep. Sander Levin (D-MI), quoted in "How Your Tax Dollars Help Do Term Papers," *New York Times*, May 28, 1986, p. B6.

30. Luther Patrick, "What Is a Congressman?" *Congressional Record*, May 13, 1963, p. H2978.

31. John R. Johannes, *To Serve the People: Congress and Constituency Service* (Lincoln: University of Nebraska Press, 1984), pp. 19–20.

32. Rep. Joel Pritchard, statement in U.S. Congress, House, *Administrative Reorganization and Legislative Management*, Hearings Before the Commission on Administrative Review, Ninety-fifth Congress, first session, June 2, 1977, p. 62.

33. Thomas E. Cavanagh, "The Two Arenas of Congress: Electoral and Institutional Incentives for Performance," Appendix, Tables 1 and 3.

34. Nicholas Longworth, quoted in Marjorie Hunter, "Congress and Dangerfield," *New York Times*, October 16, 1985, p. A24.

35. Quoted in Charles Clapp, *The Congressman: His Work as He Sees It* (Washington, D.C.: Copyright © 1963 by The Brookings Institution), pp. 51 and 55.

36. Senators Evans and Helms, quoted in Steven V. Roberts, "Wheels Are Spinning Over the Senate's Rules," *New York Times*, February 26, 1986, p. B8.

37. *Congressional Quarterly Weekly Report*, February 19, 1971, p. 416.

38. Ibid.

39. *Congressional Quarterly Weekly Report*, March 15, 1975, p. 545.

40. Quoted in Jack Germond and Jules Witcover, "Minority Hamstrings U.S. Senate," *Boston Globe*, February 9, 1978, p. 18.

41. Quoted in David Broder, "Byrd vs. Byrd Over Senate Rules," *Boston Globe*, February 4, 1979, p. A7.

42. Senator Harrison Schmitt, quoted in Ann Cooper, "The Senate and the Filibuster: War of Nerves—and Hardball," *Congressional Quarterly Weekly Report*, September 2, 1978, p. 2309; and Senator Harry Byrd, quoted in David Broder, "Byrd vs. Byrd Over Senate Rules," p. A7.

43. Norman J. Ornstein, et al., *Vital Statistics on Congress, 1984–1985* (Washington, D.C.: American Enterprise Institute, 1984), p. 148.

44. Louis M. Kohlmeier, Jr., *The Regulators* (New York: Harper & Row, 1969), p. 291.

45. U.S. Congress, Senate, *Congressional Tenure, Hearings Before the Subcommittee on the Constitution of the Committee on the Judiciary*, Ninety-fifth Congress, second session, March 14, 1978, p. 6.

46. Theodore Lowi, *Legislative Politics, U.S.A.* (Boston: Little, Brown, 1962), p. x.

47. William K. Muir, Jr., *Legislature: California's School for Politics* (Chicago: University of Chicago Press, 1982), pp. 52–53.

48. U.S. Congress, House, *Final Report of the Commission on Administrative Review*, Ninety-fifth Congress, first session, December 31, 1977, vol. 1, pp. 677–78.

2

Representation

The constitutional bicentennial of 1987 inspired a great deal of research on how well the political system created by that document was working two hundred years later. This is how the study by a group of political leaders and scholars known as the Committee on the Constitutional System begins:

> Government deficits, the spiraling imbalance of trade, inconsistencies in foreign policy, illegal immigration, unemployment, the decay of our cities, the abuse of the environment, the staggering cost of elections, and the piracy of special interest groups—these problems and a host of others have led thoughtful citizens to question whether our political system is capable of meeting the challenge of modern governance.[1]

The Committee on the Constitutional System considered many broad reforms in the electoral system and the government structure, most of which were directed at the problem of divided government. The congressional term of office has been one subject of reform proposals over the years. The Committee on the Constitutional System proposed that the term of office for representatives be changed from two to four years, and that of senators changed from six to eight years. Longer terms are proposed as a

39

way to improve the lawmaking capability of Congress. Because longer terms might weaken the accountability of lawmakers, however, many proposals for longer terms are accompanied by proposals for limiting the total number of terms that a senator or representative can serve. Term limitations are directed at the representative nature of Congress.

In looking at the debate over congressional terms, we see once again the problem identified by a former representative and long-time proponent of reform, Richard Bolling, as "the reconciliation of seemingly incompatible goals." "One is that you want greater efficiency for reasons that are pretty obvious. However, on the other hand, you never want to lose sight of the importance of the representative nature of the institution. That raises a lot of curious conflicts."[2] The debate over a term limitation for members of Congress gets to the heart of the meaning of representation and provides, once again, an insight into the conflicts between the goals of representation and lawmaking.

During the past two hundred years, there have been a number of proposals for limiting congressional terms, with a restriction of twelve years being the most common. Seventy term limitation resolutions have been introduced in Congress. In the Ninety-fifth Congress (1977–1978), a Senate judiciary subcommittee held hearings on the proposal but took no action. A poll taken during that Congress showed representatives and senators to be strongly opposed to any form of term limitation. By contrast, Gallup Polls in 1977 and 1982 found the general public favored a term limitation by a two-to-one margin.[3] A summary of the arguments advanced by the supporters and opponents of the term limitation proposal illustrates the underlying conflict between representation and lawmaking. Proponents of the twelve-year limit on congressional service make the following arguments.[4]

> Limited terms of service would ensure infusion of new blood from the mainstream of our communities into the American political system. New Members of Congress would bring to their jobs a fresh outlook and approach to the nation's problems. A greater number of people with diverse backgrounds would be drawn from the private sector. We would certainly be offered greater opportunity of a variety of people who wish to serve their country.

> Limited terms would counteract the recent trend toward "professional politicians." Challengers as well as incumbents

would regard public service more as a contribution to the nation, and less as a personal career goal. What our country needs, as envisioned by the framers of the Constitution, are "citizen legislators" not "career politicians."

Competition for public office would be enhanced. More people could be encouraged to run for office, many of whom may now feel as if they don't have a real chance to be elected when challenging a well entrenched incumbent.

A limitation on service is a limitation on the power of incumbency; the power of incumbency can be stagnating, unreceptive to fresh ideas and new approaches to the nation's problems.

It would strike at the heart of the seniority system, the nature of which is such that all voters do not have equal representation in Congress. Powerful committee chairmen dictate hearings and schedule consideration of bills to which they are favorable. Rotating committee chairmanships would be assured by limiting terms of service.

Many politically volatile issues and long-range problems that require solutions and immediate attention often remain unattended in the face of continual reelection campaigns. Election interests may be nurtured at the expense of these solutions; consequently, we often fail to see the comprehensive legislative remedies that are so necessary. A limitation on terms may bring these remedies about.

Members may be prompted to take a closer look at legislation and regulations proposed while they serve in Congress if they know that they would be obligated to leave Congress after a specified period of time to live with those laws and regulations implemented during their tenure.

By requiring new people to run for office after a certain interval of time, voters may be encouraged to look closer at the issues involved in a campaign, and less closely at simply the candidates' names.

At a Senate hearing on the term limitation proposal, one of the witnesses testified that he had just returned from a meeting with a large group of scholars of Congress. He polled this group and found that they were unanimously opposed to a constitutional amendment to limit the number of terms that members of Congress could serve. The witness was joined by two other leading students of the institution who voiced opposition to the resolution and demonstrated that such opposition comes not just from incumbent members of Congress with something to lose. The major arguments made by those opposing a limitation on congressional terms is summarized below.[5]

> Limited terms would deny voters the opportunity to return to Congress those Members whom they regard as worthy of office. The public should retain the ultimate power to expel from office those Members who are not performing their jobs, or to reelect as many times as it chooses those Members who are serving their constituencies well. Any limitation would be an arbitrary limitation on the public's ability to vote for the candidates of its choice.

> Experienced, seasoned, capable lawmakers would be lost automatically, and perhaps prematurely, from public service if we were to limit the number of years they can serve in Congress.

> Limited terms would create "lame-duck" Congressmen, similar to the lame-duck President created by the 22nd Amendment. Not only might a Member's legislative ability be impaired, but he/she may also feel less accountable to the public for his/her actions and decisions, causing him/her to disregard the constituency's wishes when voting.

> A regular influx of new, inexperienced Members would result in loss of cohesion and sensibility when scheduling or dealing with legislation. This would invite institutional instability and would make it difficult to formulate comprehensive policies with the Executive.

> Congressional reforms, spurred by recently elected (post-Watergate) Members have already brought about changes in the seniority system; Members, are now more likely to "speak up" and challenge their elders. Internal reforms can adequately address problems inherent in the seniority system; a Constitutional Amendment limiting terms of service would be "overkill."

The constitutional bicentennial has come and gone without an amendment limiting congressional terms being added to that document. Nor are members of Congress likely to be restricted to twelve years of service in the foreseeable future. But it is the debate on such a proposal, rather than the outcome, that is helpful in furthering our understanding of the politics of Congress. A key element in the debate surrounding this reform proposal is the meaning of the term *representation*. People may be referring to quite different things when they say that Congress is or is not the representative body it was intended to be. This chapter provides a closer look at some of the meanings of the term and applies them to the modern Congress. A useful starting point for this discussion is Hannah Pitkin's analysis in her book, *The Concept of Representation*. She talks about four different dimensions of representation—formal, descriptive, symbolic, and substantive—and provides a framework for considering how representative Congress really is.

Formal Representation: Congressional Redistricting

Formal representation is the authority to act in another's behalf gained through an institutional arrangement such as elections. The essence of representation is that the representatives are authorized in advance to act in behalf of their constituents, who agree to be bound by the representatives' collective decisions.[6] Emphasis is on the formal arrangements that precede the actual representative behavior. This notion of representation as a process requiring formal transfer of authority from many people to one delegate was a central part of Thomas Hobbes's conception of the state. In *Leviathan* (1651), Hobbes observed: "A multitude of men are made one person, when they are by one man, or one person, represented; so that it be done with the consent of every one of that multitude in particular."[7] It is the covenant between the people and the person selected to act in their behalf that establishes the latter as a representative. The formal arrangements of selection, not the behavior of the representative, define representation.

Some recent political analysts have adopted the Hobbesian concept of formal representation. The remarks of a political scientist, Joseph Tussman, illustrate this:

> The essence of representation is the delegation or granting of authority. To authorize a representative is to grant another the right to act for one-self. Within the limits of the grant of authority one is, in fact, submitting himself in advance to the decision or will of another. . . .
>
> The fact that our rulers are elected does not make them any less our rulers. . . . To say that we send our representatives to Congress is not to say that we have sent our servants to market.

> We have simply designated the person or persons to whose judgement or will we have subordinated ourselves. Nor does the fact that at a later date we must redesignate a representative alter the fact that an act of subordination has occurred.[8]

Defining representation this way leads us to focus more on the procedures for selecting representatives than on the representatives' behavior once in office. We measure representation, in this sense, by reference to the institutional procedures for selecting legislators. When the Seventeenth Amendment provided for direct election of senators, it made the Senate more representative than it had been when state legislatures were the electors. It is more representative by the standards of formal representation because its members are selected directly by the people. The focus on institutional procedures that characterizes formal representation is also found in the area of congressional redistricting.

In a landmark case on congressional districting, Wesberry v. Sanders (1964), the U.S. Supreme Court ruled that the words in Article I of the Constitution stating, "Representatives shall be apportioned among the states according to their respective numbers" and "chosen by the people of the several states" meant that "as nearly as is practicable one man's vote in a congressional election is to be worth as much as another's." Subsequent decisions by the Court in 1969 and 1983 further refined this one person–one vote standard by requiring that states "make a good faith effort to achieve precise mathematical equality" and that congressional districts "come as nearly as practicable to population equality." In the 1969 case, the Supreme Court rejected the plan for congressional districts in Missouri because of a 3 percent difference in population. In 1983, New Jersey's proposed congressional districting plan was turned down even though the population of all districts was within 1 percent of the state's average district population.[9]

As a result of these Supreme Court decisions, population equality has been clearly established as the standard of formal representation. It is a standard that affects congressional representation in many ways. The first is through reapportionment. Article I of the Constitution says that representatives shall be apportioned among the several states according to their numbers. The same article requires that a national census be taken every ten years. Because the number of House seats has remained fixed since 1929, those 435 seats must be reapportioned among the fifty states every ten years to reflect changes in state populations since the last census.

The 1980 census led to the reapportionment of 17 House seats, with northeastern and midwestern states losing seats to Sun Belt states such as Florida, Texas, and California. Reapportionment of seats among states does not produce strict equality in the population of districts. Although most of the House districts created after the 1980 census had populations of approximately 520,000, for example, the number of people in South Dakota's single House district approached 700,000, and a House district in Michigan had only 380,000 people living in it. Differences in district populations that come about as people move in and out of districts and states will generally increase as we get farther away from the reapportionment of the last census.

Before the Supreme Court entered the field of legislative districting in the 1960s, there was great stability in the demarcation of congressional districts in most states. State legislatures generally had to draw new district lines only if they gained or lost a House seat as a result of reapportionment. However, that stability was gained at the expense of suburban and urban voters who were greatly underrepresented because district lines had not been adjusted to reflect changes in population.

The 1964 *Wesberry* decision and subsequent rulings that called for precise mathematical equality in the populations of House districts have led to the correction of most errors of misrepresentation. By 1972, the populations of 385 of the 435 House districts varied by less than 1 percent from their state's average.[10] But those court decisions have also brought much instability to this area.

The drawing of district lines so as to give an advantage to one party or group is known as *gerrymandering*. The term was first used by a Boston newspaper in 1812 for a plan creating a geographically absurd, salamander-shaped district that was designed by Massachusetts Governor Elbridge Gerry and his followers in order to dilute the electoral strength of Federalist rivals. The long-standing failure to adjust congressional districts to changes in population was, in effect, a passive form of gerrymandering and is what led the Supreme Court to intervene in this area in the 1960s. But applying a one person–one vote standard to redistricting does not do away with gerrymandering.

By combining computer technology with a knowledge of local politics, state party leaders have been able to devise redistricting plans that greatly favor one party over another but still meet the standard of population equality. California Democrats under the direction of Rep. Phillip Burton did this after the 1980 census, and the California House delegation went from a twenty-two to twenty-one Democratic advantage in 1980 to a twenty-eight to seventeen Democratic advantage under the new districting plan in 1982. Careful redistricting by the Republican-controlled Indiana state legislature after the 1980 census produced similar results, changing that state's House delegation from a six to five split favoring the Democrats to a six to four Republican advantage.

The party that loses under a gerrymander often will take its case to the federal courts. Indiana Democrats and California Republicans did this in the instances discussed previously. New Jersey's congressional redistricting plan was rejected by the U.S. Supreme Court in the 1983 case of *Karcher v. Daggett*. Other states whose post-1980 redistricting came under review by the federal courts included Colorado, Texas, North Carolina, and Mississippi. In addition to applying the one person–one vote standard in reviewing congressional districting, the courts look to see that districts are geographically compact, that they do not discriminate against minorities, and that there is a correlation between the proportion of votes and the proportion of seats gained by each party. All of these standards represent an attempt by the courts to make sure that congressional districting is fair, but they do not rule out gerrymandering.

In July 1986 the U.S. Supreme Court decided that the Indiana redistricting plan did not violate the Constitution's equal protection clause even though the plan was an obvious political gerrymander that favored Indiana Republicans. The Court ruled for the first time that partisan gerrymandering could be deemed unconstitutional discrimination, but said that would be the case only if "the electoral system is arranged in a manner that will consistently degrade a voter's or a group of voters' influence on the political process as a whole." Associate Justice Byron White, who wrote the opinion for a divided court in the case, applied that standard to the Indiana plan and concluded that it was not "consistently degrading" political gerrymandering:

> The mere fact that a particular apportionment scheme makes it more difficult for a particular group in a particular district to elect the representatives of its choice does not render that scheme constitutionally infirm.

An individual or a group of individuals who votes for a losing candidate is usually deemed to be adequately represented by the winning candidate and to have as much opportunity to influence that candidate as other voters in the district. We cannot presume in such a situation, without actual proof to the contrary, that the candidate elected will entirely ignore the interests of those voters. Thus, a group's electoral power is not unconstitutionally diminished by the simple fact of an apportionment scheme that makes winning elections more difficult.[11]

The 1986 decision did not affect the one person–one vote standard of earlier cases. Partisan gerrymanders are easily accomplished within that framework. The real impact of this decision will be seen in future cases that involve minority challenges to gerrymanders. Although the Indiana Republican majority was upheld in the 1986 case, the Court did serve notice that it would hear minority challenges to partisan gerrymanders in the future and established the standards of acceptable redistricting plans.

By developing and strictly applying the standard of one person–one vote to congressional districting, the courts have made Congress a more representative institution than it had been. The standard of population equality is a politically neutral standard, which the courts could apply without getting embroiled in politics. On the other hand, the application of that standard does not preclude gerrymandering. Indeed, some critics even suggest that the standard of population equality leads to an increase in gerrymandering because achieving districts with equal population often requires splitting natural political communities into different districts. The division and allocation of these communities present a wide range of options and opportunities to benefit one party over the other. If the court broadens the standard of population equality to consider whether a districting plan is fair to all or both political parties, it might also have to address other questions of fairness. For example, candidates challenging House incumbents might question the fairness of congressional redistricting plans that favor incumbents, as most plans do.

Whatever eventually happens in this area, a number of points should be clear even from this brief review:

1. Congressional districting is an intensely political process.
2. The application of seemingly neutral standards by the courts can be viewed as adding to, rather than diminishing, the political intensity that surrounds redistricting.

3. Congressional districts in the 1980s are less stable than they had been in earlier decades,

4. The standard of population equality can lead to congressional districts being separate from existing political, economic, and social communities.

All of these considerations have to do with formal representation because they focus on the institutional arrangements of selection. But the underlying question of importance here is who goes to Congress and what do they do there. To answer that, we must consider some of the other dimensions of representation.

Descriptive Representation: Them and Us

Descriptive representation is the extent to which representatives reflect the characteristics of the people they formally represent. It is measured by looking at qualities such as ethnic background, social class, sex, age, place of residence, religion, and occupation. That is the meaning of representation implicit in John Adams's statement during the American Revolution that a representative legislature "should be an exact portrait, in miniature, of the people at large."[12] It is descriptive representation that comes through in House Speaker Jim Wright's observing:

> Congress is the mirror of the people, and it reflects the aggregate strengths and weaknesses of the electorate. Its membership might include just about the same percentage of saints and sinners, fools and geniuses, rogues and heroes as does the general populace. Congress is a highly concentrated essence of the virtues and faults of the nation as a whole.[13]

Descriptive representation rests on a belief that a legislator acts in terms of his or her own social-economic background. A black or Hispanic representative from a district that is predominantly black or Hispanic, a farmer from a district with many farms, a blue collar worker from a working class district, a professional from a suburban district with many professionals will provide a spontaneous form of representation. On many issues, there is no need for those in the district to attempt to influence the legislator's vote because the legislator's background makes him or her predisposed to vote the way most people in the district would want the legislator to vote anyway. This is not to suggest a perfect fit that covers all voters and all issues. Descriptive representation rests on a predisposition, on what one legislator describes as a tendency more than a fixed pattern:

> Basically you represent the thinking of the people who have gone through what you have gone through and who are what you are. You vote according to that. In other words, if you come from a suburb you reflect the thinking of people in the suburbs; if you are of depressed people, you reflect that. You represent the sum total of your background.[14]

To determine just how representative Congress is according to this definition, we can compare the characteristics of representatives and senators with those of the general population. In Ernest Hemingway's short story, "The Snows of Kilimanjaro," he told about how F. Scott Fitzgerald had started to write a story that began "The very rich are different from you and me," and how someone had said to him, "Yes, they have more money." As you look at the characteristics of our national legislators, you will see that in many ways they are different from the general population. What makes members of Congress different from you and me is that they possess certain background characteristics that add up to political money. These include family background, occupation, and education—all of which are generally intermingled with personality attributes and situational conditions that make the typical congressman or congresswoman quite different from the typical citizen.

EDUCATION

In Table 2–1 the educational attainments of House and Senate members are compared with those of the general population. It is clear from this table that the typical House and Senate member is different from the typical American in terms of educational background. According to the 1980 census, 17 percent of the general population had a college degree of some sort. The education level of Congress is much higher, with 87 percent of the House and 92 percent of the Senate having a bachelor's or advanced college degree.

TABLE 2-1 Educational Attainments of House and Senate Members and the General Population, 1980

Level of Education	House	Senate	General Population
No college	3%	0%	70%
Some college	10	8	13
Bachelor's degree (or equivalent)	23	19	
Law degree	45	57	17
Advanced degrees	19	16	
Total	100%	100%	100%

Source: The figures on House and Senate members are from Alan Ehrenhalt and Robert Healy, *Politics in America, 1982* (Washington: Congressional Quarterly Press, 1981). Those on the general population, for persons twenty-five years of age and older, are from the Department of Commerce, Bureau of the Census, Current Population Reports, Series P-20, no. 390, August 1984.

OCCUPATION

Table 2-2 shows the occupational background of House and Senate members in the Ninety-ninth Congress (1985–1986). The occupational backgrounds of representatives and senators over-represent high prestige professional and business jobs. Occupational groups such as factory workers, farmers, and human service workers consistently have been underrepresented in Congress. The most striking aspect of legislators' backgrounds, however, is the number of lawyers among them. While lawyers constitute about one-tenth of 1 percent of the total work force in the general population, the 255 representatives and senators who list law as their occupation represent almost half (48 percent) of the total membership of Congress.

This overrepresentation of the legal profession in Congress is not new. In 1790, 37 percent of the membership of the House were lawyers; in 1840, 70 percent; and in 1957, 54 percent.[15] The number of lawyers in the Ninety-ninth Congress actually represents a decline of six lawyers from the previous Congress; a decline that has been consistent over the last thirty years in the House while the number of lawyers in the Senate is about the same as it was thirty years ago.[16] But the overrepresentation of

TABLE 2–2 Occupations of Members of the Ninety-Ninth Congress (1985–1986)

Occupation	House		Senate	
	Percentage of Total Membership[a]	Number	Percentage of Total Membership[a]	Number
Agriculture	6	27	10	10
Business or banking	36	157	33	33
Education	9	41	13	13
Journalism	7	31	19	19
Law	44	190	65	65
Public service politics	14	62	14	14
Other[b]	9	37	7	7

Source: Adapted from *Congressional Quarterly Weekly Report,* January 5, 1985, pp. 34–43.

[a]The percentages sum to more than 100 because many members list more than one occupation.

[b]"Other" includes aeronautics, civic volunteer, clergy, engineer, labor, law enforcement, medicine, military, and professional sports.

lawyers in Congress is still high enough for students of Congress to raise questions about both the causes and effects of having so many lawyers in Congress.

The lawyers' affinity for politics is explained not only by their expertise but also by the fact that lawyers are more able than other professionals to combine politics with their professional careers. While most professionals, such as doctors, educators, architects, scientists, and engineers, would find that running for office or serving in Congress hampered their professional careers, lawyers are able to take such a leave of absence and return with new contacts and information helpful for their law careers.

Business and banking constitute the second most common occupational background of representatives and senators. These occupations, combined with the legal profession, account for close to 85 percent of the total membership in the House and Senate. Still, there is something about all of these lawyers that catches the eye of congressional critics. The fact that members from business and banking professions as a group avoid such criticism suggests that complaints about lawyers as representatives and senators are not just a reflection of antipathy toward the dominance of professions that serve middle- and upper-class interests in Congress. Many people have expressed a belief that the difficulty of comprehending and interpreting most legislation is a direct result of having so many lawyer legislators involved in drafting it. Critics suggest this difficulty as one reason why people must turn to a lawyer to interpret most of the bills that pass through Congress, and why no one else can really understand a bill's intricacies and legal nuances. If such legislation is drafted by institutions consisting primarily of lawyers, one is tempted to think that there is some professional, albeit unconscious, collusion taking place between those who are paid to make laws and those who are paid to interpret them.

Not everyone agrees with that interpretation. Author and journalist, Garry Wills, for example, says that those who talk about the negative effects of having so many lawyer legislators are "dead wrong." "No better training could be found for them." He continues:

> They, too, must struggle with each other yet be friends the next day; make maximum claims as bargaining points but aim at a compromise settlement; satisfy most people somewhat, rather than a few people fully; represent diversity by muting differences; be always more neutral than hostile; deal in increments and margins only, but deal constantly; always adjusting, hedging, giving in a little, gaining a little; creeping toward one's goals, not heroically striding there. Always leaving oneself an out, a loophole, a proviso—what (the political scientist) Willmoore Kendall used to call a "verbal parachute"—so that no allegiance is irrevocable, no opposition adamant.[17]

AGE

"Critics of Congress often picture the institution as a collection of aging mossbacks waiting patiently for the seniority system to reward them with power," wrote Congressional Quarterly's Alan Ehrenhalt in 1979. "But whatever truth the stereotype might once have contained, the fact right now is that Congress is getting younger every year."[18] Members of Congress grow older like the rest of us, of course, but the election of more members at a younger age did indeed produce a steady decline in the average age of members from the Ninety-first Congress (1969–1970) to the Ninety-eighth Congress (1983–1984). The average member in the Ninety-eighth Congress was forty-seven years old, or six years younger than the average member in the Ninety-first Congress. As can be seen in Table 2–3, the age of members at the start of the Ninety-ninth Congress in 1985 marked a reversal of this trend toward an ever-younger Congress.

Even with this increase in members' age in the Ninety-ninth Congress, it is clear that the stereotype of "aging mossbacks" does not fit the modern Congress. The impact of the election of young members during the preceding decade is felt today in the generational shift in congressional leadership. "This is our place to run," said Rep. Thomas Downey (D-NY) in 1984 as he prepared to enter his tenth year in the House at the age of thirty-five. An important symbol of that generational change, one that has already affected the politics of Congress in the 1980s, is members' attitudes toward television. Shortly after being elected leader of the House Democratic Caucus, Missouri Rep. Richard Gephardt saw that as an important difference between the old and new generations of party leadership. "I grew up watching television," said Gephardt. "I watched Howdy Doody."[19] Being comfortable with television is an important campaign skill of this new generation. As more members like Gephardt have moved into positions of congressional leadership, this ease with

TABLE 2–3 The Changing Age Structure of Congress

Year	Average Age of Members at Start of First Year		
	House	Senate	Congress
1949	51.0	58.5	53.8
1959	51.7	57.1	52.7
1969	52.2	56.6	53.0
1979	48.8	52.7	49.5
1985	49.6	54.2	50.5

Source: Adapted from *Congressional Quarterly Weekly Report,* January 27, 1979. Figures for 1985 adapted from *Congressional Quarterly Weekly Report,* January 5, 1985, pp. 34–43.

the electronic media has also changed the face of Congress presented to the public.

RELIGION

Of the total general population of the United States, about 60 percent claim some religious affiliation. In Congress, 95 percent do. Whether this means that members of Congress are more likely to attend a church or synagogue than are others, or whether it is an indication that religious affiliation for elected officials is considered good politics is unclear. An executive of the National Council of Churches seems to think that the latter is the case: "People want to have a politician identifying himself with some denomination."[20]

Table 2–4 shows the affiliations of members of the Ninety-ninth Congress for the ten most common religions. Since the 1960s, there has been a decline in the number of Protestant members, a group which has in the past dominated Congress, and an increase in the number of Catholic and Jewish members; these two groups are now represented in Congress in greater proportion than in the general population. Catholics make up 23 percent of the general population and 27 percent of the membership of Congress. About 3 percent of all Americans are Jewish, while Jews constitute 7 percent of the membership of Congress. Even with these recent increases in Jewish and Catholic representation in Congress, almost one-half (46 percent) of the members of Congress come from the four largest Protestant denominations— Baptist, Episcopal, Methodist, and Presbyterian.

GENDER

If women were represented in Congress in equal proportion to their numbers in the general population, there would be more than 218 women members of the House (i.e., half of the total House membership) and more than 50 women senators (again more than half). But that is not the case. Instead of the 270 or so women representatives and senators that equal representation would produce, the Ninety-ninth Congress (1985–1986) had 24 women legislators (22 in the House and 2 in the Senate). That number matches the record-high number of women representatives of the previous Congress, but the fact remains that women have been underrepresented in Congress for a long time. The

TABLE 2-4 Religious Affiliations in Congress, Ninety-Ninth Congress (1985-1986)

Religion	House		Senate		Congress	
	Number	Percentage	Number	Percentage	Number	Percentage
Baptist	38	9	11	11	49	9
Episcopal	45	10	21	21	66	12
Greek Orthodox	6	1	1	1	7	1
Jewish	30	7	8	8	38	7
Lutheran	20	4.5	3	3	23	4
Methodist	62	14	15	15	77	14
Mormon	9	2	3	3	12	2
Presbyterian	48	11	8	8	56	11
Roman Catholic	124	28.5	19	19	143	27
Unitarian	7	2	2	2	9	2
United Church of Christ or Congregational	8	2	5	5	13	2
Unspecified	3	1	0	0	3	1
Unspecified protestant	18	4	4	4	22	4
Other[a]	17	4	0	0	17	3

Source: Adapted from *Congressional Quarterly Weekly Report,* January 5, 1985, pp. 34-43.

[a] "Other" includes Apostles of Christ, Christian Scientist, Christian Church, Church of Christ, Christian Reformed, Disciples of Christ, Seventh-Day Adventist, Pentecostal, Unspecified Christian and African Methodist Episcopal Zion.

average number of women in Congress over the last thirty years has been 17. The 22 women representatives in the Ninety-ninth Congress account for only 5 percent of the total House membership. "Until the number of women in the House hovers around 25 percent," says the executive director of the National Women's Education Fund, "you are just playing tiddlywinks over whether the number of congresswomen is eighteen or sixteen."[21]

In his book, *Congressional Women*, Irwin Gertzog examined the changing recruitment patterns for women legislators and predicted that the number of congressional women will increase more rapidly as the representation of women in political vocations and state and local political office increases. Even if that representation increases dramatically, however, Gertzog suggested that:

> the full integration of women into congressional life will not take place until myths about women's subordinate social role are rejected. Only then will it be possible for ascribed qualities to be peeled away from the identities of men and women, for women's identities as "other" to be discarded, and for gender differences to become irrelevant while men and women are undertaking the public's business together.[22]

RACE

In the history of Congress, there have been a total of about fifty black members. All except three served in the House. The post-Civil War period of Reconstruction in the last century accounts for about half of the black membership in Congress. Between 1900 and 1928, there were no blacks in Congress, and it has been only in the last twenty years or so that the number of black members has increased appreciably. Most of these gains came in the 1960s and after the redistricting following the 1970 census. The twenty black members (not counting the nonvoting black delegate from the District of Columbia) of the House in the Ninety-ninth Congress (1985–1986) represent a decrease of one seat over the previous Congress. There are no black senators. If blacks were represented in Congress in proportion to their numbers in the general population (12 percent), there would be over fifty black members of the House and twelve black senators.

Much the same pattern holds for Hispanics as for blacks. There are no Hispanics serving in the Senate. The twelve Hispanic members of the House in the Ninety-ninth Congress represent an increase of one seat over the previous Congress, but fall far short of the twenty seats (5 percent) that Hispanics would hold if their representation were proportionate to Hispanic population in the larger society.

Most black members of Congress come from districts with a large black population, the average having a black population of almost 60 percent. These districts are likely to be in central cities and to have lost population over the last decade. To illustrate, the 1980 census showed that the seventeen House districts then represented by blacks averaged only about three-fourths of the population that they needed to equal the population in other districts in that state. To combat this problem of shrinking population, black leaders worked with state legislatures to expand the boundaries of these black districts in an effort to protect the seats of the seventeen incumbents and to carve out new black districts in the South.

During the same period, the districts held by Hispanics, unlike the black districts, did not suffer comparable population losses. Indeed, two new Hispanic districts—one in California and one in Texas—were created by redistricting. If this trend continues, we can expect Hispanics to improve their representation in Congress more than blacks. Even with those gains, however, it is clear that Congress continues to be an institution that is dominated by whites.

SUMMARY

We come away from this consideration of descriptive representation with two strong impressions. First, the notion of Congress as a microcosm of society as a whole—as one big mirror reflecting all of the traits of the citizenry—is not an accurate depiction of congressional representation. Second, unless we can systematically relate the background characteristics of legislators to varied patterns of behavior, it does us little good to know how many x's and how many y's are in Congress. Coalitions in Congress change constantly depending on the issue. Small town legislators join urban legislators, lawyers join nonlawyers, women legislators do not necessarily take the same side, and blacks join whites against other blacks and whites. Sometimes background characteristics do influence a legislator's vote, but often they are of no relevance in explaining congressional behavior.

While connections between an individual's social background and legislative behavior are often difficult to establish, the general array of backgrounds touched on in this section does permit some overall assessment of the representativeness of Congress. The general conclusion is that there is a difference between "them" and "us." When you add up the informal requirements of office, you do find a class structure in the pattern of legislative representation. A person's class is sometimes defined as the ceiling he or she puts upon expectation. Professor Donald Matthews has suggested that less than 5 percent of the country's population could reasonably expect to serve in the Senate. Although there are occasional exceptions to the rule—a barber and a pipefitter served in the Ninety-seventh Congress, for instance—political offices in the United States appear to be class ranked, with people of high social or political status holding the more important offices. Matthews's comments on an earlier Congress still serve as an appropriate summary of descriptive representation:

> As long as the system of stratification in a society is generally accepted, one must expect people to look for political leadership toward those who have met the current definition of success and hence are considered worthy individuals. Voters seem to prefer candidates who are not like themselves but who are what they would like to be.[23]

The class bias that Matthews described almost thirty years ago is even more pronounced today. One reason for that is the 1976 Supreme Court case of *Buckley v. Valeo*, in which the Court ruled that Congress could not limit the amount of money a candidate could give his or her own campaign. This lifting of limits on contributions to one's own campaign, coupled with a dramatic increase in the costs of congressional campaigns, has created what some have described as a Congress of the wealthy. The Senate, in particular, has sometimes been described as a millionaires club, with an estimated one-third of its members having assets worth $1 million or more. The House of Representatives, which likes to be thought of as "the people's House," has been changing in the direction of the Senate. The forty-three House members newly elected in 1984 had, on an average, assets worth more than $250,000. Six years earlier, the average assets of the seventy-four incoming freshmen representatives were approximately $40,000. The effect of this trend, according to the director of the study of 1984 freshmen representatives, is that "the lower chamber is going upper class." "It establishes a de facto property qualification for office that increasingly says: Lower and middle income need not apply."[24]

Symbolic Representation: Constituents' Trust

The essence of *symbolic representation* is not what the representative is but what he or she is perceived to be by constituents. Unlike formal and descriptive representation, symbolic representation is not easily measured by looking at aggregate data on district population and demographic characteristics. As Pitkin has written, according to this definition:

> The crucial test of political representation will be the existential one: Is the representative believed in? And the basis of such belief will seem irrational and affective because no rational justification of it is possible. Hence, political representation will not be an activity but a state of affairs, not an acting for others, but a 'standing for'; so long as people accept or believe, the political leader represents them, by definition.[25]

Certainly one interpretation of the high rate at which incumbent senators and representatives are returned to office is that there are a lot of believers out there. What is it that members of Congress do to generate this acceptance and belief? Congressional scholars have found elements of symbolic representation in what members do both in Washington and back home in the district or state. David Mayhew has described the ways that symbolism can become a part of the lawmaking process in Washington:

> It is probably best to say that a purely symbolic congressional act is one expressing an attitude but prescribing no policy effects. An example would be a resolution deploring communism or poverty. But the term "symbolic" can also usefully be applied where Congress prescribes policy effects but does not act (in legislating or overseeing or both) so as to achieve them.
>
> ...There is a special reason why a legislative body arranged like the United States Congress can be expected to engage in symbolic action. The reason, of course, is that in a large class

of legislative undertakings the electoral payment is for positions rather than for effects.[26]

At times, we find members themselves commenting on the symbolic representation that takes place in Washington. Former New York Sen. James Buckley did this shortly after assuming office, expressing his surprise at how many things happen in that chamber "for symbolic reasons" and citing the common practice of members' introducing amendments they recognize as having no chance of being passed.[27] In the same vein, a common form of symbolic representation in the House is for members to cosponsor a bill, and thus gain position-taking credit, even if they do not want or expect the bill to be passed. It was clear that a number of members were engaging in that practice in October 1985, when the House passed a bill restricting textile imports. The bill came to the floor with 293 representatives listed as cosponsors. When the House passed the measure, there were only 262 members voting for it. Rep. Barney Frank (D-MA), one of the bill's proponents, let his colleagues know what he thought of the thirty-one members who had cosponsored the bill but voted against it. "Some featherheads around here sponsor major bills but don't have any idea what's in them," said Frank, and accused some members of "trying to play cute, co-sponsoring legislation and then hoping it will never come up for a vote."[28]

Mayhew suggested that the motive for this type of symbolic representation is reelection, that legislators can gain support for positions taken regardless of policy effects. The impact of symbolic representation on the larger political system has been explored by Murray Edelman, in *The Symbolic Uses of Politics.* According to Edelman, much of U.S. politics is characterized by the dispensing of symbolic rewards (such as status or broad assurances regarding national security or law and order) to the inattentive mass public, while at the same time material rewards are handed out (in the form of direct government payments or contracts, tax breaks, or other economic benefits) to the attentive political elite in society. Symbolic politics in the aggregate, suggests Edelman, not only reflect a bias in U.S. politics favoring the politically active upper and middle classes, but also help to maintain the stability of the political system by giving symbolic rewards to those who benefit the least economically from the system and are thus the most likely potential sources of disruption.[29]

The congressional practices discussed in this section would seem to be a part of this larger pattern of symbolic politics discussed by Edelman. To the representative and his or her colleagues, such activity might seem to be simply a necessary part of the job of getting reelected. But when we look at the overall impact of symbolic politics, as Edelman did, we find a class bias similar to that found in descriptive representation.

In Washington, there is a policy focus to symbolic representation, even when the position taking that characterizes that representation is likely to have no real impact on policy. In the district, symbolic representation is most likely to focus not on policy issues but rather on the qualities of the person chosen to represent the people in that district. To understand this dimension of symbolic representation, one has to look at the interaction between the representative and his or her constituents. Regardless of the nature of such encounters, the representative is obliged to present to his or her concerned constituents some picture of who he or she is and why they should continue to send him or her to Washington as their representative.

Richard Fenno studied this dimension of representation by observing the behavior of eighteen House members at home in their districts. Fenno discovered that many of the ideas discussed in Erving Goffman's *The Presentation of Self in Everyday Life*, which deals with the nuances of everyday encounters between average human beings, apply to the interaction between the representative and his or her constituents in the district. The nature of this interaction captures the essence of what Fenno calls homestyle.

In all such encounters, says Goffman, the performer will seek to control the response of others to him by expressing himself in ways that leave the correct impression of himself with others. His expression will be of two sorts—"the expression that he gives and the expression that he gives off." The first is mostly verbal; the second is mostly nonverbal. Goffman is particularly interested in the second kind of expression—"the more theatrical and contextual kind"—because he believes that the performer is more likely to be judged by others according to the nonverbal than the verbal elements of the presentation of self.

Those who must do the judging, Goffman says, will think that the verbal expressions are more controllable and manipulable by the performer; and they will, therefore, read his nonverbal "signs" as a check on the reliability of his verbal "signs." Basic to this reasoning is the idea that, of necessity, every presentation has a largely "promissory character" to it. Those who listen to and watch the performance cannot be sure what the relationship between them and the performer really is. So the relationship must be sustained, on the part of those watching, by inference. They "must accept the individual on faith." In this process of acceptance, they will rely heavily on the inference they draw from his nonverbal expressions—the expressions "given off."[30]

This "acceptance on faith" is similar to the idea expressed earlier in this section by Pitkin: The crucial test of symbolic representation is whether the representative is believed in by his or her constituents. Such belief is based more on the nonverbal signs a representative gives off than it is on specific policy positions. "People don't make up their minds on the basis of reading all our position papers," observes one congressional member in Fenno's study. "We have twenty-six of them, because some people are interested. But most people get a gut feeling about the kind of human being they want to represent them."[31] Another representative comments:

My constituents don't know how I vote, but they know me and they trust me. . . . They say to themselves, "everything we know about him tells us he's up there doing a good job for us." It's a blind faith type of thing.[32]

Fenno discovered that constituents' trust in the representative was the most important part of this relationship and went on to specify some of the essential components of that trust. First, the representatives must assure their listeners that they understand the job of representative and have the necessary experience and intelligence to hold their own in a collegial body of verbal and ambitious people. Their constituents must believe that they are qualified to represent them. Second, the representatives must convey a sense of identification with their constituents. The constituents must be assured that a representative is one of them, or at least thinks as they do. Some of the qualities of descriptive representation discussed in the previous section help representatives to convey that impression. A third component, one that can exist even in the absence of descriptive or identification ties, is empathy. Even if the representatives are quite different from most of their constituents in terms of background, they can sometimes capture the trust of people in their districts by convincing them that they think as they do or put themselves in their shoes to make decisions. Successful home-style symbolic representation builds on all three of these components and is manifested in a sense of trust that constituents have for the representative as a person.

What is it about this type of representation in Washington and in the district that makes it symbolic representation? What characteristic is common to both? In her chapter on the subject, Pitkin discusses how symbols "are often said to represent something, to make it present by their presence, although it is not present in fact."[33] This is the sense in which the flag is said to represent the entire nation or the president to represent the government. What, then, is "not present in fact" in the types of symbolic representation we have discussed? In the case of symbolic representation in Washington, the answer is policy. In the case of symbolic representation in the district, the answer seems to be the government, or more specifically, Congress.

The discussion of Washington-style symbolic representation emphasized the separation between individual position taking and the passing of legislation and the separation between policy enactment and policy implementation. By simply taking positions on issues or by introducing or cosponsoring measures that will never pass, legislators are able to present the appearance of a policy that is in fact not there.

The discussion of home-style symbolic representation suggests another distinction—the one between the individual representative and the institution of Congress. In Chapter 1, we saw that constituents make separate judgments about the performance of Congress as an institution and that of their own representatives. That distinction is reinforced by the nature of symbolic representation in the district. The focus of homestyle is the individual not the institution. There is, in fact, an anti-Congress or antigovernment theme to much of that representation.[34] Members are perceived as representatives *to* the government rather than representatives *of* the government. What is lacking in both types of symbolic representation, then, is a policy accountability by elected officials that many consider to be the essence of representative democracy.

Substantive Representation: Delegate or Trustee

Substantive representation has to do more with the entire range of representatives' behavior than with district population, background characteristics, or general feelings of trust by constituents. Here is Pitkin's definition:

> Representing here means acting in the interest of the represented, in a manner responsive to them. The representative must act independently; his action must involve discretion and judgement; he must be the one who acts. The represented must also be (conceived as) capable of independent action and judgement, not merely being taken care of. And, despite the resulting potential for conflict between representative and represented about what is to be done, that conflict must not normally take place. The representative must act in such a way that there is no conflict or if it occurs an explanation is called for. He must not be found persistently at odds with the wishes of the represented without good reason in terms of their interest, without a good explanation of why their wishes are not in accord with their interest.[35]

Policies and decision making lie at the heart of substantive representation. Two general approaches to making the many choices required of representatives stand out in discussions of this topic. A representative can elect to follow either a trustee role or a delegate role in voting on policy.

Acting in the role of trustee, the representative votes for what he or she considers to be in the best interests of constituents, regardless of those constituents' own expressed preferences. Edmund Burke captured the essence of the trustee role when he said: "Your representative owes you, not his industry only, but his judgment; and he betrays, instead of serving you, if he sacrifices it to your opinion."[36] A legislator acting as a trustee will vote in accord with his or her own judgment after studying the legislation carefully and deciding what is in the interest of constituents and the country as a whole.

Senate Democratic leader Robert Byrd articulated the Burkean concept of the legislator as trustee in the 1978 Senate debate over ratification of the Panama Canal treaties:

> There's no political mileage in voting for the treaties. I know what my constituents are saying. But I have a responsibility

not only to follow them, but to inform them and lead them. I'm not going to betray my responsibility to my constituents. I owe them not only my industry but my judgment. That's why they send me here.[37]

Underlying this role is a belief that constituents' preferences and their interests are often quite different. It is pointed out that preferences fluctuate even when interests do not. The true representative, it is argued, should consistently represent those interests and not change his or her position in accord with changes in public opinion. Supporters of the trustee role say that constituents do not have the information that the legislator has and therefore cannot really evaluate the legislation at hand. "I figure if they knew what I know, they would understand my vote," is the way one legislator put it. Another says:

I am sent here as a representative of 600,000 people. They are supposed to be voting on all the legislation. I try to follow my constituents—to ignore them would be a breach of trust—but I use my judgment often because they are misinformed. I know that they would vote as I do if they had the facts that I have.[38]

The delegate role stands in sharp contrast to that of trustee. Instead of relying on his or her own judgment and conscience, a delegate is expected to vote in accordance with majority opinion in his or her constituency. Parker Godwin expressed a rather extreme conception of the delegate role in his *Political Essays:* "A representative is but the mouthpiece and organ of his constituents. What we want in legislation as in other trusts, are honest fiduciaries, men who will perform their duties according to our wishes."[39]

One of the differences between trustees and delegates is how they define the national interest. Trustees reject the notion that they best serve the country's interests by always reflecting the wishes of their districts. They will argue that by voting in accordance with their own evaluation of the national interest and by considering the cues given by the party or by the president, they are being more responsible representatives. For trustees, what is good for their districts is not necessarily what is good for the nation. Since the welfare of the district is greatly dependent on the national welfare, trustees feel they serve the former by voting for policies that help the country as a whole.

Delegates define the national interest as being that which is best for a majority of the districts. The national welfare is seen as the sum of the individual districts' welfare:

> I'm here to represent my district. This is part of my actual belief as to the function of a congressman. What is good for the majority of districts is good for the country. What snarls up the system is these so-called statesman-congressmen who vote for what they think is the country's best interest.[40]

The trustee-delegate distinction provides standards for evaluating representation and permits us to see differences in how legislators feel that they can best serve as representatives. But the distinction also oversimplifies reality. It is based on an assumption that the legislator knows what a majority of his or her constituents want. As V. O. Key has pointed out, however:

> the question of whether a legislator should be a man and vote his mature convictions in the national interest or be a mouse and bow abjectly to the parochial demands of his constituents is irrelevant, . . . generally, a legislator may hear from a few people on a few issues. He must always, as he votes, assume the risk of antagonizing some constituents, but he is rarely faced by the difficult choice of rejecting or accepting the mandate of his constituency, for he does not know what it is. And, indeed, there may be none.[41]

A solution to this problem is provided by a third representational role, that of politico, which in effect combines the trustee and delegate roles. One reason for adopting this role is the realization that the legislator often does not have information as to constituency opinion on many issues. Although the legislator is essentially a delegate, he or she may feel that this lack of information requires him or her to be a trustee in some situations. When Abraham Lincoln was running for reelection to the Illinois General Assembly, he outlined this politico role based on limited information: "If elected, I shall be governed by their will on all such subjects upon which I have the means of knowing what their will is, and upon all others I shall do what my own judgment teaches me will best advance their interests."[42]

Issues differ in importance to legislators and that provides another reason for adopting the politico role. Legislators may feel that some issues are so important that they must vote against their constituents' wishes. This occurs regardless of the amount of information about constituency opinion that legislators have. The comments of former Arkansas Sen. William Fulbright illustrate this aspect of the politico role:

> The average legislator early in his career discovers that there are certain interests, or prejudices, of his constituents which are dangerous to trifle with. Some of these prejudices may not be of fundamental importance to the welfare of the nation, in which case he is justified in humoring them, even though he may disapprove. The difficult case is where the prejudice concerns fundamental policy affecting the national welfare. . . .
>
> As an example of what I mean, let us take the poll-tax issue and isolationism. Regardless of how persuasive my colleagues or the national press may be about the evils of the poll-tax, I do not see its fundamental importance, and I shall follow the views of the people of my state. . . . On the other hand regardless of how strongly opposed my constituents may prove to be to the creation of, and participation in, an ever stronger United Nations Organization, I could not follow such a policy in that field unless it becomes clearly hopeless.[43]

These distinctions that legislators made over the years suggest that instead of classifying someone as a delegate or a trustee, it is likely to be more accurate to say that on some issues a legislator acts as a trustee and on others as a delegate. The delegate and trustee roles provide individual members of Congress with alternative styles of representation, both of which are accepted as substantive representation. These differences are seen not just in how legislators vote, but in their focus on issues and in their overall approach to the job of representative or senator.

The contrasting styles of representation displayed by New York Sens. Daniel Patrick Moynihan and Alfonse M. D'Amato illustrate some of these differences. New York officials who work with both men describe Moynihan in terms associated with a trustee role and D'Amato as more of a delegate. While Moynihan is seen as an important spokesman on national and international issues, D'Amato is highly regarded as an advocate of projects and programs to benefit state and local interests in New York. Both senators, of course, must vote on both types of issues; the difference between the two comes out in the effort and time that they give to those issues. The comments of an important county official in New York illustrate the difference: "Moynihan is more involved in philosophical things. . . . D'Amato wants to know why the heck the wheels are coming off the subways." New York City Mayor Ed Koch draws the same distinction between the state's two senators: "You would go to D'Amato if you wanted to get your passport expedited, but if you want a discussion on policy toward the People's Republic of China, you'd go to Moynihan."[44]

In seeking to explain Senator D'Amato's emphasis on the delegate role and local focus and Senator Moynihan's on a more trustee role and national orientation, observers have pointed to the different backgrounds of the two men. Before his election to the Senate in 1976, Moynihan was a government professor at Harvard who had taken leaves to serve in the Labor Department, on the White House staff, and as U.S. ambassador to India and to the United Nations. In contrast, Senator D'Amato had served for fifteen years as an official of Nassau County in New York before being elected senator in 1980. Another reason often given for the two senators' different styles of representation was the nature of their election to the Senate. Mayor Koch and other officials pointed out that Moynihan had been reelected in 1982 with 65 percent of the vote, while D'Amato had won a three-way race in 1980 with only 40 percent of the vote. A safe margin of victory, in other words, is said to give a legislator the freedom to act as a trustee.

Explaining differences in representational style by looking at elections calls attention to the importance of elections and the different activities that elections include to substantive representation. There are three types of activity implicit in Pitkin's definition of substantive representation cited earlier—the representative's actions, his or her explanations for those actions, and the independent action of those who are represented. Congressional elections serve to link all three of those activities. To understand congressional representation in this substantive sense, then, we need to have a close look at the nature of congressional elections.

Endnotes

1. Donald L. Robinson, ed., *Reforming American Government: The Bicentennial Papers of the Committee on the Constitutional System* (Boulder, Colo.: Westview, 1985).

2. Richard Bolling, U.S. Congress, House, *Hearings Before the Se-*

lect Committee on Committees, Ninety-third Congress, first session, vol. 3, September 21, 1973, p. 215. Richard Fenno also discussed the lawmaking-representational conflict in Homestyle: House Members in Their Districts (Boston: Little, Brown, 1978), pp. 244–45.

3. Ann Cooper, "Congressional Term Limits Get More Support, but Still Unpopular on Hill," Congressional Quarterly Weekly Report, February 25, 1978, p. 533. The 1982 Gallup poll is cited in Robinson, Reforming American Government, p. 284.

4. The arguments here are from Catharine W. Trauernicht, "Pro and Con Arguments for Limiting Congressional Terms," Foundation for the Study of Presidential and Congressional Terms, Washington, D.C., correspondence to the author, February 26, 1979. Additional information on all these points may be found in U.S. Congress, Senate, Congressional Tenure, Hearings Before the Subcommittee on the Constitution of the Committee on the Judiciary, Ninety-fifth Congress, second session, March 16, 1978; and Ann Cooper, "Congressional Term Limits Get More Public Support, but Still Unpopular on Hill," p. 534.

5. Ibid.

6. Hannah Fenichel Pitkin, The Concept of Representation (Berkeley: University of California Press, 1967), p. 43.

7. Thomas Hobbes, Leviathan (New York: Collier Books Edition, 1962), p. 127.

8. Joseph Tussman, "The Political Theory of Thomas Hobbes" (Ph.D. dissertation, 1947), quoted in Pitkin, The Concept of Representation, p. 43.

9. Kirkpatrick v. Preisler, 394 U.S. 526 (1969), and Karcher v. Daggett, 462, U.S. 725 (1983).

10. Elder Witt, "As Some Justices Seek Equal Districts, Others Dispute 'Pursuit of Precision,'" Congressional Quarterly Weekly Report, September 28, 1985, p. 1941.

11. Davis v. Bandemer (1986), in Frederick Schauer, 1986 Supplement to Constitutional Law, 11th ed. (Mineola, N.Y.: Foundation Press, 1986), pp. 183–84. See also: Phil Gailey, "Justices Uphold Partisan Lines in Redistricting," New York Times, July 1, 1986, pp. 1 and 17; and Elder Witt, "Court Settles Voting Issues, Other Major Controversies," Congressional Quarterly Weekly Report, July 5, 1986, pp. 1523–27.

12. John Adams, "Letter to John Penn," quoted in Pitkin, The Concept of Representation, p. 60.

13. Jim Wright, You and Your Congressman (New York: Coward-McCann, 1965), p. 15.

14. John Wahlke, Heinz Eulau, William Buchanan, and Leroy Ferguson, The Legislative System: Explorations in Legislative Behavior (New York: John Wiley and Sons, 1962), p. 253.

15. George B. Galloway, History of the House of Representatives (New York: Thomas Y. Crowell, 1968), p. 35.

16. Norman Ornstein et al., *Vital Statistics on Congress, 1984–1985* (Washington, D.C.: American Enterprise Institute, 1984), pp. 21, 24.

17. Garry Wills, "Hurray for Politicians," *Harpers*, September, 1975, p. 49.

18. Alan Ehrenhalt, "Congress Is Getting Younger All the Time," *Congressional Quarterly Weekly Report*, January 27, 1979, p. 154.

19. Representatives Downey and Gephardt, quoted in Steven V. Roberts, "The New Wave Starts to Crest on Capitol Hill," *New York Times*, December 9, 1984, p. 2E.

20. Alan Ehrenhalt, "Most Members of Congress Claim Religious Affiliation," *Congressional Quarterly Weekly Report*, January 3, 1981, p. 3.

21. Christopher Buchanan, "Why Aren't There More Women in Congress?" *Congressional Quarterly Weekly Report*, August 12, 1978, p. 2108.

22. Irwin N. Gertzog, *Congressional Women* (New York: Praeger, 1984), p. 251.

23. Donald R. Matthews, *U.S. Senators and Their World* (New York: Vintage, 1960), p. 45.

24. Mark Green, quoted in Steven V. Roberts, "The Rich Get Richer and Elected," *New York Times*, September 24, 1985, p. A26.

25. Pitkin, *The Concept of Representation*, p. 102.

26. David R. Mayhew, *Congress: The Electoral Connection* (New Haven: Yale University Press, 1974), p. 132.

27. Richard L. Madden, "Buckley after 100 Days in Washington: At Ease in Senate Role," *New York Times*, May 2, 1971, p. 20.

28. Representative Frank, quoted in John Robinson, "Textile Quotas Get House O.K.," *Boston Globe*, October 11, 1985, p. 12.

29. Murray Edelman, *The Symbolic Uses of Politics* (Urbana: University of Illinois Press, 1967).

30. Fenno, *Homestyle: House Members in Their Districts*, pp. 54–55.

31. Ibid., p. 95.

32. Ibid., p. 152.

33. Pitkin, *The Concept of Representation*, p. 92

34. Fenno, *Homestyle*, pp. 244–47.

35. Pitkin, *The Concept of Representation*, pp. 209–10.

36. Edmund Burke, "Speech to the Electors of Bristol," *Writings and Speeches of Edmund Burke* (Boston: Little, Brown, 1901), vol. 2, pp. 93–98.

37. Senator Byrd, quoted in "Senate Debators Call Canal Treaty Unpopular Issue," *Boston Globe*, February 10, 1978, p. 5.

38. Charles O. Jones, "The Agriculture Committee and the Problem of Representation," in Robert Peabody and Nelson Polsby, *New Perspectives on the House of Representatives*, 3rd ed. (New York: Rand McNally, 1977,), p. 181.

39. Quoted in Alfred de Grazia, "The Representative Ought to Consult the Majority," in Neal Riemer, ed., *The Representative* (Lexington, Mass.: D. C. Heath, 1967), p. 38.

40. Lewis Anthony Dexter, "The Representative and His District," in Peabody and Polsby, *New Perspectives on the House of Representatives*, pp. 5–6.

41. V. O. Key, Jr., *Public Opinion and American Democracy* (New York: Alfred A. Knopf, 1964), pp. 482–83.

42. Quoted in T. V. Smith, "Congress Must Follow the Popular Will," in Neal Riemer, ed., *The Representative*, p. 44.

43. Senator Fulbright, quoted in *The Elite and the Electorate* (Santa Barbara, Calif.: Center for the Study of Democratic Institutions, 1963), p. 6.

44. Nassau County Executive Francis T. Purcell and New York City Mayor Ed Koch, quoted in Frank Lynn, "Two Senators: More Than A Contrast In Styles," *New York Times*, September 13, 1983, p. B1.

3

Elytions

"I basically really like campaigning," declared one House member, and then went on to say why it was good that he did. "I am in a situation where I think, as everybody does, the first thing you start to worry about after you win the last one is winning the next one."[1] A former representative now in the Senate had this observation: "People say to me, 'Aren't you glad you're in for six years?' I say, 'No.' I always liked campaigning. I always won big in elections. I'll campaign just as often as a senator as I did in the House and in exactly the same way."[2] Members of the House and Senate, particularly those senators who are nearing the end of their six-year term, often describe their job as a never-ending campaign. And just as military leaders are said to be always planning to fight the last war, congressional campaigners look to past elections in trying to figure out how to win the next one.

Congressional campaigns are built on both a looking backward in order to draw lessons from past elections and a looking forward in trying to determine which issues, candidates, and events will be important in the coming election. The congressional elections of any particular year will be decided by voters who have been influenced by the past behavior and anticipated future behavior of challengers and incumbents. How those candidates behave will, in turn, be influenced by the behavior of candidates and voters in previous elections and judgments about the anticipated behavior of voters on election day. As a result, any analysis of the congressional elections of November 4, 1986, for example, must consider not only what voters decided on that particular day, but a wide range of activities by voters and candidates before and after that date.

The 1986 election results can be expressed in different ways. Democrats gained eight Senate seats and a 55 to 45 majority in that chamber, despite vigorous personal campaigning by President Reagan in behalf of Republican candidates. Democrats also added to their margin in the House of Representatives by picking up five additional seats to give them a 258 to 177 House majority in the One-hundredth Congress. Voters returned 75 percent of the incumbent senators and 98 percent of the incumbent representatives running for reelection. Unlike the midterm elections in 1982, when a recession had made the economy an overriding national issue, there was no dominant national issues in 1986. The total of $342 million spent on House and Senate races in 1986 was $80 million more than the amount spent in 1984. However, only half of the top spenders among Senate candidates won their races, and patterns of campaign funding continued to favor incumbents. Only three of every eight persons eligible to vote did so in 1986— one of the lowest turnout rates in more than forty years.

All of those considerations relate to what the voters decided on November 4, 1986. But the day after the 1986 elections, political analysts were discussing the effects of those results on presidential and congressional campaigns for 1988; and members of Congress were considering how the 1986 results should influence their own behavior as public officials and candidates in the future. That activity is some of the looking forward that is involved in any election. But analysis of the 1986 results must also include a looking backward and an evaluation of earlier events that had some effect on the outcome of the election. In the next section, we will consider some illustrations of that point.

Past Elections, Congressional Votes, and Future Elections

The House of Representatives passed an omnibus trade bill on May 22, 1986, which called for a strong response to countries that discriminated against U.S. exports. The House passed the bill by the overwhelming margin of 295–115, with only 4 Democratic representatives voting against it. And even though the Reagan administration had denounced the bill as protectionist legislation that would create a world-wide trade war, 59 House Republicans—almost one-third of that chamber's Republican membership—voted against the president and for the bill. *Congressional Quarterly's* Steven Pressman had this to say about that vote: "The lopsided margin seemed to reflect the election-year zeal of many members to stake out a get-tough attitude toward the nation's trade problems."[3] The head of the Democratic Congressional Campaign Committee, California Rep. Tony Coelho, had in fact called for House Democrats to take what he called "an aggressive stance" on trade issues in their 1986 campaigns, and the Republican vote on the bill was interpreted as a recognition of foreign trade policy as a campaign issue.[4]

Why was trade policy considered to be a campaign issue in 1986? At least in part, because it was one of the lessons that Coelho and other representatives had drawn from a special election which was held in the First District of Texas in August 1985, to replace an incumbent who had been named a federal judge. In that election, Democrat Jim Chapman defeated Republican Edd Hargett even though the national Republican party had given Hargett's campaign the highest priority and over $1 million. Responding to a campaign discussion of the nation's foreign trade deficit, Hargett was quoted in a local newspaper as saying, "I don't know what trade policies have to do with bringing jobs to East Texas." Chapman hammered at Hargett's statement in his campaign ads and personal appearances and blamed the Reagan administration's trade policies for the loss of jobs at a local steel plant and a nearby telephone manufacturing facility. Traditional Democratic voting in the district and differences in the two candidates' political experience were said to have some influence on the outcome, but knowledgeable political observers in the district were said to agree that "foreign trade gave Chapman the edge, the chance to overcome a previously hopeless-seeming deficit in all the polls."[5] That was the message of the 1985 special election that was incorporated into the campaigns of many House Democrats in 1986.

Farm policies represented another campaign issue in 1986, one that was of particular importance to many representatives and senators from the Midwest. A depressed farm economy characterized by low crop prices, high debt, and declining land values made farm policies a salient issue in a number of 1986 congressional races.

In addition to immediate causes, the memories of a midterm election nearly thirty years earlier increased the saliency of farm policies to the campaigns of some midwestern senators and representatives in 1986. Discontent with the farm policies of the Eisenhower administration was the major reason given for the loss of twenty-three Republican House seats and four Senate seats in the 1958 election. That election gave the Democrats a huge 283–152 majority in the House and a 66–34 margin in the Senate. Two years later the Democrats also won the presidency.

The farm policies of the Reagan administration reflected a free market approach similar to that of the Eisenhower administration, and they were similarly unpopular among farmers. Seeing these parallels led a midwestern senator to conclude, "1986 has 1958 written all over it," and a Republican state official from that region warned his colleagues that "the writing is on the wall," because the similarities between 1958 and 1986 "are indeed startling, with one glaring exception—this year the problems are real, not simply perceived."[6]

In 1958, Republican legislators from the Midwest supported the Republican administration's position of cutting prices supports. But midwestern Republicans holding office three decades later knew of that history and sought not to repeat it. Midwestern House Republicans voted 45–6 against the Reagan farm bill in October 1985, and midwestern Republican senators up for reelection in 1986 voted against key provisions of the administration's farm policies in that chamber a month later. A similar pattern could be seen back in the home districts, where many midwestern Republican legislators found different ways to follow the advice of an Iowa Farm Bureau official: "Anyone that wants to stay in office here better get the heck away from Reagan."[7] Kansas Republican Rep. Pat Roberts did that with bumper stickers saying "I'm Mad Too, Pat." Newspaper petitions under the heading, "Wake up Washington," represented one approach used by House Republican Vin Weber of Minnesota. In addition, Weber changed from a "town meeting" format of district visits to one-on-one sessions to hear the problems of individual constituents and actively courted protest groups representing angry farmers and rural interests. "I think most of what I have done is true of incumbents across the farm belt," said the

Minnesota Republican. "This is not a problem that snuck up on us. All of us have changed our behavior."[8]

The Ninety-ninth Congress (1985–1986), like any Congress, provided other examples of the ways in which members' behavior in Washington and at home is continually being influenced by both past and future campaigns and elections. One reason given for the June 1985 House defeat of the Democratic alternative to President Reagan's request for $100 in aid for antigovernment rebels in Nicaragua was that the Democrat's proposal required a House vote on military aid in October, just before the 1986 elections. In his analysis of House action on tax reform, *New York Times* reporter Steven Roberts wrote that Democratic leaders knew that the party had mishandled the tax issue in the 1984 campaign and that House members in the 1985 debate "advanced themes and arguments that were aimed as much at next year's congressional elections as at tax overhaul."[9]

What is clear in all of these discussions is the critical role that elections play in the politics of Congress. What should also be evident is that the impact of elections goes far beyond the decisions made by voters on a particular election day on who will represent them in Congress. For the behavior of senators and representatives will be based on how they answer questions about a whole series of elections rather than just one. What made the 1986 elections different from those of 1958 for incumbent Republicans from the Midwest? Why did the foreign trade issue help the Democratic candidate in Texas in 1985 and that party's candidates in some districts in 1986 but not in others? Did congressional action on tax reform help Democrats to overcome their liability on the issue of taxes that was clear in the 1984 election?

Elections have a direct effect in that they determine who will sit in Congress for the following term. But the interpretations of elections, especially senators' and representatives' interpretations, are what give elections such a lasting effect on the politics of Congress. Those interpretations depend, to some extent, on the questions being asked. For example, do we (and they) want to know:

1. Why did the 1986 elections produce an eighty-one seat Democratic margin in the House of Representatives and Democratic control of the Senate?

2. Why were 98 percent of the House incumbents and 75 percent of the Senate incumbents running for reelection returned to office in 1986?

3. What impact did certain issues, candidates, and campaigns have on voter preferences expressed in the 1986 congressional elections?

There is a different focus to each of those questions. The first question focuses on the collective choice of the electorate in determining the makeup of the whole Congress. The second focuses on how much real competition there is between incumbents and challengers. The third question is concerned with the campaigns of individual candidates and how voter preferences are influenced by the candidates and issues in those campaigns.

Answers to all three questions give us a sense of how representative an institution Congress really is. For it is elections that provide a link between the legislature and citizens and that induce Congress and its members to act "in the interest of the represented, in a manner responsive to them." (See "Substantive Representation" in Chapter 2.) The electoral responsiveness of Congress depends on how members and certain other people interpret congressional elections, on the answers they give to the questions of collective choice, competitive change, and voter preferences.[10]

Collective Choice: Elections as National Referenda

Congressional elections can be regarded as national events, in which voters register their opinions about the current administration, about party programs, and about the economic and general well-being both of themselves and of the country as a whole. That view of congressional elections focuses on the collective choice of voters on election day. Together, voters determine what the overall makeup of the legislature will be and provide some policy direction to Congress as a whole. What do midwestern farmers think of the Reagan administration's farm policies? Do voters see a connection between a foreign trade deficit and jobs in the state or district? Which party is considered more capable on economic and foreign policy issues? Do the election results increase or decrease the chances of the president's military budget being approved by the next Congress? As we have already seen, those are some of the questions about congressional elections often asked by political observers and members themselves.

If the behavior of congressional candidates and incumbents is affected by the answers to such questions, then it is important to understand this view of congressional elections. A collective-choice view of congressional elections can be seen in assessments of congressional elections that link those elections with presidential performance and those that consider the collective decisions of particular elections as policy mandates. We find these kinds of evaluations even for elections in which there is little evidence of a national trend. For example, Democrats claimed that the Republican's loss of twenty-six House seats in the 1982 election signaled voters' rejection of Reagan administration policies, while the president and Republican leaders said they were pleased because they lost fewer House seats than the president's party traditionally loses in midterm elections. Four years after that election, House Democrats of the class of 1982 were still voting and talking in terms of their shared "mandate" to reduce budget deficits. The striking unity on this issue among the fifty-one Democrats of the class of 1982 still serving in May 1986 was an important factor in the House passage of a fiscal 1987 budget cutting the budget deficit for that year $7 billion below the Gramm-Rudman requirement of $144 billion.[11]

As the House vote on the fiscal 1987 budget suggests, collective-choice explanations can be applied both to electoral outcomes and to congressional policies. Table 3–1 provides aggregate data on party gains and losses in congressional elections from 1946 to 1986. The 1958 Republican losses still influencing the behavior of midwestern Republicans in 1986 can be seen in Table 3–1, as can the Democratic gains that helped to produce the unified class of 1982 discussed previously. Congressional passage of the administration's budget and tax programs in 1981 was linked to the "Reagan mandate" of 1980. The source of the large "Reagan class" of Republican senators up for reelection in 1986 was also evident in the 1980 figures shown in Table 3–1.

It is the explanations of the historical shifts seen in Table 3–1, rather than the patterns themselves, that illustrate the collective-choice view of congressional elections. Political leaders and scholars have explained the patterns seen there as follows.[12] Inflation and other economic problems associated with demobi-

TABLE 3-1 Net Party Shift in House and Senate Seats, 1946–1984

Year	House	Senate	President's Party
1946	56 R	13 R	D
1948	75 D	9 D	D
1950	28 R	5 R	D
1952	22 R	1 R	R
1954	19 D	2 D	R
1956	2 D	1 D	R
1958	49 D	15 D	R
1960	22 R	2 R	D
1962	1 R	3 D	D
1964	37 D	1 D	D
1966	47 R	4 R	D
1968	5 R	6 R	R
1970	12 D	2 R	R
1972	12 R	2 D	R
1974	49 D	4 D	R
1976	1 D	0	D
1978	15 R	3 R	D
1980	33 R	12 R	R
1982	26 D	1 R	R
1984	14 R	2 D	R
1986[a]	5 D	8 D	R

Source: Gary C. Jacobson, *The Politics of Congressional Elections* (Boston: Little, Brown, 1987), p. 142.

[a] Figures for 1986 compiled by author.

lization after World War II led many voters to turn against the incumbent Democrats and support Republican challengers in 1946. The Democratic gains of 1948 reflect voters' response to President Truman's campaign and their dissatisfaction with the economic policies of the Republican Congress. The unpopularity of the Truman administration and a positive response to the candidacy of Dwight Eisenhower worked to the advantage of Republican congressional candidates in 1950 and 1952. A major recession and a rejection of Republican farm policies accounted for the strong shift to the Democrats in 1958. President Lyndon Johnson's landslide victory over Barry Goldwater in 1964 and growing dissatisfaction with Johnson administration foreign policy in 1966 help to explain the shifts seen in those years. The Watergate scandal of the Nixon administration and a sluggish economy worked to the Democrats' advantage in 1974. Voters' rejection of the Carter administration in 1980 and the combination of high popular approval of President Reagan and satisfaction with the economy in 1984 are reflected in the Republican gains of those years. These are some of the conventional explanations for the patterns in congressional elections reflected in Table 3–1.

But the collective behavior of voters in congressional elections represents only one part of the collective-choice perspective. For Congress to be considered electorally responsive, there must also be collective action on the part of Congress. We have already seen how the 1986 House vote on the foreign trade bill, the 1985 House and Senate votes on farm policy, and the 1981 budget and tax cut policies were linked with elections. Similar explanations have been offered for a number of the major policies adopted by Congress over the years. Social Security and other New Deal programs were a direct product of Democratic victories in the 1932 and 1934 elections. The Eighty-ninth Congress elected in 1964 passed Great Society legislation such as Medicare and the Voting Rights Act. Many of the congressional reforms of the 1970s have been attributed to the priority given government reform in the campaigns of House Democrats first elected in 1974—a group of seventy-five members collectively known as "the Watergate babies." And the program and budget cuts of the Ninety-seventh Congress (1981–1983) reflected the Republican gains and the perceived mandate of the 1980 elections. In all of these cases, the collective action of Congress is linked to members' perceptions of the collective choice of voters in congressional elections.

A question of interest to both scholars and candidates is what factors have the greatest impact on election outcomes? The state of the economy and presidential approval are two answers often given to that question. Edward Tufte's research on congressional elections confirmed what political leaders and candidates had been saying for some time—the number of seats won by the president's party in congressional elections was systematically related to the state of the economy and presidential popularity. Tufte found that the percentage change in per capita income in the year preceding the election and the president's Gallup poll standing at election time directly affected the outcome of congressional elections in both midterm and presidential election years. "The difference between a mediocre and a buoyant election-year economy," Tufte concluded, "has counted for shifts of three or four percentage points in the vote, which translates into an equivalent swing of 25 to 45 House seats. And that is a very big difference."[13] Congressional elections, according to this research, are collective decisions that reflect voters' judgments about the president and his party's management of the economy. A number of studies subsequent to Tufte's have found, among other things, that economic conditions have even more effect on Senate elections and that congressional incumbents from the president's party are the ones whose electoral fortunes are most directly affected by the state of the economy.[14]

Collective-choice studies, in fact, are often directed at the traditional loss of House seats in midterm elections by the president's party, a pattern that is evident in Table 3–1. Since 1946, the party that controlled the presidency has lost an average of just under thirty House seats in midterm elections. But the actual number of seats lost by the in-party has ranged from four to fifty-five during that period, and the average seat loss in the midterm election in a president's second term (forty-four) has been three times that of the first term (fourteen). Economic and presidential-approval explanations appear whenever analysts try to predict the expected losses of the president's party, or to explain why those losses are above or below average.

But there are limits to this view of congressional elections. One limit is, that this view is based on an assumption that voters' decisions about congressional candidates are influenced primarily by evaluations of the economy and administration performance. Yet most studies of individual voters and how they make up their minds have found that local issues and judgments about the local campaign and candidates override national considerations. Another limit on collective-choice explanations results from the impact that incumbency has on congressional elections. The great advantage that incumbents have in congressional elections serves to insulate them from the effects of national trends. A collective-choice view of congressional elections can lead us to expect more change in congressional elections than is normally the case. Republican losses in 1982, for example, were noticeably fewer than the number predicted on the basis of the economy and presidential approval ratings of the time. More than 90 percent of the incumbent representatives and senators running for reelection in that year were returned to office. That pattern of incumbency success sets limits on the impact of national forces on congressional elections.

Competitive Change: Incumbent Success

The 1986 congressional elections consisted of 435 elections for seats in the House of Representatives and 34 for Senate seats. But as Alan Ehrenhalt pointed out early in that election year, "there are almost as many real contests in the Senate as there are in the House." The estimates of congressional campaign directors from both parties that only 40 House districts would have real contests led Ehrenhalt to describe the House campaign for the One-hundredth Congress (1987–1988) as "a laboratory event, waged in a relative handful of places, where both parties seem to agree the outcome is in doubt."[15] Since the Republican Congressional Campaign Committee had enough funds to give the legal maximum of $50,000 to GOP candidates in 200 districts and the Democratic Committee only enough to cover 40 districts, the shortage of genuine House contests worked to the advantage of Democrats. The smaller the playing field, to use the argot of campaign specialists, the greater the impact is of the Democrat's limited campaign funds.

This lack of real competition in nearly 400 House districts also helped Democrats because of that party's nearly seventy-seat advantage over Republicans going into the 1986 elections. But the fact that so many incumbents could win their races essentially by default raises additional questions about the electoral responsiveness of Congress. Competitive elections can increase congressional responsiveness by increasing the incidence of turnover among members and by making incumbents accountable for their actions, even if voters decide to return them to office.

Elections do bring new blood into Congress. It is true that nine of every ten House members seeking reelection have been successful over the past forty years, and that even though they are more vulnerable to defeat, seven of ten incumbent senators seeking reelection have been returned to office during that same period. But members of Congress leave the institution through retirement, resignation, or death in office, as well as through defeat at the polls. And congressional elections without incumbents in the running are more likely to be competitive races. All of these factors have helped to produce a regular turnover of members over the same forty-year period, one that is reflected in the fact that freshmen legislators have accounted for an average of 15 percent of the total House membership and of 40 percent of the total Senate membership at any given time.

Membership change is one of the ways that competitiveness can enhance the electoral responsiveness of Congress. Incumbents' success in winning reelection clearly limits the degree of responsiveness that can be achieved through turnover. But competitiveness can help to make Congress a responsive institution even if it produces little change in membership. Close races make candidates careful listeners. Congressional elections with a 90 percent incumbent reelection rate may still improve legislative responsiveness and member accountability as long as enough of those elections are in fact competitive races. We need to ask not only "Who wins?" but "By how much?" in order to get a true sense of the competitiveness of congressional elections.

Table 3–2 and Figure 3–1 help to answer the second question. The data in Table 3–2 clearly show that most House races are not competitive elections. In seven out of ten races, House incumbents are able to capture more than 60 percent of the vote. The greater competitiveness of Senate elections is also evident in Table 3–2. We have already noted that the reelection success rate of Senate incumbents has consistently been below that of House incumbents. Table 3–2 shows that even Senate incumbents who win reelection are likely to do so with less than 60 percent of the vote.

Figure 3–1 is a graphic illustration of the declining competition in House races over the past forty years. The concentration of House races toward the middle of the graph in 1948 reflects a high level of competition in those races; the elections in most House districts in that year made them marginal districts—those in which there was close to a 50–50 division of the vote. By 1972, that pattern had been dramatically reversed. The bimodal distribution for that year shows a huge dip in the number of marginal districts. Candidates either won or lost by substantial margins. This pattern led political scientist David Mayhew and other congressional scholars to find explanations for the decline in competition—to solve what Mayhew called the Case of the Vanishing Marginals.[16]

The observations of campaign specialists about the 1986 elections and the data in Figure 3–1 from recent House elections illustrate the same point: In most congressional races, there is little or no true competition between candidates and parties. The 1984 data in Figure 3–1, for example, show one cluster of House races on the left of the figure, which are districts where Republican candidates won with 60 to 75 percent of the vote; and

TABLE 3–2 House and Senate Elections Won by 60%

Year	House Incumbents Running in General Election	Percentage Won by 60%	Election Period	Senate Incumbents Running in General Election	Percentage Won by 60%
1956	403	59.1	1944–1948	61	39.3
1958	390	63.1	1950–1954	76	35.5
1960	400	58.9	1956–1960	84	42.9
1962	376	63.6			
1964	388	58.5	1962–1966	86	44.2
1966	401	67.7			
1968	397	72.2			
1970	389	77.3	1968–1972	74	44.6
1972	373	77.8			
1974	383	66.4			
1976	381	71.9	1974–1978	70	41.4
1978	377	78.0			
1980	392	72.9	1980–1984	84	40
1982	383	68.9			
1984	410	71.0	1982–1986	87	57
1986	393	85.0			

Source: Adapted from Norman J. Ornstein, Thomas E. Mann, Michael J. Malbin, Allen Schick, and John F. Bibby, *Vital Statistics on Congress, 1984–85* (Washington, D.C.: American Enterprise Institute, 1984) pp. 53 and 54; and *Congressional Quarterly Weekly Reports,* 1985–1986.

FIGURE 3–1 Patterns of Competitiveness in Congressional Elections, by Percentage of Two-Party Votes Received by Democratic Candidates, Selected Years, 1948–1984

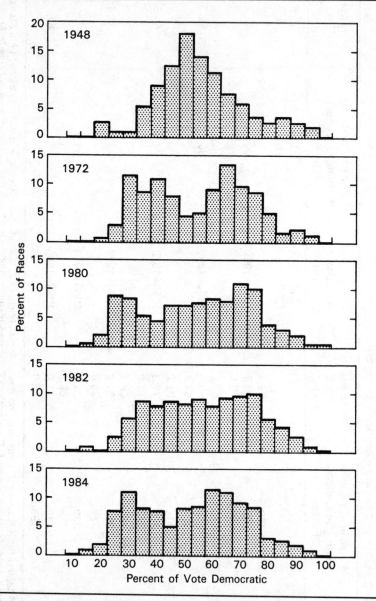

Source: John A. Ferejohn and Morris P. Fiorina, "Incumbency and Realignment in Congressional Elections," in John E. Chubb and Paul E. Peterson (eds.), *The New Direction in American Politics* (Washington, D.C.: Brookings Institution, 1985) p. 97.

another cluster on the right of the figure, which are districts where Democratic candidates won with 55 to 70 percent of the vote. The dip in the middle of the figure is a result of there being competitive elections, those in the 45 to 55 percent range, in only 48 of the 435 House districts that year. Most incumbents not only win, they win big. Incumbents' success is the single most important factor determining the nature of House elections.

How much is incumbency worth to a candidate? One way to answer that question is to look at two aspects of congressional elections—the "sophomore surge" and the "retirement slump." The sophomore surge refers to the increase in margin of victory that incumbent freshmen legislators enjoy in their second, or sophomore, election. The retirement slump refers to the falloff in the margin of victory in an election following the voluntary retirement of an incumbent.

Research on both the sophomore surge and the retirement slump suggests that the benefits of incumbency increased during the early 1970s. The average gain in percentage of the vote for House sophomores reelected in 1962–1966 was 2.7 percent, but for those reelected between 1968 and 1974, the average benefit for sophomores was a 6.6 percent increase in their vote. The other side of this same pattern, the retirement slump, showed an average loss of 2.2 percent of the vote in 1962–1966 and an average of 7.7 percent in the 1968–1974 period. What is true for House elections, however, is not the case with Senate elections. Senators running after one term do not appear to benefit from a sophomore surge the way that representatives do, although there are often retirement slumps in the first elections to replace retiring senators.[17] These and other differences between House and Senate elections suggest that the value of incumbency is greater for House candidates than it is for senators.

What accounts for the great success that incumbents have in getting reelected? Why is it generally true, in the words of political scientist and unsuccessful congressional candidate Sandy Maisel, that "if one's goal is electoral success, it is not rational to challenge an incumbent."[18] One reason for incumbents' success has been discussed in Chapter 1. Public opinion polls, you will recall, have consistently found high ratings for individual members as representatives even when Congress as an institution is rated unfavorably. Of course, the personal popularity of individual members is the result of many of the same forces that produce votes in elections. Because the public's high regard for incumbents seems to focus on personal characteristics and constituent-service activities rather than party or policy considerations, it is difficult for challengers to overcome incumbent advantage.

A number of other factors help incumbents in their reelection efforts. One factor is the number of perquisites or "perks" of office that incumbents receive as part of their job. These include a personal staff of about fifteen people for representatives and twice that for senators, a franking privilege that permits members to send mail at no cost to them, and travel allowances that pay for trips home almost every weekend. The total value of these various perquisites is generally placed between $500,000 and $1 million a year for incumbent representatives and senators. No one would argue that a representative or senator must have office and staff support and an easy means of communicating with constituents in order to carry on his or her duties. But those same activities are obviously helpful to a reelection campaign. If a challenger wished to match an incumbent's free mailing of a newsletter to each "postal patron" in a House district, that challenger would have had to spend an average of $17,000 for each mailing in 1985. The equivalent figure for any challenger seeking to match the free mass mailings of Sen. Alan Cranston, just for a three-month period in 1985, would have been $1.6 million.[19]

These resources are obviously valuable to the reelection campaigns of incumbents. They help a representative or senator to respond to constituent requests and to be a visible presence in the state or district. Another effect of incumbent perks is to increase the cost of running a credible challenger campaign in which the outside candidate seeks to provide those support services and activities that an incumbent gets free.

More than a year before the 1986 elections, a Republican and veteran of the Reagan administration named Marc Holtzman had four staff members operating a "constituent service organization" in Pennsylvania's Eleventh House District. The staff's job, said Holtzman, was "to help local residents cut federal red tape."[20] One aspect of this casework operation made it different from those seen in districts all over the country: Marc Holtzman was not an incumbent congressman.

This "casework" approach to campaigning shows a strong belief in the electoral impact of constituent services that are routinely provided by incumbents. The large House class of 1974, in particular, is credited with perfecting constituent services by such means as soliciting casework business, expanding casework staff in district offices, sending mobile offices throughout the district, and installing toll free telephone lines. On the one hand, this casework emphasis permits members to build support in the district that is not dependent on voting patterns and policy positions. On the other hand, the routinization of the casework function, especially since 1974, might limit the electoral impact of constituent service. Constituents now expect that any member of Congress will help them to solve individual problems with the government. In addition, most constituents who contact a congressional office about such a problem are already favorably disposed toward the incumbent. A study of the electoral efficacy of casework by John Johannes found that for these and other reasons the actual impact of casework on the vote is limited. Casework alone does not win votes, nor does it seem to have a lasting effect. But Johannes suggests that casework is similar to district mailings and staff resources in its being another indication of district attentiveness, and it is in that sense that it works to the advantage of incumbents.[21]

The nature of congressional districts provides incumbent House members with yet another advantage over challengers. As we saw in Chapter 2, the Supreme Court has established a strict population equality requirement for House districts. To comply with that requirement, state legislatures often must create districts whose borders do not fit with those of other political units such as cities, counties, or state legislative districts. That requirement makes these House districts separate and distinct from other political units, and it means that the incumbent House member is the only elected official who regularly deals with the House district as a whole. Any mayor, state representative, state senator, or county official who seeks to challenge an incumbent is therefore likely to have strong political ties with some parts of the House district, but not all.

All of the advantages of incumbency discussed to this point help to make incumbents known to voters in the district. Members have resources that permit communication through the mass media and through mass mailings. Constituent service and casework bring a member's staff and office into direct contact with thousands of constituents every year. And the House member is the single elected official to communicate with all constituents in terms of the district itself. Table 3–3 shows an overall effect of

TABLE 3–3 Incumbency and Voter Familiarity with Congressional Candidates, 1980–1984 (in percentages)

	Recalled Name			Recognized Name			Neither		
	'80	'82	'84	'80	'82	'84	'80	'82	'84
House Elections									
Incumbents	46	54	45	92	94	91	8	6	9
Challengers	21	26	18	54	62	54	46	38	46
Open Seats	32	29	32	82	77	80	18	23	20
Senate Elections									
Incumbents	61	61	—[a]	99	97	—	1	3	—
Challengers	40	37	—	81	78	—	19	22	—
Open Seats	47	73	—	89	95	—	11	5	—

Source: Gary C. Jacobson, *The Politics of Congressional Elections,* 2nd ed. (Boston: Little, Brown, 1987), p. 111. (Data from American National Election Studies, 1980–1984.) Copyright © 1987 by Gary C. Jacobson. Reprinted by permission of Little Brown and Company.

[a] Data not available.

these incumbency advantages—greater visibility of incumbents in congressional elections.

As the table shows, twice as many voters could recall or recognize the name of incumbent representatives than could recall the name of challengers. Senate incumbents also enjoyed an advantage over challengers in this regard, but the difference was not nearly as great as it was in the case of House races. The greater familiarity of voters with incumbents was also found to extend beyond recognition or recall. Voters were more likely to mention something they liked about incumbents than they liked about challengers, while negative comments were about evenly divided.[22] What this suggests is that the advantage of incumbent candidates grows out of their being both better known and liked by voters and not from an awareness and rejection of challengers' campaigns.

Incumbents seek to use the many resources and advantages they have to create what Rep. Jim Kolbe (R-AZ) described as "an invincible shield around you."[23] The high reelection rate of incumbents suggests that most of them are successful at doing that. But the experience of Senate incumbents in certain years and the fact that twenty to thirty or more incumbent House members are defeated every election year also suggest that incumbency alone cannot guarantee reelection. The effect of incumbency on House races certainly accounts for the low level of competitive change in that body. The impact of incumbency also serves to dampen the effects of national tides on House elections. The electoral responsiveness of Congress is determined not only by the collective-choice and competitive-change aspects of congressional elections, but also by the candidates and campaigns in individual districts.

Voter Preference: Candidates and Campaigns

In the 1984 elections, 241 House Democrats and 151 House Republicans were reelected and 13 Democratic and 3 Republican incumbents were defeated. The quality of challenger candidates was one explanation for why so few of them were able to unseat incumbents in 1984. Joe Gaylord, executive director of the National Republican Congressional Committee, felt that one difference between 1984 and preceding elections was "the awareness that incumbents could be defeated was strong in 1980 and 1982," which was not the case in 1984. Former party official and Republican consultant Ed Mahe agreed with that assessment: "We did burn up a bunch of really fine candidates in 1982." Mahe described the Republican candidates challenging House incumbents in 1984 as "less qualified, less able, less everything."[24] The 1986 Senate races, in which 16 freshman Republicans were up for reelection after six years in office, provoked a similar assessment of the quality of candidates from another Republican consultant, John Sears. Referring to the 1980 Republican sweep that carried in those 16 new Republican senators, Sears admitted: "In the wee small hours of election night, we thought, 'Had all of us known the Republicans were going to do so well, we would have run some different guys.' "[25] Gaylord and Mahe were focusing on House challengers in 1984, while Sears's analysis was based on Republican Senate candidates as both challengers in 1980 and incumbents in 1986. But the message in both cases is clear: Candidates and campaigns do make a difference in congressional elections.

In order to determine the effects of candidates and campaigns, it is necessary to look at the choices offered to voters in particular states and districts. It is also important to recognize that those choices are affected both by the national trends that produce a collective choice in elections and by the incumbency factor that limits competitive change in congressional elections. Consider, for example, a point discussed in the collective-choice section of this chapter. It was mentioned there that most political analysts and congressional candidates believe that congressional elections are greatly influenced by national issues and the state of the economy. Yet survey research has consistently found that voters look more to candidates and local considerations in deciding how to vote.

Gary Jacobson and Samuel Kernell have proposed a theory of congressional elections that can perhaps reconcile these seemingly contradictory explanations.[26] Voters may not pay much attention to national conditions and national issues, say Jacobson and Kernell, but those people who are most active politically do pay attention. These political elites, including potential candidates, make strategic decisions about who will run for a House or Senate seat on the basis of national political and economic conditions. Will it be a good year for Republicans? Does the state of the economy benefit the "in" party? Will presidential campaigning help the party's congressional races? Those are the questions that potential candidates ask in deciding whether to risk challenging an incumbent. They are also the considerations evident in Ed Mahe's observation about burning up really fine candidates in 1982 and John Sears's second thoughts about the selection of Senate candidates in 1980, which opened this section. National conditions help to determine who runs for Congress, and the quality of candidates helps to shape voters' preferences in congressional elections.

What determines whether someone running for Congress is a "good" candidate? Answers to that question are likely to be highly subjective and to depend on the nature of the district or state, the style of the incumbent, and a variety of other factors. Political scientists have tried to measure candidate quality objectively by looking at two variables—experience in electoral office and campaign spending.

Candidates who have had previous success at winning elective office are likely to be strong candidates for a number of reasons. The experience in office can be cited as a qualification, especially in the case of a state legislator running for Congress or a U.S. representative running for the Senate. Holding office also gives a candidate a certain degree of visibility. Past electoral success testifies to the campaigning abilities of the candidate and to the existence of a campaign organization. Jacobson's study of the impact of candidate quality (measured by the percentage who have held elective office) on election results from 1946–1980 led him to conclude: "The relative quality of each party's candidates is quite strongly related to how well the party does in the election."[27]

Whether experienced candidates run for Congress, in turn, depends on answers to some of the questions presented earlier. The Jacobson-Kernell "strategic politicians" thesis, you will recall, suggests that experienced candidates decide whether to challenge incumbent senators and representatives at least partly on the basis of their reading of national tides and predictions about whether it will be a good year for challengers and/or for the party. The number of experienced nonincumbent candidates will therefore vary from election to election. For example, there were 118 experienced nonincumbents running in the 1980 House elections (37 incumbents were defeated) and 88 experienced nonincumbents running for the House four years later (19 incumbents were defeated).

Potential challengers from both parties had reasons for avoiding races in 1984. Democrats could see advantages to running in a year in which Ronald Reagan was not. Republicans were more cautious in 1984 after what Ed Mahe referred to earlier as the burning up of many fine candidates in 1982; a year in which the party was thought to have sparked a high Democratic turnout and to have damaged many Republican campaigns for other offices by recruiting and running House candidates in a number of districts, particularly southern ones, where there really was no chance of that party winning a House seat. Another explanation for why there were fewer experienced House challengers in 1984 than in 1980 is that state legislatures generally favored incumbents in drawing new district lines following the 1980 census.[28]

In most congressional elections, voters are asked to choose between an incumbent member of Congress and a challenger. The "strategic politician's" approach of the preceding discussion has led us to focus on the quality of candidates and on the decisions that different potential challengers make about running. Incumbent representatives and senators do not simply sit back and wait for those decisions to be made, however. By skillfully drawing on their many resources and building that "invincible shield" around them, incumbents can discourage potentially strong challengers from entering the race. And to an incumbent seeking reelection, having no opponent is even better than having a weak opponent. As we saw earlier in the chapter, senators and representatives make strategic decisions in positioning themselves relative to the president and national issues. They can also concentrate on what we identified as the second major ingredient of a strong candidacy, campaign spending, in attempting to discourage serious opposition.

"Too many guys have big money and no opponent," suggested House Speaker Tip O'Neill during the Ninety-ninth Congress. "The idea is to get as much money as possible and scare any potential opponent away."[29] The Speaker's comments suggest a number of important points about campaign spending in congressional campaigns. One is that incumbents want large campaign treasuries not only to finance their campaigns but also to discourage potential strong challengers from entering the race. To do that, incumbents particularly need money early in the election cycle. O'Neill's comments were made some eleven months before the 1986 elections.

An experienced politician contemplating a run against an incumbent is also aware of the many resources of incumbency and the need for a challenger to do more than simply match an incumbent's campaign spending. Indeed, how much the nonincumbent candidate spends in a congressional election has been found to influence the outcome more than any other aspect of congressional campaign finance.[30] Heavy spending by an incumbent, in fact, may reflect the presence of serious opposition, and that sort of reactive spending is often associated with those incumbents who are defeated. The Speaker's phrase, "big money and no opponent," succinctly characterizes the preemptive fundraising that incumbents engage in as a way of keeping strong opponents out of the race. Preemptive fundraising has two important effects: It raises the ante for entering the race, and it cuts down on the sources of funds available to challengers.

The average price of a winning House campaign in 1984 was $325,000; in 1976 it was $87,000. The average price of a winning Senate campaign went from $600,000 in 1976 to $2.9 million in 1984.[31] Those averages serve to give a general idea of the level of spending in congressional campaigns, but it is the variation among different candidates and races that is most instructive. An example of that variation can be seen in patterns of campaign contributions by political action committees (PACs).

The growth of these organizations, whose sole function is to raise and distribute campaign funds, has made them one of the major forces of American politics in the 1980s. In the ten-year period, 1974 to 1984, the number of PACs went from 600 to 4,000; the total amount contributed by PACs to congressional campaigns increased from $12.5 million in 1974 to $104 million in 1984.[32] Who gets most of that money? Figure 3–2 clearly shows that most PAC money goes to incumbents. In 1984, House and Senate incumbents received 73 percent of the total contributed by PACs. Challengers collected only 16 percent, and 11 percent went to candidates in districts with open seats.

The incumbent advantage seen in Figure 3–2 no doubt reflects the preemptive fundraising discussed earlier and, in at least some cases, results in incumbents having no strong opponent or no opponent at all. It is not surprising that the pattern seen in Figure 3–2 carries over to campaign spending. Although spending a lot of money in a campaign can be a sign that an incumbent is in trouble, most incumbents do outspend their opponents, and they do so by a wide margin. In the 1982 elections, for example, House incumbents outspent challengers by an average of about 100 percent. Senate challengers are usually better financed than House challengers, and the 1982 spending advantage for incumbent senators was about half that of incumbent representatives.[33] But spending margins tell only part of the story.

Keep in mind that the real purpose of preemptive fundraising and campaign spending by an incumbent is not to run an expensive campaign but to weaken or to scare off opposition. And the test of such a strategy is not the relative amount of campaign spending, but whether a challenger is able to raise and spend enough money to be competitive. But in 1982, when the average cost of winning a House seat was $263,000, more than a third of the challengers in House districts spent less than $25,000—or less than one-tenth of the average it took to win.[34]

Table 3–4 illustrates the importance of challenger spending to the competitiveness of House races. The top line of that table shows that none of the House races in which the challenger spent $25,000 or less was competitive; the incumbent in those races always received 60 percent or more of the vote and usually won by 70 percent or more. The table also shows that the higher the level of challenger spending, the greater the incidence of competitive races.

FIGURE 3–2 Who Gets PAC Money?

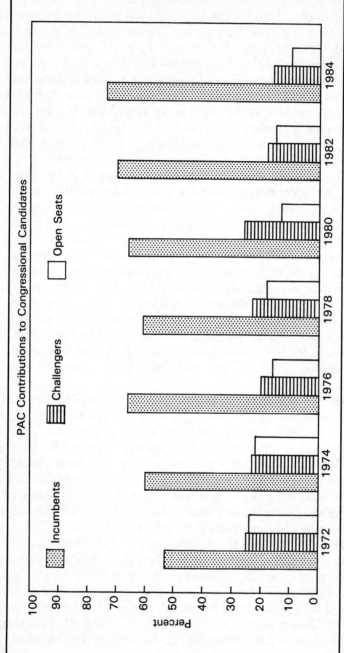

PAC Contributions to Congressional Candidates

Source: *Congressional Quarterly Weekly Report*, March 22, 1986, p. 657. Copyright 1986 Congressional Quarterly, Inc. Reprinted by permission.

TABLE 3-4 Incumbents' Share of the Vote in the 1982 House Elections, by Challenger Campaign Spending

Challenger Spending (in thousands of dollars)	Incumbents' Share of the Two-Party Vote					
	70 Percent or More	60-69 Percent	55-59 Percent	Less than 55 Percent	Total Percent	(N)
0-25	67.9	32.1	0.0	0.0	100.0	(109)
26-75	33.9	48.2	16.1	1.8	100.0	(56)
76-125	0.0	53.3	30.0	16.7	100.0	(30)
126-199	13.0	26.1	23.9	37.0	100.0	(46)
200 or more	2.7	23.3	30.1	43.8	99.9	(73)
All	32.2	34.1	16.2	17.5	100.0	(314)

Source: Paul R. Abramson, John H. Aldrich, David W. Rohde, *Change and Continuity in the 1984 Elections* (Washington, D.C.: Congressional Quarterly Press, 1986), p. 246.

Incumbency is the dominant theme of voter preference explanations of congressional voting just as it was in the preceding section on competitive change. For challengers, campaign spending is important for the consultants and media time it can buy in order to make voters aware that they have a choice. A challenger's campaign experience and holding political office is valuable for similar reasons. Generally, voters are twice as likely to recognize and to report having had some contact with House incumbents than they are with House challengers. Senate challengers fare better than House challengers on both counts and the differences between Senate incumbents and challengers in this respect is not great. What this suggests about House elections is that many voters support the incumbent because they are not aware of a choice. One reason why challenger spending is so important is that campaign spending has little effect on voters' familiarity with incumbents but a great effect on voters' awareness of challengers. Money does not buy elections, but it can help challengers to buy the attention of voters.

What effect do issues have on the choices that voters make in congressional elections. The discussion of the collective-choice aspect of congressional elections did include some consideration of the effects of the economy and other national issues on elections. The last two sections, however, have focused on the advantages of incumbency and on the quality of challenger candidates. But if elections are to be viewed as instruments of policy accountability and congressional responsiveness, some consideration must be given to the role of issues in congressional elections.

A first step in addressing the question of issues in congressional elections is to recognize a distinction that has been raised several times in this chapter. That distinction is that House and Senate elections are different. Although the reelection rate of incumbent senators has sometimes been as high as that of incumbent representatives (for example, 90 and 93 percent of the incumbent senators running in 1982 and 1984, respectively, won their races); the pattern over the years is one of incumbent senators being more vulnerable to electoral defeat: Between 1976 and 1980, the reelection rate for incumbent senators ranged between 55 and 68 percent. Senate challengers are generally more competitive than House challengers in terms of previous political experience, voter familiarity, free media coverage, contacts with voters, and campaign expenditures. Voters are also more likely to consider issue positions in evaluating Senate candidates than they are in evaluating House candidates.[35] An emphasis on personal qualities and representation in House races leads to incumbent representatives being more protected than senators from voters' dissatisfaction with policies and more insulated from issue voting. As one of the thirteen senators defeated in 1980 put it: "The congressmen all survived. If I had been a congressman, I would have survived—no doubt about it, no doubt about it. But if you're a senator, you are up there in the leadership with your ass sticking up in the air waiting to catch the lightning."[36]

One of the consistent findings of political science research on congressional elections is how little voters know about issues and the issue positions of candidates. Between 20 and 30 percent of the electorate has enough information to be considered "issue voters" in congressional elections, or only about half that found in presidential elections.[37] But other findings caution against dismissing issues in congressional elections on the grounds that 70 to 80 percent of the voters have failed a test on issues and therefore cannot be influenced by them.

One conclusion of a study of Senate elections was that an awareness of issues and a strong relationship between issue positions and the vote were found most often in those races where clear issue differences existed between the candidates.[38] How incumbents have voted on a variety of issues determines their general ideological position on a liberal-conservative scale, and it is this combination of issue positions that is often related to patterns of voting in congressional elections. A study of the 1982 House elections found that an incumbent's issue positions did affect the vote. While the ideology of challengers and candidates for open seats had little effect on the vote, it was found that incumbents who fell toward the middle of the liberal-conservative scale were the best vote getters. The authors of that study concluded that "each digit moved toward the center on the 10-point scale is worth about .80 of a percent of the vote. For example, a Republican in the center of the scale at 5 should win about 4 percent more of the vote than an extreme conservative at 10."[39]

In addition to the direct effects that issues may have on congressional voting, there is an important indirect effect suggested by the Jacobson-Kernell thesis discussed earlier. An incumbent's voting record on a particularly controversial issue is a factor that potential challengers take into account in deciding whether to run. By influencing the choice of candidates presented to voters, issues can have an effect on congressional elections even when there is little or no direct impact on the thinking of voters.

Conclusion

Congressional elections are not simply events that take place every other November. A House member's comment, "I'm never not a candidate," is also true in a general sense for elections.[40] Past elections and the anticipation of future elections exert a continuous influence on the politics of Congress. We have seen that explanations of congressional elections, whether they employ a collective-choice, competitive-change, or voter-preference focus, must necessarily examine a series of elections over time in order to have a context for understanding any single election.

Electoral responsiveness and congressional accountability is best understood in much the same way, as a process, rather than something that took place in 1986 and some other years. In U.S. politics, the institution that has been given the primary responsibility for providing responsiveness and accountability between elections is the political party. Although the influence of political parties has declined in recent years, parties still help to link together some of the key parts of the congressional system—voters with representatives and senators, legislators with other legislators, the executive and Congress, and past and future elections.

Endnotes

1. Unidentified representative, quoted in John F. Bibby, (ed.), *Congress Off the Record* (Washington, D.C.: American Enterprise Institute, 1983), p. 43.

2. Unidentified senator, quoted in Richard F. Fenno, Jr., *The United States Senate: A Bicameral Perspective* (Washington, D.C.: American Enterprise Institute, 1982), p. 42.

3. Steven Pressman, "Over Reagan's Protest, House Votes Trade Bill," *Congressional Quarterly Weekly Report*, May 24, 1986, p. 1154.

4. David S. Broder, "His Goal: No Defeats for House Democrat Incumbents," *Boston Globe*, June 8, 1986, p. 95.

5. Thomas Oliphant, "Texas Candidate Gets a Lesson on Foreign Trade," *Boston Globe*, August 7, 1985, p. 39. See also, Tom Watson, "Texas 1st Clings to Tradition, Elects Democrat," *Congressional Quarterly Weekly Report*, August 10, 1985, pp. 1605–06.

6. Former Sen. Thomas F. Eagleton (D-MO), quoted in Alan Ehrenhalt, "Specter of '58 Haunts Farm-State Members," *Congressional Quarterly Weekly Report*, October 12, 1985, p. 2087; John Parkes Cannon, executive director, Iowa Republican State Central Committee, quoted in Rob Gurwitt, "Mood of Rural Midwest Keeps G.O.P. on Edge," *Congressional Quarterly Weekly Report*, November 16, 1985, p. 2365.

7. Jan Burkhard, Taylor County (Iowa) Farm Bureau president, quoted in Rob Gurwitt, "Mood of Rural Midwest," p. 2369.

8. Representative Vin Weber, quoted in "Minn. Republican Trying To Hold House Seat Amid Farm Crisis," *Boston Globe*, November 29, 1985, p. 37.

9. Steven V. Roberts, "Tax Debate Might Foreshadow '86 Campaigns," *New York Times*, December 20, 1985, p. A32.

10. Lyn Ragsdale, "Legislative Elections and Electoral Responsiveness," in Gerhard Lowenberg, Samuel C. Patterson, and Malcolm E. Jewell, eds., *Handbook of Legislative Research* (Cambridge, Mass.: Harvard University Press, 1985), pp. 57–96.

11. Jacqueline Calmes, "Class of '82: Redefining Democratic Values," *Congressional Quarterly Weekly Report*, June 7, 1986, pp. 1269–73.

12. Gary C. Jacobson, *The Politics of Congressional Elections* (Boston: Little, Brown, 1987), pp. 142–43.

13. Edward R. Tufte, *Political Control of the Economy* (Princeton, N.J.: Princeton University Press, 1978), p. 119.

14. For more on these studies, see Ragsdale, pp. 62–66, and Jacobson, pp. 142–48.

15. Alan Ehrenhalt, "Campaign '86: Few Real House Contests," *Congressional Quarterly Weekly Report*, January 25, 1986, p. 171.

16. David R. Mayhew, "Congressional Elections: The Case of the Vanishing Marginals," in Glenn R. Parker, (ed.), *Studies of Congress* (Washington, D.C.: Congressional Quarterly Press, 1985), pp. 15–34.

17. Albert D. Cover and David R. Mayhew, "Congressional Dynamics and the Decline of Competitive Congressional Elections," in Lawrence C. Dodd and Bruce I. Oppenheimer, (eds.), *Congress Reconsidered*, 2nd Ed. (Washington, D.C.: Congressional Quarterly Press, 1981), pp. 67–72.

18. Louis Sandy Maisel, *From Obscurity to Oblivion* (Knoxville: University of Tennessee Press, 1982), p. 26.

19. The House figure is from Diane Granat, "Freshmen Find It Easier to Run as Incumbents," *Congressional Quarterly Weekly Report*, November 2, 1985, p. 2229. Senate information is from Robert M. Andrews, "Cranston Tops Franking List," *Boston Globe*, December 10, 1985, p. 1.

20. Quoted in Diane Granat, "Reagan 'Mascot' Targets Turnstile District," *Congressional Quarterly Weekly Report*, November 2, 1985, p. 2227.

21. John R. Johannes, *To Serve the People: Congress and Constituent Service* (Lincoln: University of Nebraska Press, 1984), pp. 187–211.

22. Jacobson, *The Politics of Congressional Elections*, pp. 108–15.

23. Representative Kolbe, quoted in Diane Granat, "Freshmen Find It Easier to Run as Incumbents," p. 2229.

24. Joe Gaylord and Ed Mahe, quoted in Adam Clymer, "Cost of Winning a House Seat Rose in '84, But at a Slower Rate," *New York Times*, December 4, 1984, p. A29.

25. John Sears, quoted in Maureen Dowd, "Round 2 for the 'Reagan Class,' " *New York Times*, March 28, 1985, p. B8.

26. Gary C. Jacobson and Samuel Kernell, *Strategy and Choice in Congressional Elections* (New Haven: Yale University Press, 1981). For an empirical test and critique of the Jacobson-Kernell thesis, see Richard Born, "Strategic Politicians and Unresponsive Voters," *American Political Science Review*, June, 1986, pp. 599–612. Born concluded that neither the "indirect effects" nor "challenger quality" aspects of the Jacobson-Kernell thesis were supported by his study of midterm elections from 1946 to 1982.

27. Jacobson, *The Politics of Congressional Elections*, p. 160.

28. Paul R. Abramson, John H. Aldrich, David W. Rohde, *Change and Continuity in the 1984 Elections* (Washington, D.C.: Congressional Quarterly Press, 1986), pp. 241–42.

29. Former Speaker O'Neill, quoted in David Nyhan, "Rescuing the Tax Bill from the Grasp of PACs," *Boston Globe*, December 19, 1985, p. 23.

30. Gary C. Jacobson, *Money in Congressional Elections* (New Haven: Yale University Press, 1980), p. 157.

31. Adam Clymer, "Cost of Winning a House Seat," p. A29, and Steven V. Roberts, "Some in Congress Say Money Talks Too Much," *New York Times*, November 19, 1985, p. A32.

32. Dan Balz, "Congressional Candidates Were Given $104 Million by Special Interests," *Washington Post*, January 3, 1985, p. A20, and Richard W. Bolling and Merton C. Bernstein, "A Way to Fight PACs," *New York Times*, September 21, 1985, p. 27.

33. Abramson, *Change and Continuity*, p. 244.

34. Ibid., p. 245. The 1982 average is from Clymer, "Cost," p. A29.

35. Barbara Hinckley, *Congressional Elections* (Washington, D.C.: Congressional Quarterly Press, 1981), pp. 79–82.

36. Unnamed senator, quoted in Fenno, *The United States Senate*, p. 19.

37. Hinckley, *Congressional Elections*, p. 109.

38. Alan I. Abramowitz, "Choices and Echoes in the 1978 U.S. Senate Elections: A Research Note," *American Journal of Political Science*, February, 1981, pp. 112–18.

39. Robert S. Erikson and Gerald C. Wright, "Voters, Candidates, and Issues in Congressional Elections," in Lawrence C. Dodd and Bruce I. Oppenheimer, eds., *Congress Reconsidered*, 3rd ed. (Washington, D.C.: Congressional Quarterly Press, 1985, p. 102.

40. Representative Terry L. Bruce (D-IL), quoted in Diane Granat, "Freshmen Find It Easier to Run as Incumbents," p. 2225.

4

Political Parties

A number of Senate Democrats got to talking at one of their weekly luncheon meetings in the spring of 1986 about some of the differences between Republican and Democratic members of that body. Participants reported that one topic in particular was discussed quite loudly at that meeting. Republican senators, it seemed, were being told long in advance when there would be no votes scheduled on a Friday. That permitted Republican senators to set up campaign appearances back home on those days. The party difference was that Democratic senators were not being informed about when there would be no votes and were therefore more restricted in making campaign plans.

There was no doubt about who was responsible for this selective dissemination of information: It was Senate Republican Leader Robert Dole. And there was no doubt about why he was doing it. The Republican majority in the Senate at the time was a narrow one, a fifty-three-to-forty-seven advantage over the Democrats. But Republicans had twenty-two seats to defend in the 1986 elections, while Democrats held only twelve of the total thirty-four seats at stake that year. The retirement of four Republican and three Democratic senators brought the actual number of incumbents standing for reelection in 1986 down to eighteen Republicans and nine Democrats. However one figured it, though, Senator Dole and his Republican colleagues faced a formidable challenge in trying to hold their majority.

When asked about the majority leader's favoritism in giving out scheduling information, Republican Sen. Mack Mattingly of Georgia, one of the eighteen running that year, had this to say: "Dole's No. 1 priority is Republican retention of the Senate." House Speaker Tip O'Neill, the leader of the other party in the other chamber and a person who was frequently charged of being overly partisan by House Republicans, commented on Dole's tactics. "Bob plays a tough game of politics," said O'Neill.[1] And the Speaker might have added that Senator Dole was playing that game in a number of different arenas at the same time.

First, the Kansas Senator was up for reelection to a fourth term in 1986. Kansas farmers grow more wheat than any other state, and Dole had assumed personal control of a farm bill with provisions favorable to wheat farmers, which Congress passed in December 1985. Second, the majority leader was running hard for the 1988 Republican presidential nomination. Senator Dole's playing that game of politics could be seen in his endless travels around the country to speak at fundraising events, his taking positions favored by party conservatives on issues such as abortion and responses to terrorism, and the high media visibility that he was able to maintain through C-Span's live coverage of Senate proceedings and through regular appearances on television news shows. Reelection in 1986 by his Kansas constituents was an integral part of Dole's campaign to build a national constituency for 1988. But Dole's chances of getting the Republican presidential nomination also would depend on his ability to preserve the support of another constituency—the Republican senators of the Senate majority.

For a number of reasons, then, keeping a Republican Senate majority in 1986 was of great importance to Senator Dole's political career. President Reagan and other Republican leaders also had an important stake in the Senate elections that year. With the Democrats firmly in control of the House, a Republican Senate was considered essential to achieving any legislative success during the final two years of the Reagan administration.

This situation can best be appreciated by looking at the tenuous nature of the Republican majority on committees and subcommittees in the Ninety-ninth Congress (1985–1986). Because Senate leaders agreed to have the party composition of committees and subcommittees follow the party ratio in the parent body (53–47), the Labor and Human Resources Committee consisted of nine Republicans and seven Democrats. But the position of committee member Sen. Lowell Weicker (R-CT) on the Reagan administration's proposals for cutting back social programs was consistently at odds with the administration and the Republican party. The nine to seven Republican advantage thus became an eight to eight tie when the committee dealt with those programs. The importance of a single vote was also evident in subcommittees such as the the Constitution Subcommittee of the Senate Judiciary Committee with its slim three to two Republican margin. The difficulty of governing with such a fragile majority brought to mind an earlier period in Senate history, when a changing one-vote margin between November 1952 and June 1954, made lawmaking in that body almost impossible.[2]

A fear of the 1986 Senate elections resulting in either stalemate or a Democratic majority was even mentioned as one of the unstated reasons for Chief Justice Warren Burger's retirement in June 1986, which cleared the way for Senate approval of President Reagan's new appointments to the Court before the November elections.

The importance of the 1986 Senate elections to the 1988 presidential race and to the governing capability of the Reagan administration was enough to focus more attention on races for the Senate than on the House that year. What is also evident in all of this is the important role that political parties play in the politics of Congress. Speculation about these elections produced disagreement on which party would end up in control of the Senate but agreement on the responsibility of political parties for exercising that control. The significance of political parties in a democracy stems from the linkage they provide between voters and the policies of government. Legislative control and lawmaking is at one end of that democratic linkage, and the representation of voters' policy preferences is at the other end.

What the 1986 Senate elections had to say about voters' preferences provided yet another reason why so many people were so closely watching those races. Republicans would find it harder to argue that they were the emerging majority party for the 1980s and beyond unless they could hold on to the Senate in 1986. The Democratic counterargument and hopes for a restoration of that party to the presidency in 1988 would also wax or wane with the outcome of the 1986 Senate elections. As we saw after the results were in for 1986, the debate goes on regardless of the outcome. It is the debate itself that testifies to the importance of political parties both for voters and for legislators.

Parties and Voters

How much time and effort should a voter give to deciding how to cast 1 out of 200,000 or more votes in an election to choose who will represent that district as 1/435 of one-half of one-third of the national government? Or a Senate race to determine 1 percent of the other one-half of that legislative one-third of the three branches of government? For that is what is at stake, after all, in congressional elections. A short answer to those two questions might be, "not much." For a majority of Americans, the question is answered by not voting in congressional elections. Some political scientists have incorporated those questions into studies of those who do vote and analyzed voting decisions in cost-benefits terms. At what point, for example, do the costs of gaining additional information on the candidates outstrip any benefits that the voter might receive by casting a vote one way rather than another.

An early exponent of this approach to voting behavior was Anthony Downs, whose book, *An Economic Theory of Democracy*, outlined how a perfectly rational human being might go about voting.[3] Downs's rational voter, defined only in terms of means, was said to be one who tried to vote efficiently by maximizing output for a given input (casting a vote in such a way that it has the greatest impact in bringing about policies he or she favors), or by minimizing input for a given output (not spending scarce resources such as time and money on gathering information in order to cast an "informed" vote that really will not make any difference in the political system).

To cast a rational vote for every candidate, the individual citizen would have to spend most of his or her working hours evaluating the policy positions of all candidates. Such behavior, while insuring an informed voting decision, would be grossly inefficient in terms of payoffs the voter would receive. The likelihood that his or her one vote will elect the chosen candidates and produce the desired policies is not great enough to justify the tremendous costs of gathering the information. A rational solution to this problem is to delegate the evaluation and analysis of political information to another person or agent.

If you have a friend who knows a lot about income taxes and has similar political goals, then it makes sense to rely on that friend's analysis of which candidate would be more likely to vote for tax policies that are in line with those goals. By relying on the superior information your friend has in this area, you greatly reduce your own costs of gaining the information needed to cast a rational vote. Similarly, if you know that one political party is committed to particular groups or segments of the electorate, you may cast a rational ballot by voting in terms of party labels. As was the case with a friend who knows about taxes, you are able to support candidates who share your policy goals without having to expend a great deal of time and energy gathering information.

The most important requirement of such delegation of analysis and evaluation is that the delegated agency share the policy goals of the delegating individual. It is irrational to delegate such analysis to a political party if that party is likely to change its base of group support or policy goals in order to broaden its political appeal.

Another view of voters' decision making exhibits some similarities to the cost-benefit approach of Downs. Stanley Kelley and Thad Mirer outlined the following process, which they call the *Voter's Decision Rule*, to explain how voters make up their minds:

> The voter canvasses his likes and dislikes of the leading candidates and major parties involved in an election. Weighing each like and dislike equally, he votes for the candidate toward whom he has the greatest net number of favorable attitudes, if there is such a candidate. If no candidate has such an advantage, the voter votes consistently with his party affiliation, if he has one. If his attitudes do not incline him toward one candidate more than toward another, and if he does not identify with one of the major parties, the voter reaches a null decision.[4]

A "null decision," according to Kelley and Mirer, means that the person does not vote. Barbara Hinckley applied this model to congressional voting and concluded that party affiliation has an effect similar to incumbency: "Many people do not pay attention to the congressional race or care much about the outcome, but they still manage to vote in the contest. We can now understand why this occurs. Both *party* and *incumbency* supply low-cost information cues to voters and help them make a general-choice decision."[5]

As we noted earlier, a certain degree of stability is needed for party affiliation to serve as a reliable cue in congressional voting. Table 4–1 shows the pattern of party affiliation at the individual

TABLE 4–1 Party Identification in the United States

	1952	1956	1960	1964	1968	1972	1976	1980	1984
Democrat									
Strong	22%	21%	20%	27%	20%	15%	15%	18%	17%
Weak	25	23	25	25	25	26	25	23	20
	47	44	45	52	45	41	40	41	37
Independent									
Democratic leaning	10	6	6	9	10	11	12	11	11
Independent	6	9	10	8	11	13	15	13	11
Republican-leaning	7	8	7	6	9	11	10	10	12
	23	23	23	23	30	35	37	34	34
Republican									
Strong	14	15	16	11	10	10	9	9	12
Weak	14	14	14	14	15	13	14	14	15
	28	29	30	25	25	23	23	23	27
Apolitical	3	4	3	1	1	1	1	2	2
Total	100%	100%	100%	100%	100%	100%	100%	100%	100%
Number	1784	1757	1911	1550	1553	2694	2850	1612	2236

Source: American National Election Studies, Center for Political Studies, The University of Michigan.

level for 1952–1984. Political scientists first started to employ the concept of a person's self-described affiliation with one party or the other in studying elections in the 1950s. In retrospect, it seems that this same period was one in which the importance of the effect of party identification on electoral outcomes was greatest. A person's identification with the Democratic or Republican party was found to be a remarkably stable phenomenon that he or she acquired early in life. This early established party attitude was found to act as a perceptual screen through which all political stimuli were given meaning. Information about issues and candidates generally took on meaning as it was related to party identification. Most important, party identification was found to be the single-most significant variable in predicting electoral outcomes during that period.

One trend that can be seen in Table 4–1 is the recent shift toward Republican party identification. While Democrats still outnumber Republicans, the gap has narrowed enough in recent years to support arguments of an emerging Republican majority discussed previously. Another trend in Table 4–1 that has drawn a lot of attention is the increase in the percentage of the population that defines itself as independent. In 1984, slightly over one-third of those in the sample described themselves as independents, as compared to one-fourth thirty years earlier. Those who describe themselves as strong Democrats or Republicans are also fewer in number than in earlier years. The decline in the number of strong party identifiers would be expected to produce an increase in the number of voters who desert their party and support candidates from the other party. That effect is what we see in the increase in "defectors" shown in Table 4–2.

A number of studies have shown that the increase in defectors shown in Table 4–2 can be attributed primarily to the advantages of incumbency, which were analyzed in Chapter 3. Most of the increase in defections was produced by voters of one party supporting an incumbent of the other party. Candidates who challenged those incumbents were much less likely to receive the support of voters who identify with the other party. The defection rate among voters whose party identification was the same as their incumbent representative in 1984 was 9 percent for Democratic identifiers and 5 percent for Republican identifiers. Conversely, when the incumbent belonged to the other party, the defection rate went to 60 percent among Democrats and 38 percent among Republicans.[6] Although the pull of

TABLE 4–2 Party-Line Voting in Congressional Elections

Year	House Elections			Senate Elections		
	Party line Voters	Defectors	Pure Indepen-dents	Party line Voters	Defectors	Pure Indepen-dents
1956	82%	9%	9%	79%	12%	9%
1958	84	11	5	85	9	5
1960	80	12	8	77	15	8
1962	83	12	6	—	—	—
1964	79	15	5	78	16	6
1966	76	16	8	—	—	—
1968	74	19	7	74	19	7
1970	76	16	8	78	12	10
1972	75	17	8	69	22	9
1974	74	18	8	73	19	8
1976	72	19	9	70	19	11
1978	69	22	9	71	20	9
1980	69	23	8	71	21	8
1982	77	14	6	77	17	6
1984	74	22	4	75	20	5

Source: Gary C. Jacobson, *The Politics of Congressional Elections,* 2nd ed. (Boston: Little, Brown, 1987), p. 107. Copyright © 1987 by Gary C. Jacobson. Reprinted by permission of Little, Brown and Company.

incumbency in Senate elections is not as strong as it is in House elections, a pattern of defections favoring incumbents is found in elections for that chamber as well. Generally speaking, however, the party cue is more important in Senate elections than it is in House elections.[7]

While the evidence presented in Tables 4–1 and 4–2 clearly indicates that party identification is not as important as it once was, it continues to be an important determinant of how people vote in congressional elections. Table 4–1 shows a decline in strong party identifiers and an increase in independents, but it also shows a certain degree of stability in the partisan composition of the electorate. Table 4–2 shows an increase in the number of voters who defect from their party in congressional elections, but even at the point of the greatest defection, over two-thirds of the electorate were casting a party-line vote.

One factor that helps to account for the stability of party identification is the party's group base. Certain religious, racial, income, education, age, and residential groups traditionally associate with either the Republican or the Democratic party, and one's membership in these groups is generally a stable phenomenon (with the obvious exceptions created by time, money, or moving). Indeed, the basic difference between the two parties is often expressed more as a difference in the groups represented by each than as a difference in ideology.

Tables 4–3 and 4–4 illustrate the group bases of the two parties as they are reflected in constituency characteristics asso-

TABLE 4–3 Constituency Characteristics and Party, Ninety-eighth Congress (1983–1984)

Characteristic	Percentage of All Democratic Seats (n = 268)	Percentage of All Republican Seats (n = 167)
Median Income in District		
Under $10,000	3 (7)	1 (1)
$10,000–$19,999	79 (213)	71 (119)
$20,000 and over	18 (48)	28 (47)
Percentage of Owner Occupied Housing Units in District		
Under 50%	13 (34)	3 (5)
50%–69%	55 (147)	46 (77)
70% and over	32 (87)	51 (85)
Percentage of Black Population in District		
Under 10%	54 (144)	79 (132)
10%–19%	17 (45)	11 (19)
20% and over	29 (79)	10 (16)
Median Years of School Completed (Adults, 25 Years and Over)		
Under 10	19 (50)	15 (25)
10–12	43 (115)	33 (55)
Over 12	38 (102)	52 (87)

Source: Data compiled from *Congressional District Data Book,* Ninety-eighth Congress (U.S. Government Printing Office, 1984).

TABLE 4–4 Group Voting in Two Congressional Elections

	1978		1984	
Group	Percentage Voting Democratic	Percentage Voting Republican	Percentage Voting Democratic	Percentage Voting Republican
Race				
White	52	48	44	50
Nonwhite	84	16	86	10
Religion				
Protestant	50	50	44	51
Catholic	62	38	54	41
Sex				
Men	53	47	46	49
Women	57	43	50	44
Age				
18–29 years	58	42	47	46
30–49 years	54	46	50	45
50 and over	54	46	47	47
Education				
Some College	46	54	42	53
High School	56	44	47	48
Grade School	70	30	59	34

Source: Percentages for 1978 from the Gallup Poll 17, 1978. The figures are based on personal interviews with 1,564 likely voters out of a total sample of 2,844 adults aged eighteen years and older. Percentages for 1984 from the Gallup Poll October 28, 1984. The findings are based on in-person interviews with 3,140 likely voters out of a total sample of 4,629 aged eighteen and over.

ciated with Democratic and Republican congressional districts and in patterns of group voting in congressional elections.

As the tables indicate, groups traditionally associated with the Democratic party are voters with lower incomes, those who rent rather than own their own homes, blacks, Catholics, younger voters, and those with no college education. City dwellers and blue collar workers are two additional groups, not included here, which have traditionally been associated with the Democratic party. The Republican group base, conversely, is made up of higher-income, home-owning, Protestant, white, older, college-educated, white collar, and suburban voters.

There are, of course, many exceptions to these general patterns of group affiliation and group voting. Many of the factors discussed in Chapter 3—the state of the economy, presidential popularity, and the appeal of local candidates and issues—will outweigh party in the minds of some members of these groups. And as we have seen, the incumbency factor may lead to many of those who belong to groups that traditionally favor Republicans, in fact, supporting a Democratic incumbent and vice versa. But the traditional alliance of certain groups with either the Democratic or the Republican party does help to explain both the stability in party identification and party voting seen in congressional elections. A candidate's party affiliation, like incumbency, is information that a voter can acquire without much effort. And both incumbency and party appear to be important cues for voters in congressional elections.

On the other hand, to say that political parties serve as a voting cue in congressional elections is not enough to support a conclusion that parties are providing the linkage between voters and policymakers that is required in a democracy. Choosing one candidate over another on the basis of party affiliation makes little sense unless there are policy differences between parties. In a similar vein, the affiliation of a group with a particular party would be meaningless unless elected officials from that party consistently sought policies that would favor the group. We might find, in fact, that a Republican representative from Massachusetts supports policies favorable to traditionally Democratic groups more often than does a Democratic representative from Georgia. Or that a Republican senator from Connecticut votes more often with a Democratic colleague from New York than he does with a fellow Republican from North Carolina. Unless party affiliation means something to legislators, it does not matter that it means something to voters.

Parties and Legislators

When we move from the setting in which a voter makes a decision to one in which a legislator acts, we are struck by obvious differences. The average voter cares little about politics; a legislator's entire life centers around it. While most voters do not have much information on which to base a voting decision, legislators are flooded with information provided on every issue by the press, interest groups, executive agencies, and their own staffs. It would seem, therefore, that the process by which a member of Congress makes up his or her mind about a legislative vote would be quite different from that of the voter in elections. The party cue would not seem to be such a reliable basis for casting a rational vote. The legislator not only has information available; he or she also has a great interest in using this information to cast a knowledgeable vote. The costs of casting uninformed votes are great enough to the legislator to justify his or her assuming the costs of gathering information.

These differences between the citizen's voting decision and the legislator's voting decision seem not so great, however, when we consider the number and scope of decisions legislators must make. A voter makes a political decision every two years; a legislator is constantly called on to make such decisions. Figure 4–1 shows the number of record votes taken in both chambers since 1947. The effects of reforms discussed in Chapter 1, which made it easier to call for a record vote and provided the electronic voting system, can be seen in the dramatic increase in record votes beginning in the mid-1970s. In the Ninety-sixth Congress (1979–1980), for example, the total number of record votes was 2,304—more than five times the 417 recorded two decades earlier in the Eightieth Congress. Although the number of record votes has dropped off somewhat in the 1980s, the average is still around 700 to 800 recorded votes per year.[8] Keep in mind, too, that the number of recorded floor votes represents only a fraction of the total number of decisions that must be made by each representative and senator. Add to this total the great number of unrecorded decisions the legislator makes on the floor, in committees and subcommittees, in the office, and simply through answering constituent mail. Even when the legislator is simply stating a position on some issue, he or she often must acquire some information through the normal cue sources of party leadership, interest groups, colleagues, and staff.

The scope of these decisions is mind boggling. Consider, for example, the variety of issues that members had to deal with in one day in a recent Congress—energy legislation, a major tax bill, a full-employment bill, airline deregulation, endangered species legislation, creation of a wilderness area in Minnesota, regulation

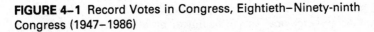

FIGURE 4–1 Record Votes in Congress, Eightieth–Ninety-ninth Congress (1947–1986)

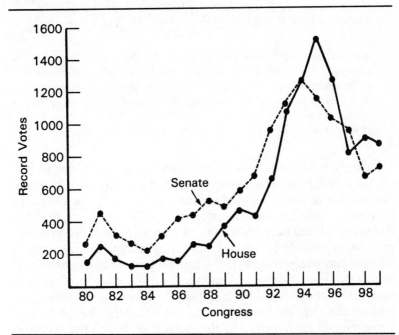

Source: Adapted from data in Norman J. Ornstein, et al. *Vital Statistics on Congress, 1984–1985* (Washington, D.C.: American Enterprise Institute, 1984) pp. 144–46, and *Congressional Quarterly Weekly Review,* Nov. 15, 1986, p. 2902.

of banking practices, maternity coverage for health insurance programs, federal funding of abortions, federal water projects, price supports for sugar, federal aid for middle-income families with college students, aid for elementary and secondary education, federal housing assistance, highway and mass transit funding, school busing, White House staff size, veterans' pensions, meat import quotas, and textile tariff levels.[9] Because of the number and variety of issues that arise, legislators often find themselves in a decisional situation with a low level of information, not unlike the voter. One House member, on his way to the chamber to cast his fourth roll call vote in about an hour, paused and had this to say about the bill he was to vote on: "I don't know a goddamn thing about the Amateur Sports Act of 1978. So I'll just have to ask someone on the floor. And frankly, I couldn't care less."[10] Two other representatives' comments:

I have to vote on 150 different kinds of things every year— foreign aid, science, space, technical problems, and the Merchant Marine, and Lord knows what else. I can't possibly become an expert in all these fields.

It's not uncommon for me to go on the floor with the bells ringing, votes being taken, and it's on a bill or issue that I have never heard of before. I haven't the remotest idea of the issues involved. You've got to make up your mind; you can't vote "maybe" and you can't vote "present"—you don't want to. So you have to make a decision on the best basis you can.[11]

Members of Congress seek to make rational decisions in voting on issues even when they have little knowledge or information on that issue. Because of the number and scope of decisions, it is impossible for the legislator to avail her- or himself of the technical information needed to cast an informed, independent vote on the merits of every issue. Donald Matthews and James Stimson have suggested that the normal process of congressional decision making follows a low-information strategy of seeking cues from fellow members and from certain external sources of information.[12] These cues serve the same function for the legislator as they do for the voter in elections. They permit the decision-maker to make rational voting decisions without having to incur great costs of gathering information. The sources of these cues will vary a great deal from member to member and from issue to issue. They may include state delegations, parties, subject matter experts, the president, those who come from similar districts, and other members with whom the legislator has apolitical, informal ties.

By building a network of cuegivers for different issues, the legislator assures her- or himself of fairly reliable information on how to vote without having to expend a great deal of time and effort arriving at an independent decision. Instead of trying to determine the impact on his or her constituency of a proposed tax reform bill by extensive research on constituency opinion, the legislator may simply follow the advice of a Ways and Means Committee member whose district is similar. A legislator might find it more reasonable to vote with the other members of his or her state delegation than to run the risk of notoriety that comes with being "the only congressman from Illinois to vote against the interests of her citizens."

In their study of normal decision making in the House, Matthews and Stimson distinguish between two important types of cuegivers—initial and intermediary. The legitimacy of initial cuegivers is based on their technical expertise. This is developed by serving on the committee reporting the bill to be voted on or by tapping the expertise of the executive branch. While there is never much doubt about the reliability of the technical expertise of initial cuegivers, members may sometimes question their underlying value preferences.

The second set of cuegivers, the intermediaries, consists of groups of members who have examined the technical information supplied by the initial cuegivers and arrived at a collective decision as to how to vote on the issue at hand. A representative looking to these groups for cues as to how to vote puts trust in the value preferences he or she shares with them and in their having attained some modicum of technical information about the bill from initial cuegivers.

Matthews and Stimson asked members to indicate the sources of information or cues they would turn to when called upon to vote on a matter about which they know nothing. Table 4–5 shows what they found.

This ranking of cue sources illustrates the importance of the political party in the cue network of congressional voting. Even if we attribute the listing of partisan committee leaders to the expertise that comes from serving on the committee rather than party resources, we find that the legislative party occupies a dominant position in the legislative cue network. The most frequently cited sources of cues are party colleagues from the state delegation and congressional party leaders. If we combine the three party cue sources (state party delegation, party majority, and party leaders), we find that 41 percent of the total cue sources cited by members of Congress are party ones. Matthews and Stimson looked at initial cue sources in greater detail and concluded that party leaders represented the single most important source of initial cues for members involved in a low-information decision.[13]

It is clear that the political party occupies a central position in the cue-seeking network within Congress. This influence is achieved both through the party leadership's control over certain kinds of information (such as advance knowledge about how members plan to vote on an issue) and through the attachment the legislator has to the party label. The impact of party leader-

TABLE 4-5 The Relative Importance of Cue Sources in the House

Cue-Givers	Number of Mentions	Percentage of All Mentions
Initial		
Chairman of Relevant Committee	34	13
Ranking Minority Member of Relevant Committee	29	11
President	35	14
Intermediary		
State Party Delegation	44	18
Party Majority	19	7
Majority of the House	9	4
Democratic Study Group or Wednesday Club	32	13
"Conservative Coalition"	12	5
Not Classified		
Party Leaders	40	16
Total	254	101

Source: Donald Matthews and James Stimson, *Yeas and Nays: Normal Decision-Making in the U.S. House of Representatives* (John Wiley and Sons, 1975), p. 94. Copyright © 1975 John Wiley and Sons, Inc., reprinted by permission.

ship and the party organization as an intelligence network will be discussed later. Here, we are more interested in the way the party acts as a cue for the legislator's vote.

Members of Congress indicate a desire to support their party even when other pressures, such as constituency opinion or ideology, lead them to oppose their party in floor votes. Randall Ripley found that more than 90 percent of the representatives from both parties responded affirmatively to the question: "Do you want to act in accord with your party's position?." More than 70 percent from both parties said that this was generally their first consideration in deciding how to vote.[14] The impact of party affiliation as a major cue source is reflected in voting on the floor. Despite a decline in partisan voting in the 1970s, studies of congressional voting over the years consistently found party affiliation to be the single most important predictor of legislators' votes.[15] And party affiliation appeared again to be more relevant to congressional voting in the 1980s. For Congress as a whole, partisanship increased during the Reagan administration, and the degree of partisanship seen in congressional voting in 1985 was the highest since the first year of the Kennedy administration in 1961. A majority of Democrats opposed a majority of Republicans on 56 percent of all recorded votes in the House and Senate in 1985. That is noticeably above the average of 40 percent of recorded votes on which Congress divided along party lines in the 1970s. Party unity also increased along with partisanship. The average Democratic member voted with his or her party on 79 percent of all partisan votes in 1985, which represented the highest degree of Democratic party unity in Congress in over twenty-five years. The average Republican voted with his or her party on 75 percent of all partisan votes in 1985.[16] What all of this suggests is the important influence that the party cue has on congressional behavior and how the saliency of party affiliation changes over time.

The importance of the party cue also varies from issue to issue. Aage Clausen found five general policy dimensions along which legislators were arrayed in terms of their roll call voting behavior. These five dimensions, which included a wide range of specific issues and roll call votes, were civil liberties, international involvement, social welfare, agricultural assistance, and government management. The study showed that the member's political party was basically irrelevant to his or her position on issues of civil liberties and international involvement, while it was a relatively strong indication of how the member would vote on social welfare, agricultural assistance, and government management issues.[17] Issues relating to government management—such as government ownership and/or regulation of economic enterprises, spending on public works as opposed to private business incentives, public versus private development of natural resources, business regulation, distribution of the tax burden, interest rates, and a balanced budget—were found to be those that most clearly differentiated congressional members of the two parties. It would be incorrect to say that a legislator's party identification always signals how he or she will vote on every issue. Clausen's study clearly showed that the importance of party varied from issue to issue. The underlying importance of the issues raised by the government-management dimension and the fact that party is found to be such an important determinant of voting on that dimension tend to reinforce the importance of the party cue for congressional voting.

Another study by Jerrold Schneider that looked at ideological coalitions in Congress, found a great deal of consistency in members' voting on foreign policy, economic policy, racial policy, and civil liberties issues. Schneider's findings portrayed a Congress that was more regularly ideological than the pluralist picture of shifting coalitions described by earlier voting studies. Although the impact of parties on congressional voting was not a major concern in this study, the author did note that "the ideological character of congressional parties, or factions within them, was implicitly confirmed by the findings of this study."[18]

What these and other studies suggest is that in the absence of strong pressures from the constituency or from committee leaders, the average legislator is predisposed to support his or her party on issues. However, in cases where the opinion or interests of a member's constituency is at odds with the party position, the demands of representation might require a vote against party. Lawmaking, too, can lead to a representative or senator not voting with the party if, for example, a party vote would run contrary to that member's own ideology. For the most part, though, it is representational rather than lawmaking reasons that are used to justify members' defections from the party fold. Because party is only one consideration that goes into a member's vote, and because the relevance of party varies from issue to issue, party leaders are required to build coalitions of support for individual bills. Lewis Froman and Randall Ripley have suggested that six conditions in particular seem to determine whether legislators will follow party leaders.[19]

1. *Party leadership is committed and active.* Because of limits on time and other resources, party leaders cannot become actively involved in every bill that is introduced in Congress. Party leaders therefore trim the list of legislation that they will give an all-out effort to push. The importance of a bill as part of the president's program, as an expression of party principles, or in straightforward policy terms will influence the degree of party leaders' efforts. A senior leadership aide's comment, "We don't want to waste effort on a losing cause," suggests another important criterion for deciding how involved party leaders will become.[20] Little or no party effort will be expended in cases where it seems that a bill will easily pass anyway or in cases where there is no chance of winning. Exceptions to the latter case are those instances where even doomed counterproposals to

an administration program might be put forward by opposition party leaders. Party leaders are not equally committed to all bills brought forward by members of their party, and initial decisions about the degree of involvement will determine whether a bill is perceived as a party issue. By terming a particular issue a party vote, by disseminating information as to the importance of the vote through the interpersonal cue-giving networks, and by polling legislators to gain information and a commitment, the legislative party leaders can make it more difficult for a member of Congress to vote against his or her party.

2. *The issue is procedural rather than substantive.* The difference between a procedural and a substantive vote was illustrated by an incident during the Ninety-sixth Congress (1979–1980). Rep. John Ashbrook (R-OH) appealed a ruling by the chair that an Ashbrook amendment was out of order and was able to force a roll call vote on the appeal. The Democratic majority upheld the ruling of the chair, but forty-four Democrats voted against the party leadership on that vote. Each of those defecting Democrats received a letter from House Speaker Tip O'Neill, in which the Speaker informed them: "It is elementary to our procedural control of the House that the Chair be supported by members of our party. That is basic to a parliamentary body. In other countries if such a vote were lost, the government would fall." O'Neill went on to say that he would not call for disciplinary measures against those defectors, that he understood the pressures on members, "but I believe members have to be ready to support the orderly process when a member seeks to confuse procedure with issue."[21] That difference helps to explain why parties achieve their greatest cohesion on the most procedural measures such as the election of the Speaker and the greatest number of defections on narrowly substantive measures such as votes on conference committee reports and amendments to bills.

3. *The visibility of the issue is low.* Like many of these conditions, visibility is not something that party leaders can fully control. Some issues, such as income tax reform or comprehensive spending cuts, will lead to highly visible votes regardless of what party leaders do. On the other hand, procedural votes generally have less visibility than substantive ones. For members who must decide whether to follow party leaders, it is the visibility of an issue in their district or home state that is important. Quite often, constituents might have no awareness of, or interest in, an issue that generates headlines in Washington,

D.C., and is of great concern among those in government. This is illustrated by the fact that the most partisan issue in the House in 1985 was a contested election in Indiana's Eighth District. After a recount of the votes in the 1984 election, Indiana's secretary of state, a Republican, had declared Republican candidate Richard McIntyre to be the winner over Democrat Frank McCloskey. But Democrats refused to seat McIntyre when the Ninety-ninth Congress convened in January 1985, and called for an investigation by the House Administration Committee. A task force of that committee recounted the votes and concluded that the Democrat, McCloskey, had won the election by 4 votes out of more than 233,000. One week later, a party-line vote to seat McCloskey precipitated a Republican walkout and a series of partisan skirmishes over normally routine procedural matters for the rest of 1985. Of the 286 recorded partisan votes in that year, 71 of them (26 percent) were related to the McIntyre-McCloskey dispute.[22] The most partisan issue in the House during 1985, then, was one that received a lot of media attention, yet was a low-visibility issue in most House districts. Members from districts outside of Indiana could support party leaders on these partisan votes and would know that most of their own constituents did not know or did not care how their representative voted.

4. *The visibility of the action is low.* Paul Light has described how the low visibility of congressional action can support party cohesion and party differences even when the issue itself is highly visible. The issue that Light wrote about is Social Security, a program that has been a major point of contention in national campaigns and one with which most Americans are familiar. Light analyzed 138 votes on Social Security between 1935 and 1982. He found clear party differences on those votes, with Democrats almost always supporting expansion of the program and a majority of Republicans consistently voting for benefit cuts and a smaller program. Yet most descriptions of congressional action on Social Security portrayed it as one of bipartisan support. The reason for this, said Light, is that Republican opposition to the program came early in the legislative process in votes to consider the bill and in votes on amendments. Republicans were more likely to join Democrats at the end in the more visible votes on final passage of the bill. Light suggests that this pattern of voting was one in which "Congress was able to hide most of the conflict from the public spotlight," and that "it was a technique that worked well only until the

1970s." "With changes both inside and outside Congress, the party differences on Social Security could no longer be so easily disguised."[23]

Nothing is mysterious about the relationship between visibility and party voting, especially when constituency influence is taken into consideration. On low-visibility votes, members can support party leaders without having to worry too much about criticism back home, because people back home are often unaware of their representative's vote. That is not the case, however, in major floor votes on prominent issues when party leaders are likely to face stiff competition from the demands of constituency opinion and pressure from constituent groups.

5. *There is little counterpressure from constituencies.* While the average northern Democrat in the Senate supported the Democratic party on 80 percent of the roll call votes in 1985, the average southern Democratic senator supported the party on only 64 percent of these votes. The same pattern held in the House, with northern Democrats supporting their party on 84 percent of the votes, and southern Democrats supporting it on 71 percent of the votes.[24] The lower party support by southern legislators is generally explained by their coming from constituencies different from those of the northern Democrats. Indeed, most deviations in party votes are explained in terms of constituency factors.

Lewis Froman suggested that differences between northern Democrats and northern Republicans are a function not just of party but also of different types of constituencies. Looking at such variables as percentage of owner-occupied dwellings, percentage nonwhite population, average population per square mile, and percentage urban population, Froman found that Democrats tended to represent constituencies that were more urban, were more racially mixed, had a lower percentage of owner-occupied dwellings, and had more people per square mile than Republican constituencies, a pattern similar to that shown in Table 4–3.[25] In supporting the programs of Democratic presidents, these northern Democrats were voting both for party and for the interests of most constituents.

The 1986 Senate races provided some additional illustrations of how constituency can outweigh party as an influence on policy positions. In Missouri, for example, Republican candidate Christopher Bond ran a campaign that was critical of the Republican administration's positions on farm policy, international trade, and military spending. When asked why he was trying to help the Republicans maintain control of the Senate by running against the policies of a Republican president, Bond replied: "I'm talking about the issues that sell in Missouri." Rep. Ken Kramer's campaign for the Colorado Senate seat vacated by Gary Hart was in some ways similar to Bond's campaign. Although he usually supported his party and president in his House votes, Kramer did stress his differences with the Republican administration on international trade and the defense budget. Kramer's explanation: "If I have to choose between where the people of Colorado are and where the President is, unless there's an awfully compelling reason, I'll go with the people of Colorado."[26]

6. *State delegations are not engaged in collective bargaining.* Members of Congress from the same party and the same state are an important reference group for legislators. State delegations are a primary socializing agency for freshmen legislators and continue to play an important cue-giving role throughout their tenure in the legislature. This role can be seen in Table 4–5, where state party delegation is the cue source legislators mention more often than any other. Voting in line with party colleagues from the same state provides a member with an automatic rationalization for his or her vote. He or she need only point out to those who challenge this position that every member of his or her party from the state delegation voted the same way. By acting in unison, the state delegation can be an effective bargaining agent in winning concessions from the party leadership.

Large state delegations such as those of Texas, California, and New York can exert great influence in the House of Representatives when they are united on state or regional issues. For example, Texas representatives succeeded in blocking a 1986 proposal by the National Aeronautics and Space Administration to transfer a major space project from Houston, Texas, to Huntsville, Alabama. The influence and unity of the Texas delegation on issues affecting the oil and gas industries has given it an almost legendary status among representatives over the years. California Democrats have displayed similar unity on federal education programs and on legislation providing agricultural aid to the states. The New York delegation has often been more divided than those of Texas or California, a reflection of the division between New York City and the more conservative areas of upstate New York. Even so, New York representatives have drawn together on votes with an impact on the fiscal health of

New York City and on military programs important to the state's economy.

As a potent source of cues conflicting with the legislative party, the state delegations may weaken the effectiveness of the party in much the same way that constituencies do. About half of the state delegations in the House meet on a regular basis and seek unified issue positions. They represent about half of the total membership of the House. Roll call analyses show that state delegations are most influential on two quite different sorts of issues: (1) "tough questions, controversial both within the party and within the House," and (2) "matters of trivial or purely local importance."[27] The party's strength as a cuegiver is greatly enhanced when state delegations either are co-opted to support the party leadership position or are not separated from the party position on the issue.

The congressional party is most correctly conceived as an effective source of voting cues within a complex network of competing cue sources. At times, the constituency cue or state delegation cue is more important in determining the legislator's vote, but political party continues to be the single most important factor in congressional voting decisions. The party organizations and party leaders in Congress are responsible both for establishing and maintaining reliable cue networks to facilitate representation and for providing the structure needed for congressional lawmaking.

Party Organization

House Republican Leader Robert H. Michel of Peoria, Illinois was first elected to Congress in 1956. The last time that his party had a majority in that chamber was 1954. For a while, in 1981 and 1982, Michel had been able to put together a working majority of Republicans and "Boll Weevil" conservative Democrats that were able to pass Reagan administration programs, but the Democrat's gain of twenty-six seats in 1982 put an end to that. As the Ninety-ninth Congress was drawing to a close in 1986, Michel talked about what it was like to be part of a permanent minority: "I haven't chaired a subcommittee or full committee in my thirty years in Congress. It's a pretty doggone discouraging and debilitating thing." A somewhat different view was offered about the same time by Henry J. Hyde, Michel's Illinois colleague first elected to the House in 1974: "If you come to understand your role is to be a gadfly, a conscience factor, and try to work some influence in committee . . . if that's enough and you don't need to be chairman of a committee or subcommittee or see your name on a bill, this can be very rewarding." Moreover, House Democrats expressed little sympathy for members of the opposition. The chairman of the Democratic Congressional Campaign Committee, Rep. Tony Coelho said, "Republicans will continue to be non-players in the legislative arena." Henry Waxman, a fellow Democrat from California agreed. "If we have a united Democratic position," said Waxman, "Republicans are irrelevant."[28]

At the time these assessments were being offered in the House, party fortunes were just the reverse on the other side of the Capitol. When Republicans took control of the Senate in 1981, it was for the first time in twenty-six years. Democrats no longer had the power to set committee schedules, to select issues for committee hearings and investigations, and to control proceedings on the floor. According to some members of the former majority party, being a Democrat in the Senate was now similar to being a Republican in the House. Louisiana Democrat J. Bennett Johnston said that after 1981, "Many of us felt neutered, totally powerless, like fifth wheels around this place." On the other hand, Republicans held only a six-seat majority in the Senate. The narrowness of that margin and the nature of the 1986 elections led to a different perspective among some Democrats. "If you want to see a silver lining in this dark cloud," said Kentucky Sen. Wendell Ford, "we'll have been able to see what the Republicans had gone through for 26 years." "Maybe when we do take the majority, we'll do things differently from what they've done, what we've done in the past." Democrats in the Senate could take this long view not only because many regarded their being in the minority as a temporary status, but also because both the party split and Senate rules permitted members of the Senate minority to play a more active role than Republicans could in the House. This difference was evident in House and Senate action on tax reform legislation. House Republicans protested against what they regarded as their exclusion from the bill-writing process with a 14-to-164 vote against bringing tax reform legislation to the floor in December 1985. Extensive lobbying by President Reagan turned around fifty-four Republican votes, but even when the House did reverse itself and bring the tax bill to the floor a week later, 110 Republicans still voted against the measure. Senate passage of the tax reform measure in June 1986 was strikingly different from the earlier House action. Committee leaders presented the bill as a bipartisan measure; the Republican chairman of the Finance Committee gave full credit to the work of key Senate Democrats, and the Senate passed the bill by a 97-to-3 vote. Minority participation in the Senate is greatly enhanced by Senate rules that permit any senator to bring an amendment to the floor without first having to go through a committee and that enable a single senator to delay action by threatening a filibuster. The effect of these rules on minority participation was clear in May 1986, when the threat of a Democratic filibuster convinced Republican leaders to delay a vote on selling arms to Saudi Arabia. In criticizing party leaders for that decision, Sen. Barry Goldwater (R-AZ) expressed a clear view of the majority party's responsibility for organizing each chamber of Congress: "I think we ought to vote tonight, frankly. That is what the majority party is for. We are supposed to run this place, but I am beginning to think we do not."[29]

House Party Organization

The four key elements of the Democratic organization in the House of Representatives are the Speaker, the whip organization, the Democratic Steering and Policy Committee, and the House Democratic Caucus. The Republican equivalents, who are charged with organizing the opposition rather than the business of the House, are the Republican leader, the Republican whip organization, the Policy Committee, and the Republican Conference.

When Tip O'Neill left the House at the end of the Ninety-ninth Congress (1985–1986), he had served in that chamber for thirty-three years and been Speaker for ten. Only former Speaker Sam Rayburn had held that office longer than O'Neill, but Rayburn's service as Speaker between 1940 and 1961 had twice been interrupted by Republican majorities in the House (1947–1949 and 1953–1955). The departure of Tip O'Neill after establishing a record for the longest consecutive tenure as Speaker invited comparison with Rayburn and with others who had held that office. Congressional scholar Ronald M. Peters, who was completing a book on the office, had this to say: "I don't think he will be regarded as an institution, the way Sam Rayburn was, or as a great political leader, like Henry Clay. But Tip was a Speaker who filled the shoes of that office."[30] And O'Neill himself offered this assessment:

> Sam Rayburn could do things that I could never think of doing today. He didn't know 20 guys in Congress, but he was an amazing power. Today, if I call a committee chairman and say, "Let's do this," he says, "I have to talk to my subcommittee chairmen, and they have to talk to their members, and they have to talk to their staffs." But it's all better now. It's not dictatorial like it used to be.[31]

Tip O'Neill's tenure, first as majority leader and then as Speaker, coincided with the decentralization of power and increased participation of junior members brought about by the reforms of the 1970s. The decreased power of committee chairmen, which O'Neill suggests makes the Speaker's job more difficult and time consuming, also had the effect of weakening committee leaders as competitors of party leaders for institutional power. In that relative sense, then, the power of the Speaker and of other party leaders has actually been enhanced by those decentralizing reforms.

In addition, a number of specific reforms during this period centralized power under the Speaker. A 1973 reform made the Speaker the head of the Committee on Committees and created a new Steering and Policy Committee, with members appointed by the Speaker and selected by regional caucuses. In 1975, the Speaker's discretion in referring bills to committee was broadened by permitting the Speaker to send a bill to two or more committees concurrently or sequentially, to divide a bill and send different sections to different committees, to create ad hoc committees for considering a particular matter, and to set time limits on committee consideration of a bill. Additional reforms in 1975 gave the Speaker the power to nominate Democratic members and the chairperson of the House Rules Committee and gave the Democratic Steering and Policy Committee the power to make all committee appointments. The Ninety-fifth and Ninety-sixth Congresses (1977–1978 and 1979–1980) saw a continuation of this trend toward a stronger Speaker in a number of procedural rules changes that made it easier for the leadership to control floor proceedings and prevent delaying actions by the minority. All of these centralizing reforms have given the modern Speaker a wide range of tools for exercising party leadership, but they in no way guarantee success.

The term *whip* came to Congress from the strong party organizations found in eighteenth century British Parliament and had been derived from "whipper-in," the person in charge of keeping the hounds together in a fox hunt. The majority whip organization has grown from just a few members in the 1930s to more than sixty today. The majority whip occupies the number-three position in the party organization and until January 1985 had been appointed by the number-two officer, the House majority leader, who in turn, was elected by the House Democratic Caucus. In 1985, however, the caucus voted to elect rather than to appoint the majority whip. Proponents of an elected whip argued that because the whip often spoke for the party and because that position had been part of a leadership ladder (Tip O'Neill had moved up from whip to majority leader to Speaker and Tom Foley had been the whip before his election as majority leader), it was important that all members of the party have a say in choosing the whip. In addition to the majority whip, the whip's organization consists of a chief deputy whip, seven deputy whips, thirty-two at-large whips, twenty-three assistant whips, and ad hoc task forces to deal with particular bills. Assistant whips are elected by the Democratic members from a particular geographic area, while the deputy and at-large whips are chosen by the Democratic leadership (Speaker, majority leader, and majority whip). The whip organization is an intelligence organization for the party leadership. Whips collect and disseminate information important to House consideration of a bill. The whip organization disseminates information by issuing whip notices, which summarize the major issues involved, on all important bills and by informing all Democratic members of the upcoming legislative schedule. The collection of information is conducted primarily by the assistant whips through whip checks in which all Democratic members are asked "Will you vote for" or "Will you oppose" a particular measure; it is implicit in these whip checks that a "yes" response is the leadership position. The tally from these polls is a key resource for party leaders as they attempt to build majorities. A whip meeting held every Thursday morning and regularly attended by fifty or more Democrats provides another intelligence source for the leadership. The two-way nature of those meetings is captured in a staff member's description: "Very often there are screaming matches. It's not a tea party."[32]

The Democratic Steering and Policy Committee was created as part of the broad reforms adopted in 1973. In the Ninety-seventh Congress (1981–1982), the membership of the Steering and Policy Committee was increased from twenty-four to twenty-nine by adding the chairmen of the Appropriations, Budget, Rules, and Ways and Means Committees and the secretary of the Democratic Caucus to the existing membership of elected and appointed party leaders. While the Speaker obviously will have a great impact on Steering and Policy Committee decisions, the committee is intended to function not simply as an extension of the Speaker but rather as an independent and representative formulator of party policy. Political scientists Lawrence Dodd and Bruce Oppenheimer consider this committee a key to strong party government in Congress. "Ideally, the Steering and Policy Committee will become a representative body that keeps the Speaker in touch with the general sentiments of the party, provides healthy debate and innovative direction on public policy, gives guidance to committees and subcommittees, and spurs the party leadership into an articulate, persuasive policy role that reflects the dominant sentiment of the party."[33] Although the committee has not yet reached that point, it has played an increasingly active policy role in recent years. Beginning with the Ninety-sixth Congress (1979–1980), the Democratic Steering and Policy Committee put more effort into the earlier stages of legislation than it had previously by creating ad hoc task forces to work with subcommittees and committees to develop and pass specific bills. In addition to its policy role, the Democratic Steering and Policy Committees serve as the Democratic Committee on Committees, a function it was given in 1975. Although the Democratic Caucus must give final approval of those assignments and has on occasion overturned them, the Steering Committee's committee-on-committees role has met with general approval in the House.

The House Democratic Caucus is made up of all Democratic representatives meeting as a group to discuss procedural matters such as reviewing committee assignments, voting on committee chairpersons, electing party leaders, and recommending changes in House rules and procedures. Unlike the Steering and Policy Committee, the caucus is supposed to concern itself with procedural rather than policy matters. As we shall see, however, this is not always the case. During the 1970s, the Democratic Caucus emerged as a major force in the House both as an instigator of sweeping reforms that changed the structure of the House and as an important check on theretofore independent committee chairpersons. Two rules adopted in 1969—one requiring monthly caucus meetings and the other giving any member the right to bring an issue before the caucus for debate and possible resolution of a policy position—laid the groundwork for this development. Reforms in 1971 and 1973 gave the caucus the power to review nominations for committee chairpersons coming from the Committee on Committees, and, in 1975, the caucus deposed the chairmen of three major committees. In January 1985, the caucus voted to remove the chairman of the Armed Services Committee and instead of going to the next senior member, it elected the seventh-ranking member as chairman. This influence over the committee system gives the caucus an obvious, but indirect, toehold in the policy process. A more direct policy rule was exercised by the caucus when it instructed the Rules Committee to permit a House vote on the oil depletion allowance in 1975 and passed a resolution opposing military aid to Cambodia and Vietnam in the same year. The strong negative reaction of both policy opponents and the House leadership to these caucus policy votes led to the caucus backing off from its new policy role. It did not have another direct vote on a policy matter until 1978, when it passed a resolution opposing a Social Security tax increase. The policy focus of the caucus was revived after Republicans captured the White House in 1980, however, and in recent Congresses, the caucus has adopted party positions on issues ranging from U.S. policy toward Nicaragua and South Africa to budgets and tax reform. The tradition of junior members pushing for a stronger and more active caucus has continued and was evident in proposals offered in 1985. The proposals would require the caucus to meet at least twice a month and would ban standing committees from meeting when the caucus was in session.

The structure of the Republican organization in the House roughly parallels that of the Democrats, but it has not been as stable a hierarchy in terms of advancing leaders through the ranks. The official House Republican leaders are the chairman of the conference, vice-chairman of the conference, secretary of the conference, floor leader, whip, and chief deputy whip. In addition to these officers, the chairpersons of the Policy Committee and the Research Committee and the ranking minority member of the House Rules Committee are important figures in the House Republican leadership. The Republicans have a separate Committee on Committees for making all Republican committee assignments rather than having the Policy Committee do this as the Democrats do.

The Republican floor leader heads that chamber's party in the same sense that the Speaker leads the majority party. When Robert Michel was elected Republican floor leader in December 1980, he changed the title of his office from minority leader to Republican Leader. The Republican's long-term status as the minority party has been frustrating to Michel and to other party leaders and has also produced a great deal of conflict and debate over what the role of the opposition party should be. To illustrate, in the years before they won the presidency in 1980, most Republican leaders saw their role as one of offering alternatives to House Democrats' programs and of attempting to weaken the other party's incumbents by forcing roll call votes on social and economic issues that they thought would hurt Democrats at the polls. A different approach was employed during the first two years of the Reagan administration, however, because House Republicans and the Boll Weevil conservatives from the Democratic party had a working majority in the House. This majority permitted Republican leaders and representatives to act as lawmakers in getting the economic programs of the Reagan administration through Congress. After losing that working majority in the 1982 elections, House Republicans split over what the proper role of the party should be. One side of that division was represented by a dozen junior members organized as the Conservative Opportunity Society (COS). Georgia Rep. Newt Gingrich and Minnesota's Vin Weber, two of the most vocal COS leaders, favored a strategy of confrontation with Democratic leaders and engaged in what they called guerilla tactics to block House proceedings. The conflict over whether McCloskey or McIntyre won Indiana's Eighth District provided many opportunities during 1985 for conservative Republicans to engage in confrontational tactics. They did so, as often as possible, with an eye toward the television cameras in the House. Their goal was high visibility and the widest audience possible for the representation of their views. On the other side of the debate within the Republican party were moderates who felt that bipartisan compromise was a better strategy for a minority party. Rep. Bill Green (R-NY) and Mickey Edwards (R-OK), both of whom serve on the House Appropriations Committee, which has a strong bipartisan tradition, exemplify this wing of the party. "Conservatives are not part of the process of shaping legislation," said Green, and he argued that moderates "have a lot more to show in terms of legislative products." And here is what Edwards had to say about the COS strategy of confrontation: "I don't want to change the United States Congress into a high school fraternity, always looking for ways to throw pillows and have water fights, always looking for ways to attack the Democrats."[34] In 1985, Republican Leader Michel supported COS tactics as a form of protesting Democrats' behavior in seating McCloskey from Indiana. Overall, however, Michel's service as floor leader has been more in line with the lawmaking approach of GOP moderates. The debate over strategy in the minority party, like much of the disagreement within the Democratic party as well, seems to turn on the value that each side gives to lawmaking and to representation.

Senate Party Organization

In his first press conference after being elected majority leader of the Senate, Robert Dole was given an early Christmas present by his wife, Secretary of Transportation Elizabeth Hanford Dole. The present was a schnauzer puppy with a large sign announcing "Leader" hanging around the puppy's neck. The new majority leader stood at the podium holding the puppy and waited for the questions to begin. "Is it housebroken?" asked one reporter. Without missing a beat, Dole shot back: "He's housebroken, but not Senate broken." Beneath the humor, Dole's message was clear: He intended to be a strong leader of the Senate. "If we really want the discipline, I'm willing to help provide it," he told reporters. "And sometimes," he added, "if we really don't want the discipline."[35] A veteran of sixteen years in the Senate, the new majority leader understood well the independent nature of senators, regardless of party.

A membership of 100 rather than 435 makes a big difference in the structure of party leadership in the Senate. The fact that an estimated 10 percent of all senators at any given time are seriously pursuing higher office in the form of the presidency or vice-presidency means that a large number of them are more interested in leading than they are in being led. These differences in size and members' goals help to account for the Senate party leadership's being a smaller, more informal, and more collegial structure than the House. The key elements of the Senate party leadership are the majority leader or floor leader, the majority whip and assistant whips, the party conference (which includes all senators of that party), and the Policy Committee. Senate Republicans also have a Committee on Committees while Senate Democrats use the Democratic Steering Committee for making committee assignments.

The majority leader in the Senate might be considered the equivalent of the House Speaker in the sense that they both are responsible for controlling floor proceedings. Unlike the Speaker, the Senate majority leader is not a constitutional officer nor does he or she preside over the Senate. Like the Speaker, however, the majority leader is responsible for scheduling legislation, organizing the chamber, and for developing and building support for party positions on legislative issues. The responsibilities and powers of the majority leader have developed by custom and usage over the years, and are based more on informal agreement than on written rules.

When Sen. Robert Dole was elected majority leader at the end of 1984, he replaced Sen. Howard Baker, who had held the position for four years. Baker's election came as a result of the Republicans being a majority in the Senate for the first time in twenty-five years. It was also the first time since 1933 that the Senate was controlled by one party and the House by another. The divided chamber control in the Ninety-seventh Congress (1981–1982) served as an incentive for the majority party in each chamber to follow a path of moderation and coalition building rather than one based on partisanship. Minority Senate Democrats could appeal to the Democratic majority in the House to overcome blatantly partisan actions in the Senate, and minority House Republicans could make the same appeals to the Republican majority in the Senate. Senator Baker's low-key leadership style fit in well with the demands generated by this divided party control. Senators from both parties came forward with praise for what one senator called Baker's "even-handed, orderly" approach to being majority leader. "I think he's misguided as a Republican," said a liberal Democratic senator, "but I've taken to calling him Glue Baker, because he's holding the whole thing together for them." A Republican colleague described Baker as "the best leader we've had in the Senate in a half-century."[36] Senator Baker's bipartisan approach was most clearly evident during his first year when he gained Senate approval of the Reagan administration's sale of AWACS to Saudi

Arabia in October 1981. Throughout the first session of the Ninety-seventh Congress (1981–1982), Baker's leadership and the Reagan administration together produced the highest level of Republican party unity in Senate voting since 1953.[37] Despite this early success, Baker became increasingly frustrated by the difficulty of controlling the Senate schedule and became more and more the target of conservative Republicans who rejected his centrist approach. In 1984, Howard Baker announced that he would leave the Senate in order to pursue the presidency in 1988 or some later year.

Although Dole won the majority leader's position by a margin of only three votes, he quickly established himself as a forceful and independent leader of the Senate. Dole had this to say about the man he succeeded in that office: "Howard is an easygoing guy, with a lot of patience—a lot more than I have."[38] An aide to the Republican leadership compared the two majority leaders along these lines: "Bob Dole is much more of a freelancer than Howard Baker ever was. I think he'll try to help the Administration, but I don't think he'll be the Administration's point man in the Senate the way Baker was. He's going to call his own shots."[39] Senator Dole's approach to the majority leader's job was made clear soon after he assumed office: "I'm not going to be confrontational, but I'm not going to be a patsy for the White House staff either." He suggested that a shared feeling that the Senate was not working very well after 1982 had produced a climate in which "most senators want leadership—if they wanted someone to just call meetings, or someone who will always check with each and every senator, they wouldn't want me."[40]

Robert Dole's record as majority leader during the Ninety-ninth Congress (1985–1986) displayed this independence from the White House on such issues as farm policy and the budget. At the same time, however, Dole's leadership and his own votes favored the Reagan Administration to the degree that Dole ranked as the most reliable Senate supporter of the president's programs in 1985.[41] The fit between Senator Dole's leadership style and the Senate of the 1980s is implicit in the announcement of Alaska Sen. Ted Stevens, whom Dole had defeated in 1984 by only three votes, that Stevens might again try for the majority leader's position. The Alaska senator said that he had no complaints about Dole's record as majority leader, and his only reason for contesting the office was Dole's use of the position as a steppingstone to the presidency.[42] His tenure as majority leader in the Ninety-ninth Congress showed Robert Dole to be capable as both the inside leader who sets the Senate schedule and works toward compromise and the spokesperson for the Senate who represents that institution to the outside world.

Senate Democrats have been more unified in their minority status than have their House Republican counterparts. The small margin of the Republican majority, the Senate's emphasis on full participation by all members, and the bipartisan development of major bills such as tax reform have all made being in the minority less frustrating for senators than for representatives. Senate Democrats have been able to take an active part in lawmaking and to maintain their influence in that chamber. However, a number of Senate Democrats have indicated a dissatisfaction with their leader's performance in the outside role of party spokesperson. Sen. Robert Byrd (D-WV) was challenged in 1984 and again in 1986 for the position of minority leader, a post he has held since 1981, when Republican control of the Senate ended his four-year stint as majority leader. Both challengers conceded that Senator Byrd was a master at the inside game of the Senate, and both stressed a need to improve the outside game. In announcing that he would run for minority leader in 1986, Louisiana Sen. J. Bennett Johnston said that now that Senate proceedings were televised, Senate Democrats "need a brand new image." "I think we need a little passion out there on the floor." A similar message came from the man who had challenged Byrd in 1984, Florida Sen. Lawton Chiles: "I think we need somebody who can communicate like Robert Dole can, who can articulate ideas and concepts and is ready to do that. We're talking about a new media day, where you've got to be proactive, thinking about getting our message out there."[43] What is evident in these assessments of Baker, Dole, and Byrd is a standard that party leaders be effective both at the inside game of lawmaking and at the outside game of representation.

Party Leadership

The primary responsibility of majority party leaders and the chief function of the majority party organization in both the House and the Senate is to see that policy proposals favored by the majority are passed by Congress. To achieve that goal, the party organization must bring together both the party and the chamber in order to conduct legislative business. Once organized, the party leadership's major functions are gathering and disseminating information relevant to the policies under consideration, scheduling the business of the House and the Senate, and controlling the floor proceedings of both chambers.

House and Senate party leaders have gone about meeting these responsibilities in a variety of ways. Underlying this variety is the fact that any party leader has an established source of resources from which he or she can draw. All party leaders dip from this same pool of resources, but the specific techniques of leadership that they can employ will depend upon such factors as personalities, the legislative structure as changed and shaped by reforms, the party occupying the White House, and the general political climate. Rather than going through a long list of party leadership techniques and cases illustrating such techniques, let us close this section with a quick look at the general sources of leadership party leaders have at their disposal as they attempt to provide a centralizing force and reliable cue network in Congress.

Randall Ripley has suggested that all successful tactical maneuvers and leadership ploys are connected to four basic resources of party leaders' influence. These four resources are: (1) the leaders' ability to use congressional rules to their own advantage because of their expertise in such matters; (2) the power to bestow or withhold tangible rewards such as appointments to special committees and commissions, office space, and material support for reelection campaigns; (3) the ability to influence members' standing in the informal hierarchy in each chamber and thereby help to determine their position in the cue network of that chamber; and (4) control over the intelligence and communications network in Congress.[44] Structural reforms, the personal style of elected leaders, and the political variables related to the larger political system all affect the relative importance of each of these resources. But taken together, these four resources of power represent a stable base from which all party leaders draw whatever influence they have over the legislative process.

A quick rundown of the impact of these resources on congressional behavior includes the following observations. The first resource—ability to use rules effectively—works primarily to the advantage of the majority party. Minority party leaders can employ chamber rules to obstruct passage of unwanted legislation, but the majority party—because it controls scheduling (both when and under what conditions a bill will be brought to the floor)—can exercise great influence in pushing legislation through Congress. This is particularly true in the House, where structural controls over the floor are more important. House rules facilitate quick passage of noncontroversial legislation under procedures such as "suspension," which are designed to maximize the lawmaking function and thus enhance the party leaders' control over the floor proceedings. Senate rules put greater emphasis on individual representation and provide more opportunities for delay.

The remaining three resources of leadership influence—control over tangible rewards, ability to affect each member's informal position, and control over the communications network in Congress—have all been affected by sweeping reforms that took place in the 1970s. When it comes to horse trading, party leaders find that they have less control over dispensing many of the tangible rewards—public works projects or geographically targeted programs—than they had prior to the reforms of the 1970s. "You have a hunting license to persuade—that's about all you have," is the way House Speaker Jim Wright described the situation.[45] Party leaders attempt to persuade members by promising assistance in gaining a sought-after committee assignment or by favorably scheduling a member's bill. But all of that takes place in what Barbara Sinclair has described as "a context of limited resources and high uncertainty."[46]

The party reforms discussed throughout this chapter can be said to have cut in two directions. First, they enhanced the relative power of party leaders by reducing the potential for challenges to that power by independent committee leaders. Second, the reforms opened up the congressional process and by doing so increased the number of decisional arenas in which party leaders have difficulty gaining compliance because members are subject to counterpressures from constituents and from outside interests.[47] The reforms, in other words, had both a centralizing effect in their adding to the powers of party leaders and a decentralizing effect brought about by the increased demands for representation that comes when decisions are made in the open. In all cases, however, political parties and party leaders serve as brokers. Internally they build coalitions among individual members, committees, and the two chambers in order to pass legislation. They also serve as brokers by linking elections and the activities of interest groups to what happens in Congress. Without the coordination that political parties can provide, elections would be a representational activity with little or no effect on lawmaking.

Endnotes

1. Senator Mattingly and former Speaker O'Neill, quoted in Steven V. Roberts, "In the Matter of 'Disenchantment' With Dole," *New York Times*, April 24, 1986, p. A20

2. Alan Ehrenhalt, "A 50–50 Senate: Prescription for Confusion," *Congressional Quarterly Weekly Report*, April 19, 1986, p. 891.

3. Anthony Downs, *An Economic Theory of Democracy* (New York: Harper & Row, 1957).

4. Stanley Kelley, Jr., and Thad W. Mirer, "The Simple Act of Voting," *American Political Science Review*, June, 1974, p. 574, and Stanley Kelley, Jr., *Interpreting Elections* (Princeton: Princeton University Press, 1983), p. 11.

5. Barbara Hinckley, *Congressional Elections* (Washington, D.C.: Congressional Quarterly, 1981), p. 75.

6. Paul R. Abramson, John H. Aldrich, David W. Rohde, *Change and Continuity in the 1984 Elections* (Washington, D.C.: Congressional Quarterly Press, 1986), p. 269.

7. Hinckley, *Congressional Elections*, pp. 69–70.

8. Stephen Gettinger, "Hill Voting Participation Hits 33-Year High," *Congressional Quarterly Weekly Report*, January 11, 1986, p. 81.

9. Richard L. Lyons, "Marathon Adjournment Session Leaves Members Groggy," *Washington Post*, October 16, 1978, p. A8.

10. Ann Cooper, "House Use of Suspensions Grows Drastically," *Congressional Quarterly Weekly Report*, September 30, 1978, p. 2693.

11. Donald R. Matthews and James A. Stimson, *Yeas and Nays: Normal Decision Making in the U.S. House of Representatives* (New York: John Wiley and Sons, 1975), pp. 18 and 25. Copyright © 1975 John Wiley and Sons, Inc., reprinted by permission.

12. Ibid.

13. Ibid., p. 103.

14. Randall B. Ripley, *Party Leaders in the House of Representatives* (Washington, D.C.: The Brookings Institution, 1967), p. 141.

15. William R. Shaffer, *Party and Ideology in the United States Congress* (Lanham, Md.: University Press of America, 1980). For an analysis of declining partisanship, see Melissa P. Collie and David W. Brady, "The Decline of Partisan Voting Coalitions in the House of Representatives," in Lawrence C. Dodd and Bruce I. Oppenheimer, eds., *Congress Reconsidered*, 3rd ed. (Washington, D.C.: Congressional Quarterly Press, 1985), pp. 272–287.

16. Steve Blakely, "Partisanship in Congress Up Sharply in 1985," *Congressional Quarterly Weekly Report*, January 11, 1986, pp. 86–91.

17. Aage R. Clausen, *How Congressman Decide: A Policy Focus* (New York: St. Martin's Press, 1973), pp. 93–100.

18. Jerrold E. Schneider, *Ideological Coalitions in Congress* (Westport, Conn.: Greenwood Press, 1979), p. 199.

19. Lewis Froman and Randall Ripley, "Conditions for Party Leadership: The Case of the House Democrats," *American Political Science Review*, March, 1965, pp. 52–63.

20. Unidentified leadership aide, quoted in Barbara Sinclair, *Majority Party Leadership in the U.S. House* (Baltimore: Johns Hopkins, 1983), p. 127.

21. Former Speaker O'Neill quoted in ibid., p. 90.

22. Blakely, "Partisanship in Congress Up Sharply in 1985," p. 86.

23. Paul Light, *Artful Work: The Politics of Social Security Reform* (New York: Random House, 1985), pp. 100–101.

24. Blakely, "Partisanship in Congress Up Sharply in 1985," p. 88.

25. Lewis Froman, *Congressmen and Their Constituencies* (New York: Rand McNally, 1963), p. 92.

26. Christopher Bond and Ken Kramer, quoted in Steven V. Roberts, "Races for Open Senate Seats Held Crucial by Both Parties," *New York Times*, July 20, 1986, p. 17.

27. Ripley, *Party Leaders in the House of Representatives* (Washington, D.C.: The Brookings Institution, 1967), p. 169. Also see Richard Born, "Cue-Taking within State Delegations in the U.S. House of Representatives," *Journal of Politics*, vol. 38 (February, 1976), pp. 71–94.

28. Representatives Michel, Hyde, Coelho, and Waxman, quoted in Janet Hook, "House GOP: Plight of a Permanent Minority," *Congressional Quarterly Weekly Report*, June 21, 1986, p. 1393.

29. Senators Johnston, Ford, and Goldwater, quoted in Janet Hook, "Senate Rules, Closeness of GOP Margin Keep Democrats Influential in Minority," *Congressional Quarterly Weekly Report*, June 21, 1986, pp. 1394–95.

30. Ronald M. Peters, Jr., quoted in Steven V. Roberts, "Assessing the Record-Setting Speaker O'Neill," *New York Times*, January 12, 1986, p. 34.

31. Ibid.

32. Diana Granat, "Today's Whip: Not Just Keeping Pack in Line," *Congressional Quarterly Weekly Report*, November 30, 1985, p. 2502.

33. Lawrence C. Dodd and Bruce I. Oppenheimer, "The House in Transition: Partnership and Opposition," in Dodd and Oppenheimer, (eds.), *Congress Reconsidered* (1985), p. 58.

34. Representatives Green and Edwards, quoted in Diane Granat, "Deep Divisions Loom Behind House GOP's Apparent Unity," *Congressional Quarterly Weekly Report*, March 23, 1985, p. 537.

35. Senator Dole, quoted in Martin Tolchin, "New Leader of the Senate," *New York Times*, November 29, 1984, p. B14.

36. Sens. Edward Kennedy and Christopher Dodd, quoted in Benjamin Taylor, "Reagan's Low-keyed Senate Magician," *Boston Globe*, November 22, 1981, p. A23; and unidentified senator, quoted in Norman J. Ornstein, Robert L. Peabody, and David W. Rohde, "The Senate Through the 1980s: Cycles of Change," in Dodd and Oppenheimer, eds., *Congress Reconsidered* (1985), p. 25.

37. Irwin B. Arieff, "Under Baker's Leadership Senate Republicans Maintain Unprecedented Voting Unity," *Congressional Quarterly Weekly Report*, September 12, 1981, p. A23.

38. Senator Dole, quoted in Norman J. Ornstein, "Dole as Majority Leader: An Early Assessment," *The Dirksen Congressional Center Report* (Pekin, Ill.), December, 1985, p. 5.

39. Unidentified leadership aide, quoted in Hedrick Smith, "A Shift Toward Center," *New York Times*, November 29, 1984, p. 1.

40. Ornstein, "Dole as Majority Leader," p. 5.

41. Janet Hook, "Hill Backing for Reagan Continues to Decline," *Congressional Quarterly Weekly Report*, January 11, 1986, p. 69.

42. Jacqueline Calmes, "Stevens Eyes New Bid for Senate GOP Leader," *Congressional Quarterly Weekly Report*, July 19, 1986, p. 1611.

43. Senator Johnston, quoted in Janet Hook, "Senator Johnston Challenges Byrd for Democratic Leadership," *Congressional Quarterly Weekly Report*, June 14, 1986, p. 1316; Senator Chiles, quoted in Hedrick Smith, "For Democrats, the Medium's a Mess," *New York Times*, December 10, 1984, p. B10.

44. Randall B. Ripley, *Congress: Process and Policy* (New York: Norton, 1983), pp. 233–36.

45. "Eroding Loyalty Weakening House Leaders," *Quincy Patriot Ledger*, June 7, 1979, p. 10.

46. Barbara Sinclair, *Majority Party Leadership in the U.S. House*, p. 174.

47. For a good overview of the effects of reform, see: Leroy N. Rieselbach, *Congressional Reform* (Washington, D.C.: Congressional Quarterly Press, 1986).

5

Committees

The Tax Reform Act of 1986 represented a high point in the legislative record of the Ninety-ninth Congress (1985–1986). In rewriting the federal tax code, the bill achieved two goals long sought by reformers—a reduction in tax rates and the closing of many loopholes used to avoid taxes. All sides agreed that the 1986 act was the most comprehensive tax reform measure to pass Congress in more than forty years. But there were a number of times when it seemed that major tax reform would never be passed in the Ninety-ninth Congress. One of those came on December 11, 1985, when the House voted 202–223 against a rule to consider the bill. Intensive personal lobbying by President Reagan turned around about fifty Republican votes in the House, enough to pass the bill six days later. Hopes of approving a tax bill faded again in April 1986, when the Senate Finance Committee suspended its consideration of the bill after recognizing that by expanding a number of special-interest loopholes, the committee had produced a revenue shortfall of almost $30 billion.

What happened in both of those instances to get tax reform moving again was that proponents of tax reform found ways to get legislators to focus less on being representatives and more on being lawmakers. To illustrate, when the House of Representatives reversed its earlier vote and passed the tax reform bill on

December 17, 1985, it did so by voice vote. Usually, when the House passes such a major piece of legislation, it is by a roll call vote. In the tax reform case, procedural votes to consider the bill and the vote on an alternative bill offered by Republicans had been recorded votes. But there was no roll call on final passage of the bill in the House. One explanation for the absence of a roll call was that the vote had come around 11:00 P.M., after a long day of debates and votes on the bill, and that, in the words of a Republican opponent of the bill, "We were asleep at the switch."[1] House Speaker Tip O'Neill insisted that he had scanned the House floor at the time of final passage in order to recognize anyone calling for a roll call vote, and that he had gavelled the bill through on a voice vote only after no one called for a recorded vote. At the time, House Republican Leader Robert Michel was back in his office picking up some papers. A spokesperson for the GOP leadership later acknowledged that Republican leaders had avoided calling for a roll call vote on final passage of the tax bill in an effort to protect many colleagues from having to go on record either for or against the bill and therefore for or against the president, or business organizations who opposed the bill, or important constituency interests. The public accountability and representation implicit in a recorded vote was not there in House passage of the bill.

The choice of lawmaking over representation was even more evident in the Senate Finance Committee decision to suspend further action on the bill on April 18, 1986. At that point, the committee had held three weeks of public sessions where, under the watchful eyes of lobbyists, it had approved amendments giving tax breaks for private pensions, federal employees, municipal bonds, oil refineries, home builders, and other special interests. Finance Committee Chairman Bob Packwood said a suspension was needed because "the time has come to simply reflect on the way we are going." In order to do that, Packwood said the committee would move its deliberations behind closed doors. New Jersey Sen. Bill Bradley, a principal sponsor of tax reform, agreed. "I think we're at a predictable point in these deliberations," said Bradley. "I think we are going to be in the back room making some trades. It won't be as pure as I would like, but I think we can come out with something that reduces rates for the majority, gets low-income people off the rolls and improves the economy."[2]

The Senate Finance Committee decision to go behind closed doors was based not only on its own experience with public sessions but also on the record of the House Ways and Means Committee on tax reform. When the House Committee began its work on the bill in September 1985, it voted overwhelmingly (twenty-seven–two) to keep its meetings closed to the public. Rep. Bill Gradison of Ohio, a Republican member of Ways and Means, explained why he supported closed sessions: "I feel the committee produces a better bill behind closed doors. There is less posturing, less playing to the audiences. We are able to move much more quickly and I think, in the end, we do a better job." Ohio Democrat Don Pease, a former newspaper editor, was one of the few committee members to oppose closed sessions. Although Pease felt that legislators "ought to be willing to look the lobbyists in the eyes and make those decisions right out there in public," he recognized the lawmaking benefits of private meetings: "With a closed markup you can always say to lobbyists or constituents that you fought like a tiger for their position and asked for a record vote, but not enough members raised their hands. Members almost feel obligated to demand a record vote in public, and then you have members voting in a way they don't really want." Two close followers of tax legislation who are consistently on opposite sides of just about every substantive proposal found themselves in agreement on the closed-door procedure. One of them, a lobbyist for the Independent Petroleum Association of America (IPA) who had himself been moved out into the hallway, admitted: "In a public session there are so many different interest groups eyeballing the congressmen that they're so torn they end up doing something nonsensical." The director of The Ralph Nader Organization, Tax Reform Research Group, found that he agreed with the IPA lobbyist and that posed "a real dilemma for liberal reformers." "When you look at recent tax bills," he said, "the best ones have come out of closed sessions. You take what you can get and hope someday you can get a good bill at an open meeting."[3]

The legislative history of tax reform in the Ninety-ninth Congress includes a number of other instances where representatives and senators focused on lawmaking at the expense of representation. The positive experience gained from a private weekend retreat in the Virginia countryside by Ways and Means Committee members and staff and administration tax officials led the Senate Finance Committee to hold a similar private gathering at a West Virginia resort six months later. The justification for these weekend retreats was that they "gave the participants a chance to exchange views far removed from day-to-day pressures, the prying questions of reporters and the incessant arm-twisting of lobbyists."[4] After the House approved the tax bill, Massachusetts Rep. and Ways and Means Committee member Brian Donnelly recounted how he first came to believe that a tax bill would pass after hearing a one-on-one confrontation between Treasury Secretary James Baker and Ways and Means Chairman Dan Rostenkowski on a Friday afternoon in October 1985. Donnelly said he and three other members were meeting in the committee's library when Rostenkowski stormed past them into his office and loudly slammed the door. Baker followed five minutes later and soon Donnelly and the others "could hear both of them, right through the walls, yelling."[5] What Rostenkowski told Baker in no uncertain terms was that the administration would have to back off on its proposal to eliminate the state and local tax deduction. Baker said he could not possibly sell that to the president. Donnelly believed that the stormy private session between Baker and Rostenkowski paved the way for productive negotiations over the state and local tax deduction as well as other issues. Each side was able to make it quite clear what it wanted without being locked into a public position on specific provisions. Senate consideration of the tax bill included similar private meetings of great significance. A *New York Times* story detailing one such meeting began with the observation that "there are few secrets in Congress, mostly because senators and representatives cannot hide. Several times a day, they must leave their offices and private meetings to go to the Capitol to vote. They cannot avoid being buttonholed by almost anyone interested in what is going on." After continuing in this vein and describing the press of lobbyists outside the Finance Committee's meeting room, the *Times* reporter wrote, "That is why it is so unusual that perhaps the most important development in drafting the bill happened with hardly anyone knowing about it." The incident in question began on a Friday afternoon in May 1986 with Finance Committee Chairman Bob Packwood's announcement that the committee would recess for the weekend. Lobbyists, reporters, and most senators went home. On Saturday morning, however, Senator Packwood and a bipartisan group of five other Finance Committee senators got together with a few senior staff members and Deputy Treasury Secretary Richard G. Darman. The unannounced meeting continued well into Saturday night, and on

Sunday the group had produced a tax bill almost identical to the one passed the following month by the full Senate.[6]

What is clear in all of these instances relating to passage of the Tax Reform Act of 1986 is that legislators at times come to regard the goals of representation and lawmaking as working at cross purposes. Because committees are the workshops of Congress and because all of the events described here had to do with major legislation, the senators and representatives in all of these cases chose to sacrifice representation for the sake of lawmaking. Chapters 2 and 3 provided examples where representation was clearly the dominate value for legislators. And even though lawmaking is the primary focus of this chapter on committees, the structure and behavior of certain committees are shaped as much by representation as they are by lawmaking. Because the committee system includes both values, members of Congress always seem to be either reforming or considering changes in that system. And once again, it is the tension between representation and lawmaking that creates a dynamic for congressional change.

For the most part, however, this chapter is about lawmaking. It follows the discussion of parties in Chapter 4 in that it too considers the degree of centralization that is needed for Congress to perform its lawmaking function. On the one hand, congressional committees can exert a centralizing influence on the behavior of members and get them working toward a shared goal of lawmaking. On the other hand, many of the committee reforms of the 1970s, especially those seeking to improve representation, had a decentralizing impact on the committee system and produced what some people have called subcommittee government in Congress.

Subcommittees

One of the most important and comprehensive congressional reforms passed by Congress in the last half century was the Legislative Reorganization Act of 1946. It was a grand scheme to democratize and modernize Congress and to redress the imbalance of powers. During the war years, powers that once belonged to Congress had slipped to the executive branch. The key to streamlining and modernizing Congress to make it more efficient was to eliminate minor or inactive committees and to merge committees whose areas of jurisdiction seemed to be similar or overlapping. The Legislative Reorganization Act reduced the total number of standing committees in the House from forty-eight to nineteen and those in the Senate from thirty-three to fifteen. The 1946 reorganization was clearly intended to improve the lawmaking functions of Congress by consolidating and centralizing legislative power. With fewer independent committee fiefdoms, it was expected that party leaders would be able to exercise a tighter control and more efficiently bring forth a cohesive legislative program.

There was one side effect of this legislative reorganization that served to undercut the centralizing influence—the continuation and expansion of the number of subcommittees in both chambers. In 1945 there were 106 House subcommittees and 68 Senate subcommittees; in 1968 there were 139 House subcommittees and 104 Senate subcommittees. Table 5–1 shows the number and distribution of subcommittees in the One-hundredth Congress (1987–1988): 132 House subcommittees and 84 Senate subcommittees.

The centralization sought under the 1946 Reorganization Act has been effectively circumvented by the proliferation of subcommittees. Prior to the 1946 act, there were 81 standing committees and 174 subcommittees in Congress; in the One-hundredth Congress, there were 38 standing committees and 216 subcommittees. "Reforms have created something approaching a subcommittee government in Congress," one observer noted. The same observer commented on the policy implications of this when a hospital cost containment bill died in Congress during the Carter administration:

> A decade ago, Carter's bill would have gone to one committee in the House and one in the Senate. Last year (1978), it went to two committees in each chamber and subcommittees in each committee. Each of the four subcommittees would get to take a crack at Carter's bill. And then each of the four parent committees would have its turn. That made eight major station stops. The bill reached seven of the eight stations but at each of the stops it ran into peculiar problems of politics, power, and personalities.[7]

There are a number of explanations for this increase in the number and importance of subcommittees in Congress. First, this proliferation of subcommittees and the concomitant increase in

TABLE 5-1 Standing Committees and Subcommittees in the One-Hundredth Congress (1987-1988)

| | Number | |
Committee	Members	Subcommittees
House of Representatives		
1. Agriculture	43	8
2. Appropriations	57	13
3. Armed Services	51	7
4. Banking, Finance and Urban Affairs	50	8
5. Budget	35	0 (8 task forces)
6. District of Columbia	11	3
7. Education and Labor	34	8
8. Energy and Commerce	42	6
9. Foreign Affairs	42	8
10. Government Operations	39	7
11. House Administration	19	6
12. Interior and Insular Affairs	37	6
13. Judiciary	35	7
14. Merchant Marines and Fisheries	42	6
15. Post Office and Civil Service	21	7
16. Public Works and Transportation	50	6
17. Rules	13	2
18. Science, Space, and Technology	45	7
19. Small Business	42	6
20. Standards of Official Conduct	12	0
21. Veterans' Affairs	34	5
22. Ways and Means	36	6
Subcommittee Total		132
Senate		
1. Agriculture, Nutrition and Forestry	18	6
2. Appropriations	29	13
3. Armed Services	20	6

Continued

TABLE 5-1 *Continued*

Committee	Number Members	Number Subcommittees
4. Banking, Housing and Urban Affairs	18	4
5. Budget	24	0
6. Commerce, Science and Transportation	20	8
7. Energy and Natural Resources	19	5
8. Environment and Public Works	16	5
9. Finance	20	7
10. Foreign Relations	20	7
11. Governmental Affairs	14	5
12. Judiciary	14	6
13. Labor and Human Resources	16	6
14. Rules and Administration	16	0
15. Small Business	18	6
16. Veterans' Affairs	11	0
Subcommittee Total		84

Source: Compiled by author from data in *Congressional Quarterly Special Report,* May 2, 1987, pp. 3–65.

The table lists only standing committees and excludes select committees in both chambers. Those committees in the House are: Select Aging (64 members, 4 subcommittees), Select Children, Youth and Families (30 members, 3 task forces), Select Committee to Investigate Covert Arms Transactions with Iran (15 members), Select Hunger (26 members, 2 task forces), Select Intelligence (17 members, 3 subcommittees), and Select Narcotics Abuse and Control (25 members). In the Senate: Select Committee on Secret Military Assistance to Iran and the Nicaraguan Opposition (11 members), Select Ethics (6 members), Select Indian Affairs (8 members), Select Intelligence (15 members), and Special Aging (19 members).

specialized expertise represent a rational attempt by the legislative branch to keep pace with the increasing specialization and decentralized autonomy of executive agencies. A Senate Finance Committee Social Security Financing Subcommittee and a House Ways and Means Social Security Subcommittee are clearly in a better position to oversee and legislate in their particular area than the full committees that are also dealing with other major policy areas.

Second, we can look at the proliferation of subcommittees in terms of the party leaders' control over tangible rewards for members. Committee and subcommittee assignments are one of the most effective ways in which party leaders are able to manipulate their members. A high rate of return of committee incumbents and a fixed number of committees can limit the available resources for party leaders in this area. It is only natural that leaders would want to expand their resource base by increasing the size of committees and the number of subcommittees.[8] The proliferation of subcommittee seats available no doubt decreases the value or scarcity of such leadership resources. At the same time, it increases the base of rewards from which party leaders are able to draw.

Third, we have the notion of politics as property, of subcommittees as turf. The central idea here is that committee and subcommittee positions are a political property of value to the holder of that position. The value may be primarily symbolic and only have consequences in terms of the member's prestige and chances of reelection. Or, it might be an important position from which the member is able to affect policy outcomes. David Mayhew sees credit claiming as one of the primary activities or goals of legislators, and notes that the existence of a great number of subcommittee positions means that "every member can aspire to occupy a part of at least one piece of policy turf small enough so that he can claim personal responsibility for some of the things that happen on it."[9] The chairman of the House Commission on Administrative Review, Rep. David Obey of Wisconsin, had this notion of subcommittee appointment as political property in mind when he said:

> The problem right now is, everyone around this place is badge-happy. If you get to be a subcommittee chairman, you get to have an extra staffer, maybe even an extra secretary. So you have great pressure to expand subcommittees, the number of subcommittees; the numbers show it.
>
> We do not have an expansion of subcommittees because we have so many interesting subjects. We have expansion of subcommittees because we have a lot of people, number one, who want a badge and, number two, who want the ability to get an extra staffer.[10]

This proliferation of subcommittees, and the number of people with badges, led another representative to chuckle, "When you walk down the halls and you don't know a member's name, if you say 'Hello, Mr. Chairman' you come out right one out of three times."[11] Once members are given a piece of legislative property, in the form of subcommittee positions, it becomes difficult to take it away from them for the sake of a more efficient Congress.

All three explanations for the increase in the number of subcommittees make sense. The additional consideration of the representational function served by these multiple points of access for citizens and expanded number of podiums for articulating different viewpoints should not be ignored. But to really appreciate the lawmaking functions now being performed by subcommittees, we have to look at some of the reforms of the 1970s.

Between 1971 and 1975, a series of changes in House rules and in positions adopted by the controlling House Democratic Caucus drastically altered the relative power of committees and subcommittees and their leadership. The impact of these changes was to reduce greatly the power and authority of committees and their chairpersons and to enhance greatly the independence and real policy roles of subcommittees. A summary of these rules includes the following:[12]

1. *No House member can be chairperson of more than one legislative subcommittee.* This rule was adopted at the beginning of the Ninety-second Congress and had an immediate impact on the legislative structure. Sixteen new subcommittee chairmen were brought in through this reform in 1971 with positions on such important committees as Banking, Currency and Housing, Foreign Affairs, and Judiciary. The reform opened up subcommittee leadership positions to middle-level and junior Democrats who previously had been frozen out by conservative senior Democrats on many of these committees. One study showed that the new chairmen of the subcommittees had an average seniority in 1971 of about seven years of service, while the men they replaced had an average seniority of almost eighteen years of service.[13]

2. *Since the adoption by the Democratic Caucus of a series of new rules in 1973 known collectively as the Subcommittee Bill of Rights, committee chairpersons are required to share most of their powers with other Democrats on the committee, who are*

formally organized into a committee Democratic caucus. The committee caucus has the power to select subcommittee chairpersons, establish subcommittee jurisdictions, provide full subcommittee budgets, and guarantee that all members be given a major subcommittee assignment whenever vacancies occur. Giving the committee caucus the power to establish subcommittee jurisdictions means that committee chairpersons can no longer follow their long-standing practice of arbitrarily assigning bills to select subcommittees that will do what the chairperson wants. A final rule requires the committee chairperson to refer bills to subcommittees within two weeks after their referral to the full committee. This requirement eliminates the chairperson's power of quietly vetoing proposed legislation by simply not referring it to a subcommittee.

3. *All House committees having more than twenty members are required to have at least four subcommittees.* As Table 4–1 indicated, only the District of Columbia Committee, the House Administration Committee, the Rules Committee, and the Standards of Official Conduct Committee have fewer than twenty members. (Because of their special centralizing role in the legislative process the budget committees in both chambers have no subcommittees.) The House Ways and Means Committee, which had operated without subcommittees for over fifteen years under the tight control of former chairman Wilbur Mills, was the chief target of this new subcommittee requirement. Ways and Means now has six relatively autonomous subcommittees organized in terms of distinct policy areas within the full committee's jurisdiction. The six subcommittees are: Health, Oversight, Public Assistance, Social Security, Trade, and Select Revenue Measures.

4. *All subcommittee chairpersons and ranking minority subcommittee members are authorized to hire at least one staff person who works directly with them on their subcommittee work.* On a committee such as Foreign Affairs, which has nine subcommittees, this means that there is now a subcommittee staff bureaucracy totaling twenty professionals. By making subcommittee leaders less dependent upon full committee staff (which is under the direction of the full committee leadership), the autonomy and independence of the subcommittee is further enhanced.

5. *Committees are required to have written rules.* These rules have the effect of reducing or eliminating the great discre-

tionary power that chairpersons were able to exercise in the absence of written committee rules, and to provide another step in the institutionalization of subcommittees. (Aspects of these written rules are connected with the formal relationships between the committee and its subcommittees.)

6. *Senior Democrats are restricted to membership on only two of a committee's subcommittees as voted by the Democratic Caucus in December 1974.* This rules change was directed primarily at the Appropriations Committee, where multiple subcommittee memberships permitted a handful of senior Democrats to dominate subcommittees handling funding for such important areas as defense, agriculture, labor, health, education, and welfare appropriations. The thrust of this rules change is to open up subcommittee positions to younger and middle-level members.

7. *A final reform measure, adopted at the beginning of the Ninety-fourth Congress, required that chairpersons of all of the appropriations subcommittees be approved by the full House Democratic Caucus.* The prime sponsor of this reform, Rep. David Obey of Wisconsin, ranked twenty-second out of the thirty-seven Democrats on the Appropriations Committee during the Ninety-fourth Congress. He saw these subcommittee reforms as being absolutely crucial to loosening the control of conservative chairman George Mahon of Texas and the "college of cardinals" (the conservative subcommittee chairmen) over the full Appropriations Committee.[14] A study of the committee published in 1981 shows that this reform had the desired effect: The election of subcommittee chairpersons, elevation of a new full committee chairman, and change in party ratio on the committee greatly diminished the influence of conservatives on the Appropriations Committee.[15]

One immediate effect of these reforms was an increase in activity at the subcommittee level. Dodd and Oppenheimer point out that "during the late 1940s and early 1950s only 20 or 30 percent of committee hearings occurred in subcommittees, whereas by the first session of the Ninety-fifth Congress (1977–1978), over 90 percent of all committee hearings took place in subcommittees."[16] Another effect (though not necessarily intended) was to increase the number of resignations at the upper end of the congressional hierarchy. In the spring of 1976, the number of retirements from Congress reached a new high as fifty-two members announced that they were not running for reelection. Included in the list of House retirees were six full committee chairmen: Henderson of Post Office and Civil Service, Jones of Public Works and Transportation, Morgan of International Relations, Patman of the Joint Economic Committee, Randall of the Select Committee on Aging, and Sullivan of Merchant Marine and Fisheries. One of the reasons offered for this high rate of committee chairpersons' retirement was that "being a chairman isn't all that great now that House rules changes have spread power around and left the chairman with little but a gavel and an administrative headache."[17]

The greatest effect of these reforms was to shift the site of most congressional lawmaking from the full committee to the subcommittee level. The increased number of subcommittee hearings and the ability of the subcommittees to dig deeper into narrow areas of policy has created a level of expertise unmatched by full committees. The increasing importance of subcommittees is summed up by a full committee chairman:

> I didn't pay much attention to subcommittee chairmen before—I did it all myself. Now, the subcommittee chairmen handle bills on the floor. They know that when they're answering questions on the floor they had better know what they're talking about. They really study the legislation now: they're much better prepared and more knowledgeable. Now we go to conference and they do the talking—the Senators never open their mouths. Their staffs are the only ones who know anything. So we're more effective with the Senate.[18]

It is clear that subcommittees in the House have come into their own as new centers of power. They once again seem to be "the inner circle of an inner circle," a phrase used to describe congressional subcommittees in the last century.[19] Some of the lawmaking benefits of subcommittee government have been that more members actively participate in policymaking and develop expertise in certain policy areas, which in turn makes policy innovation more likely. But there are drawbacks as well; a point that Dodd and Oppenheimer make in their analysis of the House of Representatives in the 1980s: "At its heart, subcommittee government creates a crisis of interest aggregation in the House. It largely removes committees as arenas in which interests will be compromised, brokered, and mediated. Subcommittee government has led to increased dominance of committee decision making by clientele groups, particularly single-interest groups."[20]

Subcommittee government means more than simply the existence of many subcommittees. It means that those subcommittees govern, that they make authoritative decisions. As the previous discussion and examples have made evident, subcommittee government is a phenomenon found in the House of Representatives. The Senate has long relied on subcommittees to provide tangible rewards to its members and to enable senators to engage in representational activities. Subcommittee hearings provide senators with a forum for representation. But when the time comes to amend, revise, and rewrite a bill—a practice referred to as "marking up" the bill—the full committee becomes the locus of activity for senators. In contrast to the House, the normal practice in the Senate is one of subcommittee hearings and full committee markup. Since any decisions made at the subcommittee level are likely to be reviewed, repeated, or reversed at the full committee level, senators regard subcommittee markup as an inefficient use of their time. That feeling leads to the situation described by the staff director of one Senate committee: "We tried a subcommittee markup a couple of years ago, but we could only get two senators to show. They just decided to get together over lunch and make some recommendations to the committee without taking formal action. We haven't tried it since."[21]

A difference between the two chambers that comes through clearly in the staff director's remarks is the pronounced individualism found in the Senate. And it is that characteristic, and its detrimental effect on lawmaking, that a representative worried would be one result of the House reforms discussed earlier:

> We're going the way of the Senate. We've spread the action by giving subcommittees more power and by making it possible for members to play more active roles on them. But there's nothing at this point to coordinate what all these bodies are doing and to place some checks on their growing independence.[22]

There was enough concern in both chambers about the effects of decentralization on the lawmaking capacity of Congress to produce some movement in the other direction. A committee reorganization adopted by the Senate in 1977 established a limit on senators' assignments and reduced the number of committees and subcommittees in that chamber. A year later, the House Democratic Caucus adopted a similar limit on subcommittee assignments. However, these reforms to check the drive toward decentralization have been greatly overshadowed by changes in the policy environment of Congress. The decentralized structure brought about through reform in the 1970s has not been eliminated. But the policy environment of the 1980s, a time when government is both divided and contracting and when taxing and spending questions monopolize all policy debates, has had a centralizing effect on Congress. The 1981 budget cuts, the Gramm-Rudman Act, and the Tax Reform Act of 1986 all came about through centralized legislative activity rather than through the process of subcommittees and a decentralized committee system. Subcommittees were noticeably absent in the account of the Tax Reform Act that opened this chapter. While all that does not mean an end to subcommittee government, it does suggest that the committee system is undergoing significant change in the 1980s and that some of those changes have resulted in the important lawmaking activity taking place in committees rather than in subcommittees.[23]

Committees

The tax reform bill that passed the House of Representatives in December 1985 was almost 1,400 pages long. The Senate bill approved six months later was just under 1,500 pages. Although one of the goals of proponents of tax reform was to simplify the federal tax code, the complexity of the subject and the comprehensive nature of the legislation made for long bills in both chambers. Another reason for the length of the tax bills was the inclusion in both bills of a large number of provisions known as "transition rules." These are exceptions to the general rules of the new law that are intended to help individuals and businesses who would otherwise suffer under the new rules as a result of financial commitments made under the old rules. These special provisions are aimed at smoothing an individual's or business's transition to the new rules. The Senate bill included provisions designed to help a number of particular interests: the Associated Press; those who sell reindeer or reindeer products from herds that are held in trust; a Des Moines, Iowa truck leasing company; a housing project in Massachusetts; and corporations established under the Alaska Native Claims Settlement Act.[24] Or, consider the following transition rule in the House bill:

> An exception from the repeal of authority to issue I.D.B.'s (industrial development bonds) for convention centers would be provided for a specified amount of bonds issued for expansion of a convention center with respect to which a convention tax was upheld by a state supreme court on February 8, 1985.[25]

Anyone reading that paragraph of the House bill might have difficulty connecting it to a convention center in Miami Beach. But what that transition rule did was to exempt the Miami Beach convention center from the bill's general rule that prohibited the use of tax-exempt bonds to finance convention centers, sports stadiums, and parking garages. Miami Beach is in the congressional district of Rep. Claude Pepper, head of the House Rules Committee, the panel responsible for setting the terms of the floor debate on the tax bill. Pepper's district also benefitted from provisions in the tax bill that exempted the bonding of a new stadium for the Miami Dolphins, a redevelopment project, and two heating and cooling systems.

Claude Pepper and the Dolphins were not the only ones to get help with a stadium out of the House bill. For the legislation also included transition rules that provided exceptions for financing stadiums in Cleveland, Memphis, and New Jersey's Meadowlands—stadiums in or near the districts of Ways and Means Committee Democrats Don Pease of Ohio, Harold Ford of Tennessee, and Frank Guarini of New Jersey. Three New York representatives on Ways and Means, Charles Rangel, Thomas Downey, and Raymond McGrath, were also successful in getting special provisions that exempted waste-treatment plants, construction projects at a New York hospital and university, and the purchase of new subway cars for the Metropolitan Transit Authority. Representative McGrath was able to get a special exemption that helped an office products company from Long Island. Merrill Lynch & Company received tax advantages for its new headquarters in Manhattan. Major urban development projects in a number of cities, all developed by the nationally known firm, The Rouse Company, were also exempted from certain tax provisions. And the House bill made it possible for the Talman Home Federal Savings and Loan Association of Illinois, located in Ways and Means Chairman Rostenkowski's hometown of Chicago, to change ownership without having to comply with tax rules on operating losses.

The wording of the transition rule that helped Talman Home Federal was similar to that of the Miami convention center provision. Talman was not mentioned by name. The wording of the rules makes it difficult or impossible not only for outsiders to understand these special provisions, but also for some members of Congress, and even some of those on the Ways and Means Committee to know what is going on. A Republican on the Committee, California Rep. William Thomas said he and many of his party colleagues were not able to comprehend most transition rules because "we were never told what was what." Thomas and others were kept in the dark not only by the carefully crafted wording of these special provisions but also by the process through which they were inserted into the bill that reached the floor. After two months of drafting tax legislation, Ways and Means Chairman Dan Rostenkowski told the other thirty-five representatives on the Committee to give him their requests for special tax provisions and to be reachable by phone during the next day, the Friday before Thanksgiving 1985. Rostenkowski and a group of lawyers sorted through the requests on Friday morning, then the chairman and the committee's chief tax counsel, Robert J. Leonard, went into a committee room and began calling members. A committee staffer described the process this way: "It was just Rostenkowski, Rob Leonard, the telephone, and an enormous stack of papers." That is how committee members found out which of their requests would be in the tax bill as it came out of Ways and Means. For a few members, the phone never rang.[26]

The process of inserting special provisions into the tax bill could be regarded as a form of representation. In that sense, the process assured that Claude Pepper's constituency interests were represented in the committee bill, and so on down the line to the representation of Tallman Home Federal. When this process is coupled with the committee procedures described at the beginning of this chapter, however, we see a decline in visibility to the public that goes from open committee sessions to closed committee markup to informal weekend sessions of a handful of senators until we reach the level of two guys and a phone. That is hardly the open forum generally associated with representation. An important point to consider in all of this is that Rostenkowski's thirty-five colleagues had known for two months that it

would come down to the chairman and a telephone in the closing days of drafting the bill. Throughout the two months of drafting the bill, recalled committee member William Thomas, the
chairman reminded everyone on the committee "that those who
were cooperative could expect to be rewarded in the transition
rules."[27] That knowledge made this stage more one of lawmaking
than of representation.

One of the more influential Republicans on Ways and Means,
Rep. Bill Frenzel of Minnesota, said that all members understood
the primary rule of writing a tax bill in the committee: "The rule
is that if you're on board you get something that normal policy
wouldn't get you. No one gets punished. It's not a system of
punishment. It's a system of rewards."[28] Georgia Democrat and
committee colleague, Ed Jenkins, said that as a member of Ways
and Means, "You have to decide, with Rostenkowski to play in
the game or not. I've always found it better to be a player."[29] And
this is how Chairman Rostenkowski himself described his role:

> I'm counting votes, measuring attitudes, looking for pressure
> points, trying to build a consensus. I need 19 votes to get the
> bill out of the committee and 219 votes in the House, and if
> there's one thing that will keep one member or another from
> voting for the bill, I want to know what it is and maybe we can
> help him.[30]

The Ways and Means Committee vote to report the tax bill favorably was 28 to 8, and the crucial House vote on the rule to
consider the bill produced a 258 to 168 margin for taking up the
bill on the floor. In other words, Rostenkowski got 9 votes over
the minimum in building a coalition on the committee and 39
more than he needed for the vote on the rule.

Subcommittee reforms, which were discussed in the preceding section, led to the creation in 1975 of six subcommittees on
the Ways and Means Committee. But the committee has no subcommittee for tax policy, and the coalition-building process that
created the House tax reform bill in 1985 illustrates why. The
broad coalition assembled by Rostenkowski was based on a combination of support for the general policy goals of tax simplifi-
cation and reduced rates and of transition rules that protected
special interests in members' districts. A key to building that
coalition was Rostenkowski's ability to keep his end of all of
those bargains that required a degree of centralized authority and

coordination not found at the subcommittee level. The same general pattern of coalition building at the committee level was seen in Senate action on tax reform, a process that Finance Committee Chairman Bob Packwood described as "like a poker game. Everyone anted up to make the pot worthwhile."[31] In the Senate, the resulting coalitions were even broader than in the House: The Senate Finance Committee unanimously reported the bill favorably to the parent chamber and the Senate passed the bill by an overwhelming ninety-seven to three vote. In the face of decentralizing reforms and subcommittee government, the legislative history of the Tax Reform Act of 1986 is a clear reminder of the importance of committees to congressional lawmaking.

Woodrow Wilson had this to say about committees in his 1885 book, *Congressional Government*:

> It is evident that there is one principle which runs through every stage of procedure, and which is never disallowed or abrogated—the principle that the Committee shall rule without let or hindrance. And this is a principle of extraordinary formative power. It is the mould of all legislation.[32]

Almost eighty years later, Rep. Clem Miller described Congress as "a collection of committees that come together in a chamber periodically to approve one another's actions."[33] If the first point here is that committees are important; the second point is that committees differ a great deal in their importance, membership, structure, environment, and the degree to which they are concerned with representation and with lawmaking. One of those differences is whether a committee is in the House of Representatives or in the Senate.

House and Senate differences about the relative emphasis put on representation and lawmaking affect the roles the committees play in each chamber. Senate committees tend to maximize representational goals; House committees are geared more to decision making. House members can spend more time developing expertise relevant to the one or two committees on which they serve, while senators would find such a task impossible because they serve on many committees. Committees are generally more important to individual House members than they are to senators, for they are the member's only means of achieving power and policy goals within the lower chamber. House committees are also more important in determining the chamber's policy outcomes than are Senate committees, because House norms tend to reinforce the acceptance of committee decisions on the floor. For these reasons, most of the following discussion will deal with House committees rather than their senatorial counterparts.

Many ways are used to classify committees. Some students of Congress have focused on the pecking order and ranked committees according to their prestige among members. By looking at committees whose members most consistently transferred over a period of time and at the most commonly listed committee assignment preferences of newcomers, congressional scholars have been able to construct a relatively stable hierarchy of committees in both the House and Senate.[34] Although changes in the committee system such as the creation of Budget committees in 1974 and the Senate reorganization of 1977 will have some effect on the hierarchy of committees in each chamber, the committees that appear at the top of these hierarchies have shown a great deal of consistency. In the House, the most prestigious committees have been Appropriations, Armed Services, Rules, and Ways and Means. In the Senate, the Foreign Relations, Appropriations, Armed Services, Finance, and Judiciary Committees have been the committees most sought after by members. The rules in both chambers recognize some committees as more important, or at least more time consuming, than others and thus limit other committee assignments for members of either "exclusive" committees in the House or "major" committees in the Senate. Although members generally agree about which are the top committees, the attractiveness of particular committees among different members varies greatly. While a senator or representative from Iowa might naturally find an assignment to the Agriculture Committee to his or her liking, a colleague from New York City might consider such an assignment to be punishment for past sins. One member, who thrives on the din of ideological battles, might consider a seat on the Education and Labor Committee to be a wonderful position for influencing policy on great national issues, while another member might regard the insistent demands made by antibusing forces, educational interest groups, and labor unions to be the sure cause of a heart attack.

The prestige or attractiveness of particular committees is also likely to ebb and flow with the tides of public opinion on national issues. In the years immediately after the "Watergate Summer" of 1974, for example, an assignment to the House Judiciary Committee was considered a plum because of the high prestige the committee gained by conducting the hearings on the impeachment of President Nixon. Similarly, in the early 1970s, the high publicity given to efforts to limit the executive's war powers and the country's military commitments increased the attractiveness of service on the House Committee on Foreign Affairs. By the time of the Ninety-sixth Congress in 1979, however, both the Judiciary and the Foreign Affairs Committees had barely enough applications to fill the existing vacancies on the committee lists. The knowledge they would have to deal with such hot political issues as gun control, busing, and abortion made the Judiciary Committee, in particular, a body on which few members chose to sit. The most popular committees at the start of the Ninety-sixth Congress, as measured by members' preferences, were Appropriations, Budget, and Commerce. Responsibility for energy policy and oversight of the federal bureaucracy were said to be the attractions of Commerce, whereas the public mood of cost cutting and government economy made the money committees of Budget and Appropriations favorites of many legislators. "These Democrats want to get on here and embellish their reputation as economizers," is the way one member of the House Budget Committee explained that committee's popularity.[35] Although the particular standing any committee has in this hierarchy of committees is likely to change over time and vary from member to member, there definitely is a ranking of committees; they are not all equal. Awareness of this variation is useful because it prevents our falling into the trap of thinking that one can make general statements about *all* congressional committees with any degree of accuracy.

Another way to classify committees has been on the basis of the types of policies they handle. Donald Matthews's study of the Senate combined committee preferences and policy to come up with a fourfold typology—(1) *top committees* (Foreign Relations, Appropriations, Armed Services, and Finance); (2) *interest committees* (Agriculture, Banking and Currency, Interstate and Foreign Commerce, Judiciary, and Labor); (3) *pork committees* (Interior, Post Office and Civil Service, and Public Works); and (4) *duty committees* (Rules and Administration, Government Operations, and District of Columbia).[36]

Based on the scope of issues handled by the committee,

George Goodwin used a similar classification scheme to construct a typology of national issue committees, clientele-oriented committees, and housekeeping committees. Some examples of each committee type are (1) *national issue:* Appropriations, Armed Services, House Ways and Means, and Senate Finance; (2) *clientele-oriented:* Agriculture, Banking, and the Commerce committees in both chambers; and (3) *housekeeping:* District of Columbia, Government Operations, and Administration Committees in the House and Governmental Affairs and Rules and Administration Committees in the Senate.[37]

Classification of committees by the types of policies they handle makes possible comparisons of committees with their counterpart institutions in other branches of government. When we compare committees classified by prestige with committees classified by the scope of the issues handled, we find that the most prestigious committees are generally concerned with broad policy issues. But again, such a classifying scheme may often hide important differences among committees. For example, even though both Education and Labor and Interior have been placed in the same category of clientele-oriented committees, they often have represented opposite extremes in terms of the degree of conflict found in committee activity. Whereas Education and Labor consistently has been the scene of intense partisan and ideological conflict, Interior has been characterized more by a low-conflict, consensual pattern of decision making.

The tension between representation and lawmaking that was evident in the way the Senate Finance and House Ways and Means Committees went about drafting the Tax Reform Act of 1986 has suggested that committee behavior will depend to some degree on what members want from the committee. In the tax reform case, closed committee sessions helped members to accomplish the primary goal of lawmaking, while the process of inserting transition rules permitted some representation to take place. Members' goals, in other words, greatly influenced committee behavior. Classifying committees on the basis of members' shared goals alerts us once again to the differences among committees and provides grounds for explaining some of those differences. For example, the difference between the Interior and Education and Labor Committees might best be explained as follows: Members on the Interior Committee want it to be a low-conflict committee that can provide projects for home districts; while members on the Education and Labor committee want to focus on drafting important social policy, and they regard intense conflict as a necessary part of that process.

Richard Fenno discovered that members' committee behavior was greatly influenced by the value they attached to three goals—gaining influence within Congress, making good public policy, and being reelected. He also found that members with similar goals tended to gravitate to the same committees and that the shared goals of members helped to shape the structure of the committee, its relationship with outside groups, the patterns of committee decision making, and the committee's output. A classification scheme based on Fenno's seminal work in *Congressmen in Committees* (1973) and on research along similar lines reported in Smith and Deering's *Committees in Congress* (1984) is that of power committees, policy committees, and constituency committees.[38]

Table 5–2 provides a classification of House and Senate committees according to the reasons members give for wanting to serve on those committees.

Power Committees

Dan Rostenkowski came to Congress in 1958 from the Thirty-second Ward in Chicago, where he served as Democratic Committeeman and ward boss in the political machine of then mayor, Richard J. Daley. Twenty-seven years later, the *New York Times* was calling Rostenkowski "the most important lawmaker on Capitol Hill," because of his leadership of Ways and Means and his role in tax reform. At the same time, a disenchanted congressional aide had this to say about Rostenkowski's operation of the committee: "It's all a replica of Chicago City Hall. His obsession with patronage, with power, with boot-licking."[39] When another reporter told Rostenkowski that some of his House colleagues had suggested that he was more interested in the exercise of power than in statesmanlike policy questions, the chairman retorted: "Who *doesn't* want power?" He went on to say that "a lot of people assume that because I'm from the big city and from, quote unquote, a machine operation, that all I want to do is play politics." But Rostenkowski said that he wanted "to be a patriot, too. It sounds like corn but, if we get no credit at all on this tax reform bill, My God, we're elected to do what's right. And what's right is being fair to those people that work so hard."[40] These words, coupled with the chair-

TABLE 5–2 Types of Congressional Committees

House	Constituency		Policy		Prestige	
Congress	92	97	92	97	92	97
Prestige Committees						
Appropriations	5*	5	3	6	7	11
Budget	—	0	—	4	—	5
Rules	1	0	0	1	0	3
Ways and Means	1	0	0	6	5	7
Policy Committees						
Banking	1	14	9	17	1	1
Foreign Affairs	1	2	4	8	0	0
Commerce	3	9	16	13	1	0
Judiciary	0	0	7	3	0	0
(Education and Labor)	5	3	7	2	0	0
Government Operations	0	0	0	9	0	0
Constituency Committees						
Agriculture	10	15	3	7	0	0
Armed Services	5	11	3	7	1	0
(Education and Labor)	5	3	7	2	0	0
Interior	7	12	4	2	0	0
Merchant Marine	3	5	0	0	0	0
Public Works	7	4	1	2	0	0
Science & Technology	0	9	1	5	1	0
Small Business	—	13	—	4	—	0
Veterans' Affairs	5	2	0	1	0	0
Undesired Committees						
District of Columbia	0	1	0	1	0	1
House Administration	0	0	0	0	0	0
Post Office and Civil Service	1	1	0	0	0	0
Standards of Official Conduct	—	0	—	1	—	0

Senate	Constituency		Policy		Prestige	
	Pre-		Pre-		Pre-	
Congress	92	97	92	97	92	97
Policy Committees						
Budget	—	1	—	4	•	0
Foreign Relations	3	1	19	5	2	0
Governmental Affairs	•	1	•	3	•	0
Judiciary	•	2	9	7	•	0
Labor	2	3	4	4	•	0

Senate	Constituency		Policy		Prestige	
Mixed Constituency/Policy *Committees*						
Armed Services	4	4	4	6	•	0
Banking	•	2	•	3	•	0
Finance	4	8	13	9	•	4
Small Business	—	4	—	4	•	0
Constituency Committees						
Agriculture	4	13	•	2	•	0
Appropriations	31	6	15	3	2	2
Commerce	13	5	5	2	•	0
Energy and Natural Resources (formerly Interior)	4	6	2	3	•	0
Environment & Public Works	5	5	4	1	•	0
Undesired Committees						
Rules & Administration	•	0	•	1	•	0
Veterans' Affairs	•	2	3	0	•	0

Source: Steven S. Smith and Christopher J. Deering, *Committees in Congress.* (Washington, D.C.: Congressional Quarterly Press, 1984) p.90 (House) and p.112 (Senate).

*Frequency of particular motivation cited by members of that committee.

• N's for cells with fewer than 2 cases not reported.

man's behavior described earlier in the chapter and by others in this section, suggest that the driving force behind the congressman is a combination of wanting power in Congress and of making good policy. For a representative such as Rostenkowski, whose percentage of the vote had not fallen below 80 percent since 1974, reelection might seem more of a given than a key determinant of behavior. Even so, it is important to remember than any member of Congress is interested in all three goals—reelection, power, and policy—and that the differences among members come from the particular mix of motives and from the value assigned to each of those goals.

Members seeking to maximize their influence within the House are naturally drawn to prestigious committees such as Appropriations, Ways and Means, and Rules. By contrast, there is no committee in the Senate that draws members primarily because of the prestige and power that comes with membership on that committee. Although members of the Senate Appropriations Committee interviewed by Fenno often used terms such as influence and power to describe why they wanted a particular committee membership, further explanations revealed that the underlying motive was really a constituency one—to bring federal dollars to the state. Smith and Deering found a similar pattern. Committee prestige was occasionally mentioned in conjunction with the Senate Appropriations, Finance, and Foreign Relations Committees; but even on these committees, constituency and policy goals were much more likely to be given as reasons for wanting to be on those committees. Because it is relatively easy for any senator to get on a "major" committee, and because committee decisions are likely to be revised or reversed on the Senate floor, a senator's influence in the chamber will depend less than that of a representative on being a member of any particular committee.

Representatives who serve on the Appropriations, Rules, and Ways and Means Committees are seldom reticent about why they like being on those committees. "After all," said Rules Committee Chairman Claude Pepper, "the Rules Committee can do almost anything it wants to." Rep. David Bonior of Michigan said he liked being on the committee because as a member of the Rules Committee, "You get to do things for other members. You can get to be a patron saint." Washington Rep. Norman Dicks used similar language to describe the Appropriations Committee, on which he served: "It's where the money is. And money is where the clout is." A newcomer to Ways and Means was quite frank about his reason for switching to that committee after six years on another. "The only way I can describe what I want to be is power. I don't know what I'd do with it when I got it, but I want to have it where I can reach out and use it when I want to."[41]

Some connection between the prestige of these committees and the policies they affect is suggested by two of the three committees—Appropriations and Ways and Means—with control over important money matters, and by the Rules Committee's control over the terms of debate for all major bills. A policy motive is also evident in Rostenkowski's notions of being a "patriot" and of being "elected to do what's right." A staff member's explanation of why Claude Pepper gave up the chair of the Select Committee on Aging in 1983 to become head of the Rules Committee demonstrates again the way committee power and policy can be intertwined:

Pepper wanted a policy committee. When he was on Aging, all he had was a mouthpiece to raise his issue. Aging could not draft legislation. If Rosty (Rostenkowski) wanted to draft a conservative social security bill, Pepper had no way to stop it. Rosty didn't have to return his calls. On Rules, if Pepper doesn't like a bill, he can keep it off the floor. Now the mountain must come to Mohammed.[42]

Most members of these committees hold relatively safe seats, and they do not need to worry a great deal about serving constituency interests. They are free to devote most of their time to the committee work that maintains their power. While some members seek out these committees in order to pursue certain policy goals, as Pepper did with Social Security, most pursue institutional power that cuts across many policy areas.

The power to tax and spend is central to all of the legislative powers granted in the Constitution. As a result, the decisions of the money committees can greatly affect the position of Congress relative to other political institutions. The Rules Committee has a similar institutional responsibility in that it must control the floor in order for Congress to pass laws. All legislators want these committees to be effective because the success and influence of Congress as an institution is at stake. That was most certainly the case with tax reform, where all members—but particularly Democrats in the House and Republicans in the Senate—had a stake in supporting committee actions that would produce a bill in 1986. Prior to the reforms of the 1970s, that institutional support was reflected in House rules that gave the Appropriations and Ways and Means Committees more independence and autonomy than other committees. Lawmaking decisions made in these committees, for example, were protected by rules that proscribed or limited floor amendments.

Many of the changes in these committees since the 1970s illustrate once again the often conflicting demands of lawmaking and representation that are always present in Congress. Generally speaking, those changes have strengthened the lawmaking role of the Rules Committee and increased the representative nature of the Appropriations and Ways and Means Committees. Since the Ninety-fourth Congress (1976–1977), when the Democratic Caucus gave the Speaker the authority to appoint all of that party's members on the Rules Committee, subject to caucus approval, the

committee has become more of an arm of the House leadership and less of an independent forum for the representation of alternative views. In contrast, most of the reforms affecting Appropriations and Ways and Means have been aimed at making them more representative panels. Democrats in the Ninety-fourth Congress took away the Appropriations Committee chair's power to appoint subcommittee chairs and gave that authority to the House Democratic Caucus. Other reforms in the same Congress expanded Ways and Means from twenty-five to thirty-seven members, required it to have subcommittees, and took away Committee Democrats' power of assigning Democratic representatives to House committees. In addition to specific reforms aimed at making the Appropriations Committee more representative, the discretion of that committee has been greatly narrowed by other changes designed to enhance lawmaking. The 1974 creation of the House Budget Committee, the 1981 use of the reconciliation process provided by the Budget Act, and the 1985 passage of the Gramm-Rudman Act all served to diminish the Appropriations Committee's control over spending. As a result, the Appropriations Committee of the 1980s serves less as the lawmaking budget-cutter that it had in the past and more as a place where program advocates can gain representation. Increased representation also weakened the lawmaking capacity of Ways and Means, at least until 1984, when the closed meetings and the strong leadership of the committee chairman provided ways of checking that representation and engaging in the lawmaking that produced the Tax Reform Act of 1986. Rules, Appropriations, and Ways and Means do not enjoy the autonomy that they had prior to the widespread changes of the 1970s. And members do not gain the same degree of prestige and institutional power by serving on these committees that they did at one time. Because these committees continue to make decisions that affect all members of the House, however, they provide resources for influencing other members and will continue to attract those representatives who put a premium on power within the institution.

Policy Committees

Table 5–2 shows that House members who were motivated primarily by the goal of making good public policy tended to gravitate toward the Banking, Foreign Affairs, Commerce, Judiciary,

Education and Labor, and Government Operations Committees. The House Budget Committee appears as a mix of policy and power goals in the table. The Budget Committee's important lawmaking rule in the 1980s gives it prestige within the chamber, but that standing is checked somewhat by a rule that limits members to six years service on the Budget Committee. Policy committees in the Senate include the Budget, Foreign Relations, Governmental Affairs, Judiciary, and Labor Committees. Four other Senate committees—Armed Services, Banking, Finance, and Small Business—drew an equal number of constituency and policy reasons for members' wanting to serve on those committees. Once again, it should be recognized that senators and representatives are interested in all three goals—reelection, influence within the institution, and good policy. Serving on a committee in order to achieve certain policy goals can also provide an opportunity to shape policy in ways that will benefit the district and help a member's reelection. And as we have seen, members may justify their seeking institutional power as a means to achieving policy ends.

A policy motive is most evident in cases where a legislator's pursuit of the policy goal works against that member's achieving other goals. That conflict can be seen in the remarks of a member of the House Foreign Affairs Committee: "Politically, it's not a good committee for me. My constituents are interested in bread and butter, and there's no bread and butter on Foreign Affairs." A similar attitude was expressed by a representative on Education and Labor:[43]

> I'm the most issue-oriented guy you ever want to meet. I know there won't be a Wagner Act with my name on it during my first term. But if I can get a few of my ideas in I'll be satisfied.
>
> Legislating in Washington, for the district and in the public interest. That's what interests me the most. Serving your constituency—that's a noble effort, too. But, frankly, I consider any time spent with a constituent as time wasted that I could have spent doing more important things.

What some saw as a conflict between the reelection goal and the policy goal also came up in discussion after Senate Foreign Relations Chairman Charles Percy lost his bid for reelection to the Senate in 1984. Percy's defeat meant that three of the four senators to chair Foreign Relations in the last ten years had been

defeated at the polls, and that all members of that committee were, in the words of a former chairman, "vulnerable to being identified by voters with foreign issues and not enough with local ones."[44] And finally, while serving on the House Budget Committee assures a representative of being in the middle of important policy decisions, it also can hurt a member's relationship with both constituents and colleagues. "Being on the Budget Committee is not a pleasant experience," said one member. "You have to say no to all sorts of people."[45]

The congressional reforms of the 1970s affected the structure of many of these committees, just as they did power committees. For example, changes that gave the Democratic Caucus control over committee chairs and reforms that expanded the powers of subcommittees helped to transform the House Banking Committee and House Commerce Committee from being centralized committees under the control of autocratic chairmen into committees with active and independent subcommittees. Other policy committees, such as Government Operations and Foreign Affairs in the House and Governmental Affairs, Judiciary, and Labor in the Senate, are also characterized by active subcommittees. A decentralized committee structure provides more opportunity for individual members to pursue policy goals. The same policy orientation that favors use of subcommittees, however, also serves to check any tendency toward subcommittee government. Members who emphasize policy goals in the congressional activity want the ability to challenge subcommittee policies at the committee level and are therefore unlikely to accept subcommittee decisions as the authoritative decisions of the committee.

Even more important than congressional reforms and structural changes in determining the nature of policy committees, however, have been changes in the political agenda that are reflected in the changing fortunes of the judiciary committees in both chambers and the Education and Labor Committee in the House. Policy-oriented members were attracted to Education and Labor during the expansion of education and welfare programs in the 1960s, but the same committee offers fewer opportunities for policy innovation in the 1980s. Similarly, the attractions of the judiciary committees as a place to deal with civil rights issues have been offset in the 1980s by the electoral dangers associated with handling issues like abortion and school prayer. On the other hand, the issues that dominate the political agenda

in the 1980s—government spending, efficiency, and energy—have attracted policy-oriented legislators to the Budget Committees, Government Operations Committees, and House Commerce Committee. Because a policy motive drives the members of these committees, changes in the structure and in the relative standing of policy committees are a product of changes in the political agenda more than they are of general congressional reforms.

Constituency Committees

A representative from a western state said that being on Interior was good for him "because it's a bread and butter committee for my state." "I guess about the only thing about it that is not of great interest to my state is insular affairs. I was able to get two or three bills of great importance to my state through last year. I had vested interests I wanted to protect, to be frank."[46] A former member of the House Public Works Committee had a similar assessment of that panel: "Public Works is a sugar committee. I could always go back to the district and say, "Look at that road I got for you. See that beach erosion project over there? And those buildings? I got all those. I'm on Public Works."[47]

The constituency advantages for a member serving on Public Works are clear, even when a representative would prefer to be on a prestige or policy committee. When freshman Rep. Peter Visclosky (D-IN) came to the Ninety-ninth Congress (1985–1986), his first choice of committees was Appropriations. Visclosky had previously served as a member of that committee's staff, a former representative from Visclosky's district had been on Appropriations, and the district was considered to be a safe one for Democrats. Nevertheless, an aide to the Democratic leadership pointed out that Visclosky had "no chance" of getting on Appropriations because "more senior members have been working at it longer than he has." The Indiana representative said that the same point was made clear in a meeting he had with House Speaker Tip O'Neill: "The Speaker asked me what my second preference was." I said, "I don't have one." He said, "Well you better get one." Visclosky, in fact, got three. He informed members of the Democratic Steering and Policy Committee that his committee preferences were now Armed Services, Commerce, or Banking. Indiana already had representatives on the first two panels, however, and the region's representatives on

Steering and Policy were focusing their attention on another member's bid for Appropriations. So Visclosky wound up with an assignment to the Public Works Committee. The Democratic Steering and Policy Committee also gave the Indiana representative a position on the Interior Committee, which was seen by some as a consolation prize for losing out on a Banking Committee assignment. The freshman representative was quick to see a silver lining in all of this. "There is no way of hiding the fact that Public Works and Transportation was not my first, second, third or fourth choice," admitted Visclosky. "But from a professional aspect, it is good for northwest Indiana." He suggested that his position on Public Works would help him to get federal funds for controlling Lake Michigan shoreline erosion, for a flood control project on the district's Calumet River, and for repairs on several federal highways that run through the district. Visclosky also saw district benefits from the Interior Committee's jurisdiction over recreational areas such as the Indiana Dunes National Lakeshore, and said that the two committees provided "a nice mix for what I want to do locally."[48]

Constituency and electoral reasons are the most commonly mentioned reasons for the committee preference of both senators and representatives. But as shown in Table 5–2, some committees attract a disproportionate number of members whose motivations for serving on a committee are primarily constituency oriented. The geographical distribution of seats on some of those same committees also attests to the emphasis that members give to constituency concerns. The House Agriculture Committee has subcommittees with jurisdiction over particular regional crops such as tobacco, cotton, and wheat, and the membership of the Agriculture Committee in both chambers has exhibited a longstanding bias in favor of southern and midwestern representation. A similar overrepresentation of western representatives and senators exists on the House Interior Committee and the Senate Energy and Natural Resources Committee (which was the Senate Interior Committee prior to the 1977 committee reforms). The constituency focus of the House Merchant Marine and Fisheries Committee is also evident in its membership, which is drawn almost exclusively from districts bordered by the ocean or by the Great Lakes.

The pattern of subcommittee government described at the beginning of this chapter is most common among constituency committees. A representative on the Interior Committee described the full committee as "a rubberstamp of subcommittee decisions," and a member of the House Public Works Committee observed that "subcommittees are seldom challenged because everyone's requests are usually incorporated by the subcommittee."[49] An emphasis on constituency benefits, the patterns of representation on constituency committees, and the narrow focus of much of the legislation in these committees are all reasons why it makes sense for the full committee to accept subcommittee decisions. Subcommittees also play an important legislative role in the Senate Agriculture, Appropriations, and Environment and Public Works Committees, but the individualistic nature of Senate representation permits senators to challenge or change subcommittee decisions at the committee level.

Constituency committees have undergone change primarily as a result of attempts to balance the geographic representation on the committee or of the infusion of new members with a strong policy orientation. Changes in the Agriculture Committee during the 1970s illustrate the first pattern: The addition of western and midwestern representatives has given more geographical balance to a committee long known for the dominance of southern agricultural interests. An example of changes brought about by new members with a policy focus is the Interior Committee. Although most members of the Interior Committee still emphasize constituency benefits as a reason for service on it, at least some of the new members joining the committee in recent years have done so in order to influence environmental policy. California Rep. George Miller was one whose environmental approach upset the traditional, pork-barrel, approach to approving federal water projects. "When I first suggested there be a review of a water project," Miller recalled, "another member came up later and informed me people have been shot for less than that." The representative admitted that such an approach often had made him "the skunk at the picnic," but stressed a need for policy concerns to override narrow constituency interests: "We're trying to get away from measuring success by how much cement we pour. This is a different era."[50]

Conclusion

Committees are the workshops of Congress where lawmaking has been done for more than a century. Within that stable pattern, however, there have been major changes in the committee system. And so, too, any description of congressional committees in the 1980s will be subject to changes brought about through reforms, the movement of issues on the political agenda, and the motives of new committee members. But the dynamic that shapes the committee system—the tension created by the fact that members are always seeking to meet the twin goals of representation and lawmaking—has remained constant. That is the unifying theme that runs throughout this chapter, from the closed-door bargaining that produced tax reform legislation (and included transition rules in that legislation) to the structure of subcommittee government in the House (but not in the Senate). A recognition of that theme helps to understand both the nature of the committee system at any one time and the meaning of changes in that system.

Endnotes

1. Rep. Vin Weber (R-MN), quoted in Pamela Fessler, "House Reverses Self, Passes Major Tax Overhaul," *Congressional Quarterly Weekly Report*, December 21, 1985, p. 2705. The account of House action on the tax reform bill also relies on Thomas Oliphant, "House OKs Measure to Revise U.S. Tax Code," *Boston Globe*, December 18, 1985, p. 1, and David E. Rosenbaum, "Tax Bill Revision Likely in Senate, White House Says," *New York Times*, December 19, 1985, p. 1.

2. Senators Packwood and Bradley, quoted in Pamela Fessler, "Finance Panel Suspends Markup of Tax Bill," *Congressional Quarterly Weekly Report*, April 19, 1986, p. 840.

3. Representatives Gradison and Pease, IPA lobbyist Harold B. Scoggins, Jr., and Tax Reform Research Group Director Jeff Drumtra, quoted in Pamela Fessler, "Panel Expects to Rewrite Tax Code in Private," *Congressional Quarterly Weekly Report*, August 31, 1985, p. 1706.

4. James F. Clarity and Warren Weaver, Jr., "A Retreat for Tax Writers," *New York Times*, January 7, 1986, p. B6.

5. Rep. Brian Donnelly, quoted in Thomas Oliphant, "A Team Effort Saves Tax Revision," *Boston Globe*, December 22, 1985, p. A17.

6. David E. Rosenbaum, "Of Loose Ends and Looser Humor on the Tax Bill," *New York Times*, June 26, 1986, p. B7.

7. Ward Sinclair, "Administration's Bill Loses Out as Rules on Hill Have Changed," *Washington Post*, November 14, 1978, p. A1.

8. For an excellent discussion of this aspect of congressional leaders' behavior, see Louis P. Westefield, "Majority Party Leadership

and the Committee System in the House of Representatives," *American Political Science Review*, vol. 68, no. 4 (December, 1974), pp. 1593–1604.

9. David R. Mayhew, *Congress: The Electoral Connection* (New Haven: Yale University Press, 1974), p. 95.

10. U.S. Congress, House, *Administrative Reorganization and Legislative Management, Hearings, and Meetings Before the Commission on Administrative Review*, Ninety-fifth Congress, first session, September 8, 1977, p. 247.

11. Rep. Butler Derrick, quoted in Elizabeth Drew, "A Reporter At Large (Washington, D.C.)," *The New Yorker*, April 9, 1979, p. 104.

12. This summary is taken from Bruce F. Freed, "House Reforms Enhance Subcommittees' Power," *Congressional Quarterly Weekly Report*, November 8, 1975, pp. 2407–12. For more on these reforms and their effects, see Leroy N. Rieselbach, *Congressional Reform in the Seventies* (Morristown, N.J.: General Learning Press, 1977); Leroy N. Rieselbach, ed., *Legislative Reform: The Policy Impact* (Lexington, Mass.: D. C. Heath, 1978); and Susan Welch and John G. Peters, eds., *Legislative Reform and Public Policy* (New York: Praeger, 1977).

13. Norman J. Ornstein, "Causes and Consequences of Congressional Change: Subcommittee Reforms in the House of Representatives, 1970–1973," in Norman J. Ornstein, ed., *Congress in Change: Evolution and Reform* (New York: Praeger, 1975), p. 102.

14. Freed, "House Reforms Enhance Subcommittees' Power," p. 2410.

15. Allen Schick, "The Three-Ring Budget Process: The Appropriations, Tax, and Budget Committees in Congress," in Thomas E. Mann and Norman J. Ornstein, eds., *The New Congress* (Washington, D.C.: American Enterprise Institute, 1981), pp. 288–328.

16. Lawrence C. Dodd and Bruce I. Oppenheimer, "The House in Transition: Partisanship and Opposition," in Dodd and Oppenheimer, eds., *Congress Reconsidered*, 3rd ed. (Washington, D.C.: Congressional Quarterly Press, 1985, pp. 44–45.

17. Richard L. Lyons, "Retirements from Hill Reach a Record High," *Washington Post*, April 16, 1976, p. 1.

18. Ornstein, "Causes and Consequences of Congressional Change: Subcommittee Reforms in the House of Representatives," p. 108.

19. Lauros G. McConachie, *Congressional Committees* (New York: Crowell, 1898), p. 136, cited in Thomas R. Wolanin, "Committee Seniority and the Choice of House Subcommittee Chairmen: 80th–91st Congresses," *The Journal of Politics*, vol. 36, no. 3 (August, 1974), p. 687.

20. Dodd and Oppenheimer, "House in Transition," p. 51.

21. Unidentified committee staff director, quoted in Steven S. Smith and Christopher J. Deering, *Committees in Congress* (Washington, D.C.: Congressional Quarterly Press, 1984), p. 134.

22. Freed, "House Reforms Enhance Subcommittees' Power," p. 2407.

23. Roger H. Davidson, "Congressional Committees as Moving Targets," *Legislative Studies Quarterly*, February, 1986, pp. 19–33.

24. Eileen Shanahan, "Panel's Tax Bill Largely Intact as Senate Nears Final Passage," *Congressional Quarterly Weekly Report*, June 21, 1986, p. 1379, and Shanahan, "Tax Bill Wins Senate Approval; Post-Recess Conference Next," *Congressional Quarterly Weekly Report*, June 28, 1986, p. 1456.

25. Excerpt from House bill, quoted in David E. Rosenbaum, "The Favors of Rostenkowski: Tax Revision's Quid Pro Quo," *New York Times*, November 27, 1985, p. B6.

26. Specific transition rules and quotations from ibid.

27. Representative Thomas, quoted in ibid.

28. Representative Frenzel, quoted in ibid.

29. Representative Jenkins, quoted in Elizabeth Wehr, "Rostenkowski: A Firm Grip on Ways and Means," *Congressional Quarterly Weekly Report*, July 6, 1985, p. 1318.

30. David E. Rosenbaum, "Crafting a Tax Bill with 36 Authors," *New York Times*, September 15, 1985, p. F8.

31. Senator Packwood, quoted in Eileen Shanahan, "Finance Panel OKs Radical Tax Overhaul Bill," *Congressional Quarterly Weekly Report*, May 10, 1986, p. 1010.

32. Woodrow Wilson, *Congressional Government* (Cleveland, Ohio: Meridian, 1967), p. 66.

33. Clem Miller, quoted in John Baker, ed., *Member of the House: Letters by Congressman Clem Miller* (New York: Charles Scribner's Sons, 1962), p. 110.

34. For a hierarchy of committee preferences, 1949–1968, see William L. Morrow, *Congressional Committees* (New York: Charles Scribner's Sons, 1969), pp. 42–43.

35. David S. Broder, "Budget Becomes Popular," *Boston Globe*, January 14, 1979, p. C7. The committee prefrences in 1979 were derived from this article and from a staff interview, Majority Whip's Office, U.S. House of Representatives, Washington, D.C., January 11, 1979.

36. Donald R. Matthews, *U.S. Senators and Their World* (New York: Vintage, 1960), pp. 154–55.

37. Goodwin, *The Little Legislatures: Committees of Congress*, pp. 102–103.

38. Richard F. Fenno, Jr., *Congressmen in Committees* (Boston: Little, Brown, 1973), and Steven S. Smith and Christopher J. Deering, *Committees in Congress* (Washington, D.C.: Congressional Quarterly Press, 1984).

39. An understandably unidentified staff member, quoted in Steven V. Roberts, "A Most Important Man on Capitol Hill," *New York Times Magazine*, September 22, 1985, p. 51.

40. Representative Rostenkowski, quoted in Elizabeth Wehr, "Rostenkowski: A Firm Grip on Ways and Means," p. 1317.

41. Representative Pepper, quoted in Paul Light, *Artful Work: The Politics of Social Security Reform* (New York: Random House, 1985), p. 161; Representative Bonior, quoted in Andy Plattner, "Rules Members Gain by Helping Others," *Congressional Quarterly Weekly Report*, August 24, 1985, p. 1673; Representative Dicks, quoted in Diane Granat, "House Appropriations Panel Doles Out Cold Federal Cash, Chafes at Budget Procedures," *Congressional Quarterly Weekly Report*, June 18, 1983, p. 1209; unidentified Ways and Means Member, quoted in Fenno, *Congressman in Committees*, p. 3.

42. Unidentified aide, quoted in Light, *Artful Work*, p. 161.

43. Unidentified members of Foreign Affairs and Education and Labor Committees, quoted in Fenno, *Congressmen in Committees*, pp. 12, 10.

44. Former Sen. J. W. Fulbright, quoted in Leslie H. Gelb, "For Senate Foreign Relations Panel, More Partisanship and Less Influence," *New York Times*, November 27, 1984, p. A27.

45. Unidentified representative, quoted in Light, *Artful Work*, p. 147.

46. Fenno, *Congressmen in Committees*, p. 6.

47. Unidentified former representative, quoted in James T. Murphy, "Political Parties and the Porkbarrel: Party Conflict and Cooperation in House Public Works Committee Decision Making," in Glenn R. Parker, ed., *Studies of Congress* (Washington, D.C.: Congressional Quarterly Press, 1985), pp. 237–38.

48. Diane Granat, "First Freshman Test: The Right Committee Seat," *Congressional Quarterly Weekly Report*, February 2, 1985, pp. 172–75.

49. Interior and Public Works representatives, quoted in Smith and Deering, *Committees in Congress*, p. 143.

50. Representative Miller, quoted in Steve Blakely, "Representative Miller Poised to Assume Udall's Interior Chairmanship," *Congressional Quarterly Weekly Report*, January 25, 1986, pp. 162–63.

6

Rules and Norms

A House vote on the question of giving aid to contras in Nicaragua and a Senate vote to confirm the appointment of an Indiana lawyer as a judge on the Seventh U.S. Circuit Court of Appeals might seem to have little in common. Both are notable, however, for what they illustrate about congressional rules and the differences between the two chambers. In both cases, those who had sought to use the particular rules of their chamber to gain a tactical advantage lost on the vote that counted. As is often the case, political or tactical failures can be more instructive than successes.

The House vote on giving aid to the contras, one of many House votes on this issue, took place on April 16, 1986. Speaker Tip O'Neill and the House Democratic leadership had devised a complicated scheme making it difficult for supporters of contra aid to win that chamber's approval of the Reagan administration's proposal of $100 million in aid, which had already cleared the Senate. The Democrats' first step was to employ a "hostage strategy" designed to avoid a presidential veto by attaching the contra aid proposal, which the president wanted, to a $1.7 billion supplemental appropriations bill, which the president had threatened to veto. Any provision for contra aid that was attached to the supplemental appropriations would then have to go back to the Senate, where opposition and further delay could be expected. The second step in the Democrats' strategy came in the rule under which the House was to consider three alternative contra aid amendments.

Under the rule, the first amendment proposed by Rep. Lee Hamilton (D-IN) and backed by many liberals would have provided $27 million in humanitarian aid to Nicaraguan refugees and money for regional peace talks instead of military aid. If the Hamilton amendment failed, which seemed likely because Democratic whip counts showed that there were only 170 of the 218 votes needed for passage, the rule stated that the House would consider another proposed amendment. This second amendment, proposed by Rep. Dave McCurdy (D-OK), would have provided $30 million in nonmilitary aid, called for direct negotiations to end the war, and required another vote after July before any of the $70 million in military aid would be forthcoming.

Although O'Neill himself was opposed to any contra aid, he and the House leadership supported the McCurdy amendment as a compromise that would preclude House consideration of the full Reagan administration's package and would delay final action by Congress. Only if the McCurdy amendment were defeated would the House then be able to consider the full administration proposal as an amendment to the bill. The rule also stated that there would be a separate vote on the supplemental appropriations bill, which gave the Speaker additional room to maneuver.

Angry House Republicans complained that the complicated rule was "an example of the trivializing of issues and the way they abuse power around here," "a farce," and a "sham charade," and one of the Speaker's aides recognized that the Republicans were "unhappy that they have to go up the mountain so many times. They have to fight the rule, they have to fight the amendments to the contra package, they have to fight the supplemental." Republicans seemed to be boxed in after the House adopted the rule on the bill. But halfway into the voting period on the first (Hamilton) amendment, House Republican leader Robert Michel surprised Democratic strategists by voting for the Hamilton amendment. "There was no way around it except simply to throw a monkey wrench into the machinery," Michel said after the vote. The head of the Republican Policy Committee, Wyoming Rep. Dick Cheney, explained that when Republican leaders saw the Democrats win on the rule, that "rather than play the game, we said 'screw it.'"

With House Republicans suddenly voting 177 to 1 in favor, the Hamilton amendment was adopted by an overwhelming 361–66 margin, and the House could therefore not move to consider the McCurdy proposal. By employing a tactic that House Majority Whip Thomas Foley called "parliamentary suicide," Republican leaders had outflanked leaders of the majority party and, in effect, forced House Democrats to release the contra aid "hostage" from the supplemental appropriations bill. Knowing that there was no chance of the president's signing the appropriations bill with a Hamilton amendment in it, or without any contra aid proposal, House Democrats halted action on the bill (killing the amendment) and agreed to separate the two issues. Two months later, the House supported the Reagan administration by approving a $100 million contra aid package.[1]

On June 26, 1986, the day after the House vote on contra aid, a Senate vote resulted in a most unusual situation: A Reagan nominee to the U.S. Court of Appeals had won a forty-eight to forty-six vote in his favor, yet had not been confirmed for the position. That was the immediate result of four hours of Senate debate and of ploys and gambits that afternoon. In May, the Senate Judiciary Committee had voted to send to the full Senate the nomination of Daniel Manion to a seat on the Seventh Circuit U.S. Court of Appeals. The Committee passed on Manion's name without recommendation, after supporters were unable to win an earlier vote on a favorable recommendation. Senate Democrats opposed Manion's nomination on grounds that he was not qualified, but Senate Republicans claimed that Manion's political background and conservative views were the real reasons that Democrats opposed him. Senate Majority Leader Robert Dole anticipated a filibuster by Senate Democrats when the Senate took up the Manion nomination on June 26, and he knew from a vote count that morning that he did not have the sixty votes needed to put an end to a filibuster. The majority leader had been calling for a direct vote on Manion's nomination, where he would need fifty votes to win (with Vice-President Bush breaking a tie), and was taken aback when one of the leaders of the opposition to Manion, Delaware Sen. Joseph Biden, told Dole he was ready for a direct vote on the nominee. Surprised by Biden's offer and knowing that it must have been based on a vote count, Senator Dole told Senator Biden that he was not willing to gamble on Manion's nomination right then because of the absence of two senators thought to be Manion supporters—Florida Sen. Paula

Hawkins and Oregon's Bob Packwood. Senator Biden countered by saying that he would abstain from voting and he would get another senator from his side to abstain, thus cancelling out or "pairing," the missing votes of Hawkins and Packwood. Hawaii Sen. Daniel Inouye agreed to be the second pair for Biden. After a brief recess and some additional negotiating, the vote on Manion began. Senate Democrats figured that they had a two-vote majority against the nomination, but that margin began to fade quickly when Sen. Slade Gorton (R-WA), one of six Republicans that had been counted as against the nomination, announced that he was switching to vote for Manion in return for a promise that the Reagan administration would facilitate the appointment of a judge in the state of Washington that Gorton had been promoting. When the voting was almost over, Sen. Nancy Kassebaum (R-KS) surprised Biden and others by withdrawing her vote against Manion. She later said that she had withrawn her vote "out of respect" for Sen. Barry Goldwater (R-AZ), whom Kassebaum was told was unable to get to the chamber but who was said to be a Manion supporter. Kassebaum's pair with Goldwater produced a tie vote (47–47) on the Manion nomination. Vice-President Bush was presiding over the Senate and ready to break the tie. Just when the time limit on voting was about to expire, Senate Minority Leader Robert Byrd (D-WV) switched his vote, thereby producing a 48–46 majority for Manion's confirmation. Byrd's vote change was a parliamentary maneuver rather than a change of heart. As a member of the majority on the vote, Byrd was able to call for a reconsideration of the vote, something he could not have done as a member of the losing side. The motion to reconsider had the effect of at least temporarily delaying the confirmation of Daniel Manion. When Majority Leader Robert Dole was asked, a few days later, when he planned to have the Senate vote on Byrd's motion, this is what he said: "I'm not going to bring it up if I don't have the votes. The Democrats felt they had it locked up, so they wanted us to vote. So we voted and they lost, and now they want to vote again." The majority leader also indicated that he was considering a parliamentary move of his own. By delaying any action on Manion's nomination until the end of the session and by immediately moving to adjourn the Senate before the motion to reconsider could be brought up, Dole could win adjournment and the earlier forty-eight to forty-six vote confirming Manion would stand. As it turned out, Dole did not have to resort to that tactic. On July 23, the Senate defeated Byrd's motion to reconsider by a forty-nine to fifty margin. On this vote, Arizona Democrat Dennis DeConcini announced that, as "a personal favor," he would pair his vote for reconsideration with that of his hospitalized Arizona colleague, Senator Goldwater. In addition, Sen. Daniel Evans (R-WA) changed his vote and supported Manion's confirmation. The pair and the vote change resulted in a 49-49 tie, which was enough to defeat the motion even before Vice-President Bush's vote against the motion produced the 49-50 vote defeating reconsideration and confirming Manion for the Seventh Circuit bench.[2]

In both of these cases, Democratic congressional leaders used the rules in an attempt to win votes they would otherwise lose. In the first case, House leaders sought to avoid a straight up-or-down vote on President Reagan's contra aid proposal. In the second, Senate Democrats tried to salvage something from a surprising loss on a direct vote on a judicial nominee. Both cases illustrate ways in which congressional rules can be used to structure decision making. Another point that is manifested in the contra aid and Manion cases is that the two chambers are distinctly different institutions. In the House, the tactics employed by the leaders of both parties depended on collective action—Democrats voting together on the Rules committee and on the floor to support the rule; Republicans giving near-unanimous support to Michel's surprise vote on the Hamilton amendment. In contrast, the maneuvering of senators on the Manion nomination was an exercise in individualism. Senate leaders accepted the pairing of votes even when those matches hurt their own cause. In some of those pairs, senators were in effect voting against their own position as a personal courtesy to a colleague. That individualism makes predicting votes difficult in the Senate, as was evident in Democrats' miscalculations on the Manion vote.

House and Senate Differences

"If the Senate has been the nation's great forum," a representative has written, "the House has been its workshop."[3] People often think of Congress as a whole and discuss it in terms of characteristics shared by the two branches (a decentralized committee system, the importance of seniority in selecting leaders, an orientation toward narrow issues and local interests, and the need to achieve accommodation with a co-equal chamber). Yet important differences exist between the House and the Senate—differences that exist despite some House reforms that make the House more like the Senate by enhancing representation, and some Senate reforms that improve its lawmaking capability of and make it more like the House. These differences are reinforced by the rules and norms governing legislative behavior in the two houses. Some of the more important differences are discussed next.

SIZE

Most of the dissimilarity between the two chambers stems from the fact that the House is made up of 435 members elected for two-year terms while the Senate consists of 100 members elected for six-year terms. In the Ninety-ninth Congress (1985–1986), there were 33 former representatives serving in the Senate. Senate Majority Leader Robert Dole, who spent eight years in the House before coming to the Senate in 1968, and who still remembered what it was like to be one of 435 rather than one of 100, had this to say about the House: "You sort of get lost over there." Illinois Sen. Paul Simon, a freshman in the Ninety-ninth Congress, talked about the size advantage even though as a Democrat he went from being part of the House majority to being in the Senate minority. In 1985, at a time Republicans controlled both the White House and the Senate, the Illinois senator noted that "a senator has greater access to virtually anyone inside or outside of government." "There are very few people who won't return a phone call from a U.S. senator."[4] One of those who sounded like he might not return such a phone call, and one who makes similar points but from a different perspective is the representative who had this to say about the other chamber:

> The Senate is a zoo. I have no interest in the Senate. I like the scaled anonymity of the House. The Senate is all personality dependent. It's people who shave the face of the next president every morning. That is just ridiculous.
>
> I have no interest in being in the Senate. Is there anything senators can do that I can't? I think the only answers are that they get their calls returned by Jim Baker (then White House Chief of Staff) more easily than I can and they can get on

*network television more easily than I can. That's the maximum
that a senator can do that I can't do.*[5]

Senators, even newly elected ones, are much more visible
than representatives. There is a media bias toward covering senators that begins even before they are elected; senate candidates
are the focus of more press and television coverage than are
candidates for the House of Representatives. The national press
corps gives senators more attention for a number of reasons, and
one of them is the different size of the two chambers. As Stephen
Hess points out: "It is easier and faster to build a coherent story
with a smaller cast of characters. The House of Representatives is
too much like *War and Peace;* the Senate is more on the scale of
Crime and Punishment.[6]

In addition to differences in the visibility of members, the
relative sizes of the two chambers affects other aspects of the
politics of Congress. Because the House is more than four times
the size of the Senate, it cannot operate in the informal relaxed
manner characteristic of the upper chamber. Although the two
chambers are more similar in many ways than they were a decade ago, the House still is more formal, more impersonal, and
more hierarchically organized. There is a sharper division of labor in the House, a difference that is seen in the narrower scope
of members' participation both in committee and on the floor.

TERMS

Senators' terms are for six years, representatives' for two years.
The biennial election cycle of House members means that most
of them are campaigning all year round, every year. At a time
when the 1986 elections were more than a year away, Rep. Terry
Bruce (D-IL) admitted: "I'm never not a candidate."[7] Members of
the House talk about how senators can "afford to be statesmen,"
about the "cushion" of a six-year term, about the "squirming
room," that senators get as a result of having longer terms. One
representative referred to the two years of a House term as "a
much shorter leash." Another said that because of the two-year
term, "you are tied down a lot closer to your constituency here
than in the Senate," and that in the House "you have to be a
politician all the time because you have to run every two years."[8]

Richard Fenno's study of the behavior of House members in
their districts led him to conclude that it is often hard to distin-

guish between campaigning and representing, that "nearly everything" a representative does "to win and hold support—allocating, reaching, presenting, responding, communicating, explaining, assuring—involves representation."[9] After a comparable study of senators, Fenno wrote: "For senators, campaign styles are not necessarily home styles." Although a number of the activities that senators engaged in were campaign related, even for those in their first year of a six-year term, there was also an awareness that the longer term gave senators more freedom to engage in noncampaign activity than the two-year term gave members of the House. "The amplitude of the six-year cycle gives senators more of a choice," said Fenno. "Six years between elections is long enough to encourage a senator to stop campaigning for a while and do something else with his or her time."[10] In making the adjustment from campaigning to governing, senators make a number of decisions about their committee work, about how they want to use staff and other resources, and about the best allocation of time and resources between Capitol Hill and the home state. The six-year term permits senators to make those choices on the basis of policy goals and lawmaking as well as representation and reelection.

COMMITTEES

The size difference between the two chambers is greatly compounded by the Senate's having sixteen standing committees for 100 members and the House's having twenty-two committees for 435 members. Most representatives therefore sit on one or two committees while senators can be on four or more committees and up to a dozen subcommittees. An episode that took place not too long ago on the Senate side of Capitol Hill dramatized the meaning of those numbers. On this particular morning, the Senate Foreign Relations Committee was meeting with Secretary of State George Shultz about a proposed arms sale to Jordan. Down the hall from that meeting, the Senate Labor Committee was holding a hearing on the question of requiring food manufacturers to include the salt content of food on their labels. Just across the way, the education subcommittee of the Senate Labor Committee was meeting at the same time to discuss the program of scholarships known as Pell Grants. Rhode Island Sen. Claiborne Pell, for whom the grant program was named, was a member of all three of those panels. (In addition, Pell served on five other subcommittees, the Senate Rules and Administration Committee, and the Joint Library Committee.) He was in fact the senior Democrat on the Foreign Relations Committee and the education subcommittee and the second ranking Democrat on the Senate Labor Committee. About midmorning, Senator Pell rushed into the Labor Committee hearing on salt labeling, informed his colleagues there that he was already late to the Foreign Relations Committee session, and began to read from a prepared statement about Pell Grants. After a few moments of this, Ohio Sen. Howard Metzenbaum leaned over and whispered something in Pell's ear. The Rhode Island senator collected his papers, said "I apologize deeply" to the bewildered audience, and rushed off to his subcommittee meeting. Senator Metzenbaum tried to help his colleague out by explaining to those present: "There are too many hearings going on at the same time."[11]

That sort of thing would happen rarely, if ever, on the House side of the Hill. Over there, they talk about senators being "spread so thin that they can't hold a candle to House members in terms of substance," and about their own committees as "*the* area where you can make your most positive contribution," and "the *one* place probably where you really can have an impact on legislation."[12] Because senators serve on so many committees, they find it difficult to give as much attention to the work of any one of their committees as House members can to theirs. The membership of the Senate Finance Committee and House Ways and Means Committee illustrates this difference. In the Ninety-ninth Congress (1985–1986), there were ten majority members of the Senate Finance Committee in addition to committee chairman, Bob Packwood. Those ten members included the Senate majority leader and the chairmen of the following Senate committees and subcommittees: Government Affairs Committee; Commerce Committee; Environmental Pollution Subcommittee; Special Aging Committee; Public Lands Subcommittee; Select Intelligence Committee; Transportation Subcommittee; Monetary and Fiscal Policy Subcommittee; Administrative Practices Subcommittee; and the Labor Committee's Aging Subcommittee. The comparable committee to Senate Finance in the House, Ways and Means, is recognized in House rules as an exclusive committee, which severely restricts members' serving on any other committees. In the Ninety-ninth Congress there were twenty-two majority members of the committee in addition to Chairman Dan Rostenkowski. Only one chaired another committee or subcommittee (the Select Narcotics Abuse and Control Committee), three served as the Ways and Means representatives on the House Budget Committee, two were on the Standards of Official Conduct Committee, and the only other committee assignments of members were to minor select or joint committees. Nine members of Ways and Means had no other committee assignments whatsoever. The many competing responsibilities of senators helps to explain the difference cited by a senator who also had served for eighteen years in the House: "On committees in the House, you would sit with other members day after day in hearings. When you have hearings of a subcommittee on appropriations in the Senate, generally only the chairman is there."[13]

House committees are primarily a place for legislative work, a place for members with expertise to deal with complex matters of lawmaking. To have any consistent influence on policy in a particular area, a representative generally must be on the committee with jurisdiction in that area. While Senate committees must necessarily perform lawmaking functions, senators have a greater opportunity to play a representational role in committee, and noncommittee senators have a better chance to have some influence over a wider range of policy areas. Once again, the experience of a legislator who has served in both chambers is instructive:

> When I wanted to influence a committee's decision in the House, all I could do is testify, talk to a few friends on the committee, and then, if I didn't like their bill, cast a lonely vote on the floor against it.

> But as soon as I walked into the Senate it became clear to me that my options are better here. Even after just four years, I tend to know more of the fellows on the committee better than I often did in the House, and everyone seems to respect the fact that you can go to the floor if you're not happy about what went on in committee.[14]

Most of the differences between House and Senate committees have to do with the lawmaking orientation of House committees and the representational focus of Senate committees. Subcommittees in the House are workshops for marking up legislation; subcommittees in the Senate are forums where senators are able to articulate issues for the full committee to consider in markup. Senate committees are more accessible to nonmembers than are House committees at both the committee and floor consideration stages of the legislative process, accessibility that enhances representation but must be limited for lawmaking to proceed.

The normal tension between these two general goals led Senate leaders of the Ninety-ninth Congress to try to correct some of the excesses of representation in the committee system by strictly enforcing Senate rules limiting each senator to two major and one minor committee. In the Ninety-eighth Congress, there were thirty-one senators serving on three major committees. After seven weeks of intense wrangling, described by one senator as "like having a hangover for weeks," and by a senate aide as "the most nerve-racking experience I've ever gone through," the number of senators with three major committees was brought down to fourteen.[15] The reasons offered by senators for their resistance to giving up committees, even when they admitted that they were overextended, were generally ones of representation. Vermont Sen. Patrick Leahy, who served on sixteen committees and subcommittees at the time, sounded that theme: "You build up your own constituencies in the state, and you know that if you drop any committees it becomes a campaign issue. People say 'Pat Leahy doesn't care about us anymore.' "[16]

LEADERSHIP CONTROL

Sen. Thad Cochran (R-MS), a three-term House veteran first elected to the Senate in 1978, said that the difference between being a representative and being a senator is "like the difference between being a spectator and being a player."[17] The greater size of the House requires that it be organized in a more formal, hierarchical way than the Senate. And that, in turn, requires that the leadership in the House be given more direct control over members. Both the formal rules and the unwritten norms of the two chambers support this difference.

A leading student of the Senate once described it as a place where "no one finally can make anyone else do anything."[18] This description fits with a lighter definition of the Senate, sometimes put forward by senators themselves, as a place where a person makes a speech that says nothing, nobody listens, and then everybody disagrees. Leadership in the Senate reflects this pattern of concern for the individual senator. For instance, in scheduling floor debate on a bill, majority party leaders will generally canvass the membership and arrange the timing of the debate to try to suit all members' schedules; what one senator characterized as conducting business "for the convenience of one senator, to the inconvenience of 99."[19] Such a practice would be impossible in the House, where leaders schedule floor action after consultation only with the principal party and committee leaders. As a result, individual House members are subject to leadership control over their actions to a much greater degree than are Senate members. These differences were evident in the contra aid and Manion confirmation cases at the beginning of the chapter.

House and Senate rules reflect this difference in control over the behavior of individual members. House rules are more complex and more specific than Senate rules. It took more than 400 pages to outline the rules of the House in a recent Congress and eleven volumes to spell out precedents of interpretation and procedure; Senate rules, on the other hand, required only 90 pages, and its precedents were contained in one volume. The loose structure of the Senate encourages the full representation of all views; whereas the rules of the House, in the words of a former parliamentarian, "show a constant subordination of the individual to the necessities of the whole House."[20]

An example of a rule that limits participation in the House is the five-minute rule, under which representatives offering an amendment to a bill are limited to five minutes of speaking. Although that time can be stretched through a number of parliamentary devices, the five-minute rule in the House does present a contrast with Senate rules that permit senators to speak for as long as they want (unless sixty senators support a cloture motion to end debate) and to offer amendments quite freely. The effect of these rules on the two chambers was made evident to former representative and freshman Sen. Albert Gore, Jr., when he took part in his first Senate filibuster:

> I spoke for five minutes and realized that I had said everything I really needed to say yet I had to keep the floor for a much longer period of time.
>
> So I did something that I never had an opportunity to do in the House—back up and say the same thing over again in a different way. I ended up speaking for two hours and 45 minutes.[21]

But senators know, too, that they are responsible for making laws as well as for representing interests. That concern is manifested in the regularity with which senators propose changing the rules to improve the lawmaking capability of the Senate. When the Senate began televising its proceedings in June 1986, many senators were concerned that the public would see an institution that appeared to be incapable of passing laws. One change in the Senate rule on cloture, which does provide a way to limit debate, was accepted in 1986, but a package of reforms that would have given Senate leaders greater control over the floor was defeated. It could be said in that instance representation won out over lawmaking. However, even those who opposed major reforms in 1986 on grounds of representation recognized that the Senate also had lawmaking responsibilities. "When the country is ready for legislation," suggested Colorado Sen. William Armstrong, "[and] when the Senate is ready for legislation, we can pass something here with breathtaking speed." But the last words on the subject were those of Mississippi Sen. Thad Cochran, a member of the Republican leadership who voted with Armstrong against major reforms in 1986: "We don't want to become totally efficient. This is not the place for legislation to speed through. The rights of minorities, small minorities, should be protected."[22]

POLICY ROLES

Sen. Bennett Johnston (D-LA) said that he opposed televising Senate proceedings because "the public will never understand why it's important to this institution and to the nation for the Senate to play the role of the saucer where the political passions of the nation are cooled." Sen. Charles McC. Mathias (R-MD) favored television coverage and said that it would "add a new dimension to the public's understanding of the Senate's business." The Maryland senator said it would help the public understand why it is important "for the Senate to play the role of the saucer where the political passions of the nation are cooled." The two senators might disagree about the effects of television, but they certainly agreed on a metaphor for the Senate's policy-making role. The Senate-as-saucer metaphor has a rich tradition, going back to a breakfast meeting between George Washington and Thomas Jefferson, at which Jefferson, who had just returned from France where he had been during the Constitutional Convention, asked Washington, who had presided over the Convention, why a senate was needed. Washington is said to have answered by asking Jefferson, "Why did you pour that coffee into you saucer?" When Jefferson said it was to cool it, Washington replied, "Even so, we pour legislation into the senatorial saucer to cool it."[23]

Different words and other metaphors have been employed to

describe the Senate's policy role, but there seems to be an underlying agreement on the essential nature of that role. Woodrow
Wilson sounded much like Washington when he wrote in 1885:
"The Senate commonly feels with the House, but it does not, so
to say, feel so fast." Sen. Bennett Johnston joined the metaphor
of the senatorial saucer with one that characterized the unlimited
debates of the Senate as "a balance wheel in the constitutional
system." And Vermont Sen. Patrick Leahy, upset by the number
of roll call votes, which had increased by over 100 in one year
and brought the total in 1985 to nearly 400 recorded votes in the
Senate, told his colleagues: "We're losing sight of why we're
here. There are only 100 of us and we're expected to handle
broad issues. We should be the conscience of the nation and
instead we're ending up being the bookkeeper of the nation."[24]
These statements clearly indicate an expectation that the Senate
will do more than simply replicate the policymaking of the
House, and vice versa. And that expectation holds true even
when the direct election of senators and congressional reforms
have made the two chambers alike in many ways.

If either chamber of Congress is capable of monitoring the
details of government, of being the bookkeeper, it is the House of
Representatives. For those who believe that God is in the details,
only the House could serve as a church. That chamber, with its
well-ordered division of labor, is better able to play a policy role
of drafting legislation in conjunction with subject matter experts
in executive agencies and bureaus. The Senate's policy role is
different. Nelson Polsby has written:

> "Passing bills," which is central to the life of the House, is
> peripheral to the Senate. In the Senate the three central activi-
> ties are (1) cultivating national constituencies; (2) formulating
> questions for debate and discussion on a national scale (espe-
> cially in opposition to the president); and (3) incubating new
> policy proposals that may at some future time find their way
> into legislation.[25]

Policy incubation is the process of keeping a new proposal
alive. The process involves continuing to introduce a proposal
until it gains enough supporters to assure passage or until the
political climate has changed enough so that a proposal that at
first struck many as too extreme becomes accepted as a possibly
rational solution to some problem. To accomplish these policy

goals, the Senate must emphasize the representational values of extensive debate, of mutual deference to individual legislators rather than to committees, and of an unstructured informal legislative chamber that gives as much time to discussing ideas as it does to passing legislation.

To become a law, policy proposals must pass both chambers and emerge from Congress in one form. If the Senate gives one nickel more than the House does in a bill to finance a housing program, the program does not come into being until the two chambers agree on an identical bill. After running the gamut of these two chambers with their different policy orientations, most important bills wind up in a joint House–Senate conference committee that must reconcile the differences between the bills and produce a compromise bill that can win acceptance on both sides of Capitol Hill.

Table 6–1 summarizes the major differences between the

TABLE 6-1 Differences between the House and Senate

House	Senate
435 members	100 members
2-year term	6-year term
Constituency: about 500,000 in district	Constituency: entire state, ranges from 300,000 to 20 million
Low visibility in press and media	High visibility in press and media
Rules strictly limit participation	Rules maximize full participation by all members
Committee and subcommittee work very important	Committees and subcommittees not as important
Distribution of power is hierarchical	Distribution of power is more diffuse
Strict leadership control of floor proceedings	Less leadership control of floor proceedings
Less reliance on staff	More reliance on staff
Policy specialists	Policy generalists
Lawmaking emphasis	Emphasis on representation

Source: Adapted from Walter J. Oleszek, *Congressional Procedures and the Policy Process* (Congressional Quarterly Press, 1984), p. 22. Some items added.

House and the Senate. While it is important to understand the differences between the two chambers, it is also important to realize that the structure and procedures of both chambers have been undergoing changes that have made the House and Senate in the 1980s more alike. This similarity has occurred because representation and lawmaking have a place in both chambers. House reforms in the 1970s to improve representation on committees and in floor voting elicited other reforms that gave House leaders more control over lawmaking. When the Senate moved to begin televising its proceedings and further the goals of representation, it also considered a number of reform proposals aimed at strengthening the institution's lawmaking capability. House–Senate differences, as well as similarities, are shaped by the tension between lawmaking and representation.

House and Senate Rules

The rules that determine how bills get to the House and Senate floors directly affect only one stage of the legislative process. That stage is the heart of congressional policymaking, however, and the rules governing that stage can give us a sense of the overall impact of the rules on the two chambers. This section will provide a brief look at first the House and then the Senate rules under which bills are brought to the floor.

HOUSE RULES

In the House, when a bill has been cleared by committee and awaits floor action, it is placed on one of many lists of bills called calendars. The Union Calendar lists bills raising revenue, general appropriation bills, and other public bills that directly or indirectly appropriate money or property. The House Calendar lists public bills that do not raise revenue or directly or indirectly appropriate money or property. The Private Calendar lists bills that affect only those named in the bill. Bills that have appeared on the Union or House Calendars but are likely to be unopposed because of their minor character may be placed on the Consent Calendar. House rules include a number of procedures designed (1) to permit members to deal quickly with bills on the Private and Consent Calendars and (2) to suspend the rules in order to pass noncontroversial minor legislation. Major legislation appears on the House or Union Calendars, and a rule from the Rules Committee is required to bring a bill from those calendars to the floor. The form and content of these rules varies, but a typical rule will look something like this:

> Resolved, *That upon the adoption of this resolution, it shall be in order to move that the House resolve itself into the Committee of the Whole House on the State of the Union for the consideration of the bill (H.R. _____), entitled, etc. After general debate, which shall be confined to the bill, and continue not to exceed _____ hours, to be equally divided and controlled by the chairman and the ranking minority member of the Committee on _____, the bill shall be read for amendment under the five-minute rule. At the conclusion of the consideration of the bill to the House with such amendments as may have been adopted and the previous question shall be considered as ordered on the bill, and amendments thereto to final passage without intervening motion except one motion to recommit with or without instructions.*[26]

The Rules Committee can issue three types of rules: open, closed, and modified. Most legislation comes to the floor under an open rule that permits germane amendments to the committee bill. The second type, a closed rule, generally takes the form of prohibiting amendments except those put forward by the committee handling the bill. This type of rule is considered essential in cases such as the Tax Reform Act of 1986, where opening the bill to floor amendments would have undercut the complex bill that the Ways and Means Committee had produced only after months of work. In 1973, the Democratic Caucus changed the rules governing issuance of a closed rule from the Rules Committee and required that heads of committees give four days' notice of a request for a closed rule. During that period, fifty members of the Democratic Caucus may call for a meeting of that body, and a majority of the caucus may instruct the Rules Committee to permit certain floor amendments when the bill comes up. This procedure was used soon after it went into effect, when the Democratic Caucus instructed the Ways and Means Committee to permit amendments dealing with the oil depletion allowance in floor consideration of a tax bill in 1974, and when the caucus instructed the Rules Committee to permit amendments to the Committee Reform Amendments considered the same year.

The third type of rule, known as a modified or complex rule, imposes a high degree of structure by limiting amendments to certain parts of the bill and by prescribing who may offer which amendments and when. The Rules Committee has increasingly relied on complex rules for important legislation. When the National Energy Act of 1977 came to the House floor, for example, the rule limited the permitted number of amendments to twenty from the Ad Hoc Committee on energy and twelve from individual representatives. We saw at the beginning of this chapter, the complex rule governing floor consideration of contra aid, where the order of considering amendments was the key to the strategy of both Democrats and Republicans.

Any of these three types of rules may also have provisions that waive points of order against a particular bill. For example, bills from the Appropriations Committee often are in technical violation of House rules because they include legislative matters that are under the jurisdiction of other committees. To prevent opponents from blocking such a bill on technical grounds, the Rules Committee can provide exemptions from certain House rules and procedures as a part of the rule governing floor consideration of the measure.

The Rules Committee currently functions as an important arm of the House leadership. But the control that the committee has over the flow of legislative traffic in the House has not always been used to keep traffic moving. For years, a Rules Committee dominated by southern Democrats and Republicans and acting under the direction of chairmen such as Virginia Rep. Howard Smith (1955–1967) was able to block civil rights, education, and economic policies favored by a House majority. A series of House reforms and changes in the makeup of the Rules Committee, however, finally brought an end to that obstructionist era of the committee. In 1961, the size of the Rules Committee was increased from twelve to fifteen, giving the Democratic House leadership an effective one-vote margin on the committee. Four years later, the House adopted the twenty-one-day rule, which permitted House leaders to call for consideration of bills that had been sitting before the Rules Committee with no action taken on them for twenty-one days. In 1966, a number of rules changes eliminated the ability of the chairperson to run the committee in an arbitrary way. And in 1975, the Speaker of the House was given the power to appoint all Democratic members of the Rules Committee. These reforms, coupled with membership changes that saw liberal and moderate Democrats replace retiring or defeated conservatives, have made the Rules Committee today a strong ally of the House Democratic leadership.

The rules and procedures of House calendars and the Rules Committee are designed to increase the efficiency of House decision making. By reducing the amount of floor time spent on minor legislation, these devices seek to increase the rationality of lawmaking. Most House rules seek to achieve this rationality by providing automatic procedures for handling legislation. Instead of each representative being asked to make a political judgment on every bill, the structure of House rules leans more in the direction of a hierarchy of experts who make rational decisions after careful consideration of all factors. Specialization is reinforced by House rules that limit the participation of unqualified members in legislative decisions.

Structural reforms and membership changes have led to much wider participation of junior members in the House and have made it more like the Senate, but those changes have not altered the fundamental lawmaking structure of the House. Leadership use of House calendars and the Rules Committee still determines which matters will come to the floor for a vote, when they will come, and the conditions under which they will be considered by the whole chamber. Leadership control over the conditions of floor debates and floor voting is still formidable. House leaders and most members accept the notion that the lower chamber is the place for making laws and that the luxury of extensive debate on issues can only be afforded in the smaller Senate.

SENATE RULES

In the Senate, bills are brought to the floor in a more direct way than in the House. The Senate does not have a scheduling committee comparable to the House Rules Committee, and there are only two Senate calendars—the Calendar of Business, which lists all legislation; and the Executive Calendar for nominations and treaties. When a bill has been reported by committee it goes on the appropriate calendar to await action by Senate leaders. The scheduling of legislation for the Senate floor is a bipartisan process that involves leaders from the minority party as well as those from the majority. In the Senate, there might be as many as five bills on the floor at the same time, while the House always limits itself to consideration of only one bill at a time.

In much the same way that rules from the House Rules Committee permit the expeditious handling of legislation by setting aside certain rules and procedures, the Senate uses unanimous consent agreements. These agreements, accepted by all senators, set aside the formal rules of the Senate in order to expedite legislative consideration. There are two types of unanimous consent agreements: simple and complex.

Simple unanimous consent agreements are those made orally on the floor of the Senate by individual senators and deal with routine business. They include requests to have certain staff members on the floor during debate, for insertion of material into the *Congressional Record*, for extensions of time for roll call votes, and for permission for committees to meet while the Senate is in session. Visitors to the Senate gallery will hear endless repetitions of the phrase, "Mr. President, I ask unanimous consent," followed by a wide variety of requests.

Complex unanimous consent agreements, on the other hand, serve much the same function as rules granted by the Rules Committee do in the House, a point that can be seen in the comparison of the two in Table 6–2. They set the guidelines under which the Senate will consider major legislation. These complex agreements are developed by Senate party leaders and key senators involved in the issue. They are written agreements that indicate the order in which particular measures will be considered, which senators will control floor time during consideration of these measures, and the guidelines for debate, often including a statement about what types of amendments will be considered germane and thus be given a hearing. The similarity between a rule issued by the House Rules Committee and a unanimous consent agreement can be seen by looking at a typical example of the latter:

Ordered. *That at* _____ *P.M. on* _____ , *the Senate proceed to consideration of S.* _____ , *a bill to* _____ , *and that there be 13 hours of consideration thereon, including debate on any amendments, debatable motion appeals, or points of order which are submitted or on which the Chair entertains debate, with the time to be equally divided and controlled by the Senator from* _____ *and the Senator from* _____ , *or their designees.*

Ordered further. *That no amendment that is not germane to the provisions of the said bill shall be received, with the following exceptions: Provided, That there be 1 hour debate on each of*

TABLE 6–2 House Rules and Senate Unanimous Consent Agreements

House Rule	Senate Unanimous Consent Agreement
Specifies time for general debate	Specifies time for debating amendments and on final passage
Permits or prohibits amendments	Usually restricts only the offering of nongermane amendments
Formulated by Rules Committee in public session	Formulated by party leaders in private sessions or sometimes on the floor
Approved by majority vote of the House	Approved by unanimous approval of senators present on the floor
Adoption generally results in immediate floor action on bills	Adoption geared more toward prospective action
Covers more aspects of floor procedure	Limited primarily to debate restrictions on amendments and final passage
Does not specify date and exact time for vote on final passage	May set date and exact time for vote on final passage
Effect is to waive House rules	Effect is to waive Senate rules

Source: Walter J. Oleszek, Congressional Procedures and the Policy Process (Congressional Quarterly Press, 1984), p. 159.

the above amendments, with the time to be equally divided and controlled by the mover of such and the manager of the bill.

Ordered further. *That there be 30 minutes debate on any other amendment, debatable motion, appeal, or point of order if submitted to the Senate, with the time to be equally divided and controlled by the mover of such and the manager of the bill.*

Ordered further. *That at the conclusion of the debate, the Senate proceed to vote on passage of S. _____.*[27]

When Senate leaders are unable to get unanimous consent to set limits on debate, their job of controlling the floor becomes more difficult, because only three ways exist to end debate in the

Senate—by unanimous consent, by the simple cessation of talk-ing, and by the extraordinary means of invoking cloture under Senate Rule 22. Unless debate is limited in some way, opponents of a measure can talk it to death by engaging in the time-honored ritual of a Senate filibuster. The strength of that tradition makes the cloture rule difficult to change. A 1975 reform, for example, was the first major change in Rule 22 in almost sixty years.

Prior to the 1975 reform, a vote of two-thirds of those present and voting was required to end debate. Once cloture was voted, each senator was permitted to speak for one hour on the bill under consideration, but they could offer no additional amend-ments and could only vote on germane amendments. The 1975 reform changed the required number needed to end debate from two-thirds of those present and voting to a constitutional three-fifths of the entire Senate membership—regardless of how many members are present and voting. Under the old rule, if all mem-bers were present and voting, sixty-seven senators were required to support cloture in order to end a filibuster. Under the new rule, sixty members can limit debate by invoking cloture, regard-less of how many members are present and voting.

The cloture rule reform was a direct response to the in-creased filibustering and cloture votes that took place in the 1970s. To illustrate, in the more than fifty years between 1919 (when the first cloture vote was taken on the Versailles Treaty) and 1970, there were forty-nine cloture votes taken in the Senate. But in just over three years, between 1971 and February 1975 (a month before the reform of Rule 22), the Senate took more clo-ture votes (fifty-two) than it had in the previous fifty years. Put another way, that increase represented a jump from less than one cloture vote a year to thirteen votes a year. It was also a reflection of an increased willingness on the part of liberal senators to employ the filibuster, which had traditionally been an instru-ment that southern senators used to defeat civil rights bills.

At first glance, it might seem that the rules change did weaken the filibuster as an obstructionist tool. In 1975, the year of the change, there were twenty-three cloture votes, eleven of which were successful. In 1976, there were only four, and in 1977, there were only five. But this drastic reduction in cloture votes did not, by any means, signal the demise of the Senate filibuster. In 1976 Louisiana Sen. James Allen breached the un-written rule that a cloture vote ended a filibuster and used the Senate rules to conduct a postcloture filibuster. By taking advantage of Senate rules saying that each senator had one hour of debating time remaining after a cloture vote and that the time spent on parliamentary tactics such as calling for a quorum and introducing amendments did not count against that allotted hour, Senator Allen was able to tie up the Senate for hours after cloture had been invoked. Widespread use of the postcloture filibuster threat by both conservatives and liberals led to another reform of Rule 22 in 1979. As a result of that change, all time spent on quorum calls, roll call votes, and other parliamentary devices for stalling action on legislation is now charged against the one-hour limit of the senator(s) responsible for the delay. A number of additional cloture rule reforms were proposed in conjunction with the 1986 decision to televise Senate proceedings, and one of them was adopted—a change that reduced the overall time limit on a postcloture filibuster from one hundred to thirty hours. Because at least sixty senators must agree to end a filibuster and because a minority of senators is able to block a majority, Rule 22 clearly supports the value of representation. On the other hand, senators' acceptance of reforms that limit postcloture filibusters indicates that they also recognize the necessity of lawmaking.

House and Senate Folkways

Any organization must develop norms of behavior that provide the stability necessary for members to get their work done. Donald Matthews's study of the post-World War II Senate found six folkways or unwritten rules of the game that governed how senators dealt with one another. Similar folkways have been found to regulate members' behavior in the House. Although most of these folkways can still be found in both chambers in the 1980s, the more active role played by junior representatives and senators and limits on the sanctions available to congressional leaders have diminished the impact of these folkways on legislators' behavior. Legislative norms may be classified by the primary functions they perform. Some contribute to the chamber's lawmaking, others to representation, and still others to maintaining the existing system by regulating the level of conflict. Folkways that help Congress perform its lawmaking function are those of specialization, apprenticeship, and legislative work. The norm of reciprocity aids lawmaking in the House but seems to be more geared to achieving representational goals in the Senate. Folkways that help maintain the existing system by controlling conflict are those of courtesy and institutional patriotism.[28]

SPECIALIZATION

Norms that contribute to the function of decision making are more important in the House than in the Senate. The House must have thorough rules governing the handling of legislation. It also must have informal norms supporting the more structured decision-making process. By encouraging representatives to specialize in one or two subjects, House norms prevent the chaos that would result from every member's attempt to speak on each subject. At the same time they insure that there will be a number of experts on each subject coming before the House. One congressman noted, "There is always someone around here who's an expert on something you need to know. I dare say there is not one subject you could think of that doesn't have at least one member of the House particularly qualified to give you advice about it."[29]

Even though we find this norm in both houses, specialization means different things in the House than it does in the Senate. In the House, specialization is tied to the importance of committee work, the development of subject matter expertise, and the division of labor necessary for accomplishing that chamber's lawmaking function. In the Senate, specialization is much less committee oriented. It is mainly looked upon as expertise that enhances the senator's standing with a national constituency associated with that subject.[30] Specialization helps the Senate to play a policy incubation role by insuring that there will be at least one senator to keep debate alive on an issue that does not yet command the majority necessary to become law. In short, the specialization norm in the House helps to fulfill the lawmaking responsibilities of that chamber, while the specialization norm in the Senate helps that chamber to provide for the representation of many diverse interests throughout the country.

APPRENTICESHIP-SENIORITY

This norm aids decision making by giving members who have been in Congress (or on the committee) the longest the most influence. It also maximizes the influence of those "best qualified" to make each type of decision. Nelson Polsby has suggested that "the great advantage of the seniority system is that it decentralizes power in the House of Representatives by creating multiple centers of policy influence and increasing the number of good Congressional jobs. This adds to the incentives of the Congressional career."[31] Although apprenticeship norms in the House continue to support a system of decision making by experienced committee experts, the impact of a strict seniority system has been diminished. Patterns of committee assignments, the distribution of power within committees, conference committees, and party leadership selection have suggested that the seniority system is a flexible one that permits consideration of factors other than just tenure. Recent studies of the Senate have found that of the six norms discussed in Matthews's earlier study, apprenticeship was the only one that had essentially disappeared by the 1970s.[32] That point was brought home to Senate Majority Leader Howard Baker when a Republican senator who had just been elected came up to him shortly after President Reagan had introduced his 1981 budget and said: "I don't like the President's budget, and I have one of my own. How can I get it passed?"[33] The extent of this change was also indicated by talk about a "juniority" system that began to emerge in the 1980s:

> The idea that there is an obligatory period of quiet apprenticeship still serves its purpose, especially when members have to fight off challengers who want to know why they have so few conspicuous achievements to point to after two years. But it bears little relationship to reality.
>
> That much is clear to anyone who watched the House in the past Congress and saw Tony Coelho of California showing enough wizardry as a fund-raiser to make himself Democratic campaign manager after one term; or freshman Newt Gingrich of Georgia scribbling Republican strategy for the rest of this century in crayon on a board in his office and selling some of it to the Reagan campaign; or newly elected Democratic Phil Gramm of Texas working on his own conservative federal budget.[34]

Changes in membership and certain congressional reforms have produced this decline in the importance of seniority in both chambers. In particular, the changes in membership exemplified by the Senate classes of 1958 and 1980 and the House class of

1974 dramatically affected the seniority system. Prior to 1958, seniority in the Senate served to maintain the power of southern Democrats. The infusion of a large number of northern Democrats in 1958 and their insistence on an active role began a trend of junior members' activity that was given another boost by the large Republican class of 1980. The comments of New York Sen. Alfonse D'Amato, who became chairman of an appropriations subcommittee and a banking subcommittee in his freshman year, illustrate what it was like for the 1980 Republican class: "I remember Senator Javits (D'Amato's predecessor) telling me that in all his twenty-four years in the Senate and eight years in the House, he was a subcommittee chairman only once. And here I am walking right into two chairmanships."[35] The House class of 1974 was able to exert a similar change in seniority, but it was done by changing the rules. A number of the House reforms discussed in Chapter 5, in particular those that provided for election of chairpersons on a secret ballot by party colleagues and those providing limits on the number of subcommittee chairs that any individual might hold, had an immediate effect in the removal of three senior committee chairmen in 1975. In 1979, three senior members of important subcommittees were denied chairs, and in 1985, House Democrats dumped the chairman of the House Armed Services Committee and replaced him with a member who ranked seventh in committee seniority.

LEGISLATIVE WORK

A third norm, one that is central to lawmaking, is that of legislative work. Because most legislative work is, in Matthews's words, "highly detailed, dull, and politically unrewarding," this norm is one that rewards those who put in the long hours needed to fashion complex legislation:

> The words used to describe those senators who seem to slight their legislative duties are harsh—"grandstanders," "demagogues," "headline hunters," "publicity seekers," "messiahs." They are said to do nothing but "play to the galleries," and not to be "team players." It is even occasionally hinted that they are mentally or emotionally deranged.[36]

In the House, the norm of legislative work is most clearly demonstrated in committees such as Appropriations and Ways and

Means, where the exclusive nature of membership, the complexity of the subject matter, and members' shared goal of influence within the House all lead to an emphasis on members' legislative work.

Representatives who want to run for the Senate and senators who want to run for president will have reason to violate the norm of legislative work in order to gain a broader policy background and broader media coverage. The retirement in 1984 of former Senate Majority Leader Howard Baker was based on the conflict he saw between his run for the presidency and the legislative work requirements of being majority leader. Some senators have expressed skepticism about Senator Dole's more recent attempts to do both. Gary Hart left the Senate in 1986 for much the same reason. While the importance of media coverage to those senators and to certain other legislators cannot be denied, a recent study of U.S. Senators in the national media found that there was a strong connection between legislative work and media coverage. In addition, Stephen Hess has written that an instructive part of that study consisted of "responses to a question I often asked senators in 1984: 'If you could pick the word that reporters put before your name, what would it be?' Most often mentioned was 'hard-working,' as in hard-working John Melcher (D-Montana) or hard-working Slade Gorton (R-Washington)."[37]

RECIPROCITY

A reciprocity norm operates in both chambers, but with quite different effects. In the House, reciprocity is shown as respect for committee members' expertise. This supports lawmaking in the House. An example of this type of reciprocity is the relationship between a substantive committee and its appropriations subcommittee counterpart, one that Fenno described this way: "There normally exists a mutual recognition that the Appropriations Committee should not define programs, i.e., legislate, in an appropriation bill and that the authorizing committee must accept the dollar figure set by the appropriating committee."[38]

Reciprocity in the Senate focuses more on the interaction between individuals than between committees. Because senators serve on many committees, the membership of any one committee will represent a broad spectrum of the other Senate committees. Unlike the House, where reciprocity operates through a specialized committee structure, Senate reciprocity works through a "relatively undifferentiated, interlocking decision-making struc- ture."[39] As a result, senators will go out of their way to insure that every member's views are given a hearing and that there is "the maximum participation of a maximum number of its members" on every decision.[40] Senate reciprocity, rather than contributing to a smooth decision-making process, primarily serves the goal of representation.

COURTESY AND INSTITUTIONAL PATRIOTISM

Both of these norms are directed toward controlling the conflict that is inevitable in a legislative body. The norm of courtesy prescribes that even the most intense conflict over issues should not lead to personal conflict. One way to accomplish this is to maintain an impersonality in debate by addressing colleagues as "the distinguished senator," or "the illustrious representative," as "gentlemen" or "gentlewomen" rather than "Mickey" or "Marge." A senator admitted that these were "little things that at times look highly exaggerated," but that they were also impor- tant. "Very frankly, I don't think, if we didn't practice these, that we would have any semblance of order in the Senate. I think that it's the catalyst that maintains a semblance of order. If we didn't stand up and go through a lot of this 'my distinguished col- league' and on and on, we'd end up probably in trouble at times."[41]

The value of the norm of courtesy is perhaps most conspicu- ous when it is absent. That could be seen in a 1984 floor fight in which Speaker Tip O'Neill referred to the behavior of conserva- tive Georgia Republican Newt Gingrich as "the lowest thing that I have ever seen in my 32 years in Congress." Minority Whip Trent Lott (R-MS) immediately demanded that the Speaker's words "be taken down," which is a call for the presiding officer to rule on their propriety. And even though a fellow Massachu- setts Democrat and O'Neill friend Joe Moakley was presiding at the time, he had no choice but to respond that O'Neill's remarks were out of order, marking the first time since 1797 that a Speaker of the House had to be rebuked for his language.[42] Another heated exchange, this time in the Senate, took place in August 1986 between Senate Majority Leader Robert Dole and Minority Leader Robert Byrd. When Democrats surprised Dole by introducing an amendment on South African sanctions, the ma- jority leader asked, "What kind of game are we playing here?"

Byrd demanded an apology for the implication that he had "sneaked" his amendment onto the floor, and when Dole refused to apologize, Byrd shouted: "I have had enough of this business of having the majority leader stand here and act as a traffic cop on this floor." Which led Dole to respond, "I don't intend to be intimidated by anyone in the Senate." Although this incident did not produce any official rebuke, a number of senators complained that they had never seen such personal outbursts on the Senate floor.[43] Dramatic violations of the courtesy norm like this are instructive more by their being infrequent than by their occurrence. The impersonality of most congressional debate tends to cool the rhetoric. When there are violations of the courtesy norm, the offending senator or representative is generally quick to apologize and to strike the remark from the record.

Institutional patriotism is also a norm that helps to limit the level of conflict in Congress. Senators who disagree on everything else are likely to share a belief that they serve in the "greatest deliberative body in the world." And one sure way to irritate any member of the House is to refer to the Senate as the "upper chamber." To representatives, the Senate is always known as "the other body," as the following remarks by a senior House member in debate over a conference report made clear:

> I will say to the Members of the House that it is high time that we assert ourselves and we say to the other body that it is time we insist upon our own rules.

> The other body, in a sort of alleged rarified atmosphere, shall no longer have the right to add on to our bills non-germane amendments. They look upon us from their Olympian heights as mere mundane characters and they do not give a tinker's damn about our own rules.[44]

The norm of institutional patriotism helps to reduce conflict within Congress by providing a shared sense of values that even the most hostile opponents can agree on. When institutional patriotism comes into play in congressional conflicts, it provides a basis for unity in each chamber. Proponents of a measure can sometimes increase the size of their coalition by making it a matter of the House versus the Senate, or Congress versus the president.

Personal feuds and outbursts of temper always give rise to talk about how the institution of Congress is damaged by any breakdown in comity. And House and Senate leaders are quick to point out that they have few, if any, sanctions against members who violate House and Senate norms. Yet both chambers continue to maintain folkways that influence how members behave as much as do the formal rules. Changes in these folkways have made Congress in the 1980s a more open and a less hierarchical institution than it was two decades ago. Because each of these norms improves either the lawmaking capacity or the representational capability of Congress, members have reason to keep them. They serve to bring both chambers closer to Oklahoma Sen. David Boren's description of the Senate: "a place that operates on a handshake."[45]

Conference Committees

As he prepared to leave office after more than thirty years in the House, former Speaker Tip O'Neill got in a parting shot about the other body:

> The Senate amazes me. The appropriations come over there and bingo, in goes $3 million for a new bridge in Newport, Rhode Island. The local headline says, "(Republican Senator John) Chafee Gets $3 Million for New Bridge."
>
> And then, when we have a conference with them, it goes out of the bill, and then the headline is: "Democrats Knock Out Bridge." It's an old game that's been played around here for years.[46]

The conference to which O'Neill was referring brings together representatives and senators from the committees that handled a bill in an effort to produce a compromise bill acceptable to both chambers. In addition to the substantive differences between the two chambers' bills in conference, the House–Senate structural and functional differences that have been discussed throughout this chapter are carried into the conference committee. That is the "game," to which O'Neill refers, and the general pattern of interaction is the same regardless of which party controls which chamber.

When one chamber produces a bill that differs from the measure already passed by the other chamber, something has to give. Either the chamber that first passed the legislation concurs in the changes made in the second house and the bill goes to the White House for signing into law; or the House and Senate keep sending the bill and amendments back and forth for further amending until an identical bill is produced; or both houses agree to set up a joint conference committee to compromise the differences and to produce one bill that both chambers can approve. In any Congress, between 15 and 25 percent of the public bills that are enacted will have gone through the conference committee route. But that percentage will include every appropriations bill and just about every major piece of legislation enacted by that Congress. Conference rules in both chambers say that the presiding officer (i.e., the Speaker of the House and the president pro tem of the Senate) is given the power to appoint conferees. The actual appointment power belongs to the chairpersons of the House and Senate committees that handled the legislation in their chamber. The committee leaders make up a list of conferees that generally will consist of senior committee members and give it to the presiding officers; the latter officers then appoint those people listed. The appointment process itself can be a key part of the conference bargaining. That was the case when Ways and Means Chairman Dan Rostenkowski skipped over many senior members and handpicked the eleven House conferees on the 1986 tax reform bill in order to make sure that the House delegation was controlled by members who shared Rostenkowski's position on key issues. Following seniority is the normal process for selecting conferees, but as we also saw in the selection of committee and subcommittee leaders, it is not a hard and fast rule.

A major change in how conferences were conducted came about in 1975 when both chambers adopted reforms that required conference committees to hold open sessions unless a majority of the delegates from each chamber voted otherwise. Prior to that time, conference committees were the most secretive of formal congressional gatherings. No minutes or written records of conference proceedings were kept; and the only printed accounts associated with a conference committee were the conference report (the compromise bill) and a statement by House conferees as to the effects of the compromise on the House-passed bill. The actual conference deliberations, the votes of members, the arguments advanced for striking or retaining certain measures, and the evidence for supporting certain changes were not part of the public record. The chief rationale for having closed conference committees was to facilitate bargaining or decision making. The idea was that members would be more willing to compromise on their own public statements or on the positions adopted by their parent chambers if the machinations of such compromises (including the who and why of compromising exactly what and when) would not be known beyond the conference doors. Although most conference committees now hold their meetings in public, a majority of conferees from either chamber can vote to close the conference committee's deliberations to the public. The 1986 tax reform conference was conducted behind closed doors for the same, lawmaking, reasons given for the closed Ways and Means and Finance Committees' sessions discussed in Chapter 6.

Representatives and senators who serve on a conference committee generally behave in ways that reproduce the characteristics and behavior of their parent chamber. Conferees from the House have a generally acknowledged policy expertise and familiarity with the committee bill that exceeds that of the Senate conferees. It is the committee bill that House conferees defend in conference. Senate conferees, on the other hand, represent the position of the entire Senate, and not just the committee, in their conference bargaining. A House conferee from the Appropriations Committee has described the effect of those differences on conference bargaining:

> Someone on the other side will say, "Senator so and so wants this project or Senator so and so is interested in this item." That Senator isn't even on the Committee and hasn't attended the hearings, but he wants something and the rest look out for him. He isn't physically in the conference room but he's in there just the same.[47]

The outcomes of conference bargaining also reflect these differences between the two chambers. A number of studies that found the conference bill to be closer to the Senate than to the House bill attributed that to the broader representational base of Senate conferees, to their acting as agents of the whole chamber rather than of one committee.[48] While other research has suggested that the earlier conclusion that the Senate "wins" more conferences is misleading, the explanations offered for conference outcomes also has drawn on chamber differences in lawmaking and representation. These researchers found that the phenomenon of the Senate seeming to win more conferences than the House was tied to the normal sequence (found in more than 70 percent of the conference bills studied) in which the House would act first on legislation, and the Senate then would make marginal changes in the original bill generated by the House. Most of the Senate amendments would then be retained in conference. However, such an outcome does not mean that the Senate has a greater impact on the final legislative product than does the House. On the contrary, by creating the original bill and setting the agenda for debate on the issue, the House is judged to have more real impact on the final shape of legislation as it passes through conference than does the Senate.[49] We see, once again, that by framing legislation and acting first on final passage of most legislation, the House plays a dominant lawmaking role in the political system. By offering many marginal changes in this original legislation, the Senate plays a key representational role.

Conclusion

This consideration of joint House–Senate interaction in conference committees brings us back to the observations made at the beginning of this chapter. The rules and norms governing the behavior of representatives and senators are different because the two chambers play different roles in making policy. Congress must pass laws and at the same time serve as a forum for the representation of a wide range of interests. The structure of the House of Representatives and the rules and norms governing the behavior of its members serve to emphasize that body's concern with lawmaking. The Senate, on the other hand, is more suited to acting as a forum where the interests and the ideas of a hetero-geneous public are introduced into the political process. When these two chambers come together in conference to determine the final form of legislation, these differences are not eliminated, but maintained. House conferees come to the bargaining table to uphold bills fashioned in committee workshops; Senate confer-ees come to make sure that individual senators' provisions to help certain segments of the public are not dropped from the final bill.

Endnotes

1. House Republican leaders and Speaker's aide, quoted in Jonathan Fuerbringer, "It'll Be Heavy Going on Contra Aid," *New York Times,* April 12, 1986, p. 7; Representatives Michel, Cheney, and Foley, quoted in John Felton, "House Republicans Go for Broke on 'Contra' Aid," *Congressional Quarterly Weekly Report,* April 19, 1986, pp. 835–37.

2. Senator Kassebaum, quoted in Nadine Cohodas, "Decision on Manion Put Off After 'Roll of Dice' in Senate," *Congressional Quarterly Weekly Report,* June 28, 1986, p. 1509; Senator Dole, quoted in William Dicke, "Dole Weighs Plan on Bench Nominee," *New York Times,* July 12, 1986, p. 7; Senator DeConcini, quoted in Nadine Cohodas, "Senate Makes It Official: Manion Is Confirmed," *Congressional Quarterly Weekly Report,* July 26, 1986, p. 1685.

3. Charles L. Clapp, *The Congressman: His Work as He Sees It* (Washington, D.C.: The Brookings Institution, 1963), p. 39.

4. Senators Dole and Simon, quoted in Andy Plattner, "The Lure of the Senate: Influence and Prestige," *Congressional Quarterly Weekly Report,* May 25, 1985, pp. 991–92.

5. Unidentified representatives, quoted in John F. Bibby, *Congress Off the Record* (Washington, D.C.: American Enterprise Institute, 1983), p. 51.

6. Stephen Hess, *The Ultimate Insiders: U.S. Senators in the National Media* (Washington, D.C.: The Brookings Institution, 1986), p. 91.

7. Representative Bruce, quoted in Dave Kaplan, "Freshmen Find It Easier to Run as Incumbents," *Congressional Quarterly Weekly Report,* November 2, 1985, p. 2225.

8. Richard F. Fenno, Jr., *The United States Senate: A Bicameral Perspective* (Washington, D.C.: American Enterprise Institute, 1982), p. 37.

9. Richard F. Fenno, Jr., *Homestyle: House Members in Their Districts* (Boston: Little, Brown, 1978), p. 240.

10. Fenno, *The United States Senate,* pp. 27–29.

11. James F. Clarity and Warren Weaver, Jr., "Right Pell, Wrong Pew," *New York Times,* October 11, 1985, p. A22.

12. Unidentified representatives, quoted in Bibby, *Congress Off the Record,* pp. 51 and 15.

13. Sen. Mark Andrews (R-ND), quoted in Plattner, "The Lure of the Senate," p. 994.

14. Unidentified senator, quoted in Steven S. Smith and Christopher J. Deering, *Committees in Congress* (Washington, D.C.: Congressional Quarterly Press, 1984), p. 78.

15. Unidentified senator, quoted in Jacqueline Calmes and Diane Granat, "Senate Cuts Committee Slots; Members Assigned to Panels," *Congressional Quarterly Weekly Report,* February 23, 1985, p. 348; unidentified senate aide, quoted in Andy Plattner, "Committees Are Where

the Work Is Done," *Congressional Quarterly Weekly Report*, April 27, 1985 (Supplement), p. 4.

16. Senator Leahy, quoted in Martin Tolchin, "Senators Assail Anarchy in New Chamber of Equals," *New York Times*, November 25, 1984, p. 40.

17. Senator Cochrane, quoted in Janet Hook, "Senate Rules, Closeness of GOP Margin Keeps Democrats Influential in Minority," *Congressional Quarterly Weekly Report*, June 21, 1986, p. 1394.

18. Ralph K. Huitt, "The Internal Distribution of Influence: The Senate," in David Truman, ed., *The Congress and America's Future* (Englewood Cliffs, N.J.: Prentice-Hall, 1965), p. 80.

19. Sen. J. Bennett Johnston (D-LA), quoted in Steven V. Roberts, "Life, or Lack Thereof, in the Senate," *New York Times*, November 22, 1985, p. B8.

20. Former House Parliamentarian Asher C. Hinds, quoted in Walter J. Oleszek, *Congressional Procedures and the Policy Process* (Washington, D.C.: Congressional Quarterly Press, 1984), p. 22.

21. Senator Gore, quoted in Andy Plattner, "The Lure of the Senate," p. 994.

22. Senator Armstrong, quoted in Steven V. Roberts, "Wheels Are Spinning Over the Senate's Rules," *New York Times*, February 26, 1986, p. B8; Senator Cochrane, quoted in Roberts, "Life, or Lack Thereof, in the Senate," p. B8.

23. Senator Johnston, quoted in Jacqueline Calmes, "Senate Agrees to Test of Radio, TV Coverage," *Congressional Quarterly Weekly Report*, March 1, 1986, p. 520; Senator Mathias, quoted in Brian Nutting, "Senate Continues Undecided on TV Coverage," *Congressional Quarterly Weekly Report*, February 8, 1986, p. 285. The George Washington—Thomas Jefferson story is related in Max Farrand, *The Framing of the Constitution* (New Haven: Yale University Press, 1913), p. 74.

24. Woodrow Wilson, *Congressional Government* (New York: World, 1967; originally published, 1885), p. 155; Senator Johnston, quoted in Janet Hook, "Senate Debates Rules Changes as Prelude to TV Coverage," *Congressional Quarterly Weekly Report*, February 22, 1986, p. 467; Senator Leahy, quoted in Susan Trausch, "For Some Senate Is Too Deliberate," *Boston Globe*, December 18, 1985, p. 15.

25. Nelson Polsby, *Congressional Behavior* (New York: Random House, 1971), p. 7.

26. Lewis Froman, *The Congressional Process* (Boston: Little, Brown, 1967), p. 67.

27. Walter J. Oleszek, *Congressional Procedures and the Policy Process*, p. 179.

28. Donald R. Matthews, *U.S. Senators and Their World* (New York: Vintage, 1960), pp. 92–117. Research on the Senate in the 1970s is reported in Norman J. Ornstein, Robert L. Peabody, and David W.

Rohde, "The Senate Through the 1980s: Cycles of Change," in Lawrence C. Dodd and Bruce I. Oppenheimer, eds., *Congress Reconsidered*, 3rd ed. (Washington, D.C.: Congressional Quarterly Press, 1985,) pp. 17–20. For House norms, see Herbert Asher, "The Learning of Legislative Norms," *American Political Science Review*, June, 1973, pp. 499–513. For changes in those norms, see Burdett Loomis and Jeff Fishel, "New Members in a Changing Congress: Norms, Actions, and Satisfaction," *Congressional Studies*, Spring, 1981, pp. 81–94.

29. Clapp, *The Congressman: His Work as He Sees It*, p. 18.

30. See Nelson Polsby's discussion in *Congressional Behavior*, p. 7.

31. Ibid., p. 13.

32. Ornstein, Peabody, and Rohde, "The Senate Through the 1980s: Cycles of Change," pp. 17–20.

33. Unidentified senator, quoted in Steven V. Roberts, "Senate's New Breed Shuns Novice Role," *New York Times*, November 26, 1984, p. A18.

34. Alan Ehrehalt, "The 'Juniority' System in Congress," *Congressional Quarterly Weekly Report*, March 21, 1981, p. 535.

35. Senator Alfonse D'Amato, quoted in Francis X. Clines, "Congress Now Suffers from Loss of Memory," *New York Times*, August 2, 1981, p. 4E.

36. Matthews, *U.S. Senators and Their World*, pp. 94–95.

37. Hess, *The Ultimate Insiders*, p. 27.

38. Richard F. Fenno, Jr., "The Internal Distribution of Influence: The House," in David Truman, ed., *The Congress and America's Future* (Englewood Cliffs, N.J.: Prentice-Hall, 1965), p. 73.

39. The description is Fenno's in *The Power of the Purse*, p. 511.

40. Ibid., p. 509.

41. David Rohde, Norman Ornstein, and Robert Peabody, "Political Change and Legislative Norms in the United States Senate," paper delivered at the 1974 annual meeting of the American Political Science Association, Chicago, Ill., August, 1974, p. 32.

42. Diane Granat, "The House's TV War: The Gloves Come Off," *Congressional Quarterly Weekly Report*, May 19, 1984, pp. 1166–67.

43. Senators Dole and Byrd, quoted in Steven V. Roberts, "Why Aren't These Men Smiling," *New York Times*, August 11, 1986, p. A12, and Susan Trausch, "Burning the Midnight Oil," *Boston Globe*, August 11, 1986, p. 2.

44. Rep. Emanuel Celler, *Congressional Record*, September 15, 1970, p. 31843; quoted in Stanley Bach, "Bicameral Conflict and Accommodation in Congressional Procedure," a paper delivered at the annual meeting of the American Political Science Association, New York, N.Y., September, 1981, p. 31.

45. Senator Boren, quoted in Roberts, "Why Aren't These Men Smiling," p. A12.

46. Former Speaker O'Neill, quoted in Robert Healy, "O'Neill Talks About Issues, Power," *Boston Globe*, August 4, 1985, p. 20.

47. Fenno, *The Power of the Purse*, p. 628.

48. Gilbert Steiner, *The Congressional Conference Committee, Seventieth to Eightieth Congresses* (Urbana: University of Illinois Press, 1950), pp. 170–72; Fenno, *The Power of the Purse*, p. 662; David Vogler, *The Third House* (Evanston, Ill.: Northwestern University Press, 1971), p. 55; John Manley, *The Politics of Finance* (Boston: Little, Brown, 1970), pp. 269–94; and Arnold Kanter, "Congress and the Defense Budget: 1960–1970," *American Political Science Review*, vol. 66, no. 1 (March 1972), pp. 129–43.

49. Gerald S. Strom and Barry S. Rundquist, "A Revised Theory of Winning in House–Senate Conferences," *American Political Science Review*, vol. LXXI, no. 2 (June, 1977).

7

Staff and
Support Systems

Management has never been Congress's strong suit. That was true during the administration of George Washington, when Massachusetts Rep. Fisher Ames complained: "Our proceedings smell of anarchy." That it was also the case about 175 years later was suggested by the title of a book produced by a management consulting firm, Arthur D. Little: *Congress Needs Help.*[1] And it was the impetus behind creation of an organization called the Congressional Management Project in the 1980s. In a management guide for new members of Congress, the latter organization pointed out how the workload demands on members had increased in recent years:

> *The amount of constituent correspondence entering the House and the Senate has skyrocketed over the last few years, from 15 million pieces of mail in 1970 to 300 million pieces today—a 2,000 percent increase!*

> *Casework requests have doubled over the last decade—some offices report as many as 5,000 to 10,000 casework requests per year.*

> *The number of bills introduced in 1956 was 7,611. By 1980, that number has risen to 14,594. While this trend dropped off slightly in the last Congress, members today are expected to*

> know a great deal more about many more issues than their
> predecessors.

> The number of recorded votes is up by 1250 percent since
> 1956. You are expected to know the details of these votes and
> to be able to defend your position on them as they are scruti-
> nized by the press and the public.[2]

New members of Congress have less reason than the rest of us to
be intimidated by the information overload described in the
management guide. For most of them have already been through
oral examinations in the form of campaign debates, stump-the-
candidate interviews by the local media, and endless rounds of
question periods with voters. Besides, there is every reason to
believe that their information-management capability will improve as time goes by.

And it is, perhaps, the last point—the assumption that senior
members have fewer workload and information problems—that
really brings home the extent to which Congress and its members
need help, both for lawmaking and for representation. It was not
a freshman, but a second-term representative with considerable
expertise in the communications issue being addressed in a subcommittee hearing who uttered this lament:

> I don't know if I have been eating magic mushrooms or wan-
> dering around Alice's Wonderland, but the more I learn about
> this field the bigger it gets. I'm always losing ground. I think
> I'm going to cry.[3]

This chapter will discuss some of the resources members can use
to keep from losing ground in the tug-of-war created by an information explosion and the demands of an expanding workload.
Congressional staffs, legislative support agencies, and a variety of
congressional caucuses all serve as important support systems
for members.

Congressional Staff

A close observer of the Washington scene once noted:

> Someday a U.S. congressman will vanish from this town and
> nobody will know it. The congressman will still deliver speeches

for the Congressional Record; he will still be quoted on the
evening news; his mail will be answered, his views made
known, his legislation introduced and his coffee poured. But he
will be gone, laughing from a gazebo on the Rhone or testing
the waters off the Bahamas. . . .

The Fifth Estate is what makes such a happening quite possible. There are only 535 senators and representatives, but the
Fifth Estate consists of more than 30,000 people whom they
employ. First, there are the aides or assistants, 10 to 30 of them
depending upon the legislator's committee assignments and his
personal wealth. Then there are the office workers, letter-
writers, secretaries, memo readers and campaign staffers. The
several dozen congressional committees have staffs of up to 40
each.[4]

This commentator states that some congressmen show up in
Washington as rarely as possible, and most of them spend Mon-
days or Fridays at home. "Meantime, their speeches are inserted
in the record, their committee votes made by proxy, and press
assistants see to it that they are quoted on public issues just as
though they were in their offices."[5] While admitting that the
congressional staffers making up this "fifth estate" do play important roles in the complex political and congressional system,
the columnist quoted above sees a bit of irony in the fact that the
recent and rapid expansion in the size of this congressional bureaucracy has come at a time when most members of Congress
are denouncing the growth in the federal government bureaucracy in general.

Roles played by congressional staff vary greatly from office to
office and from committee to committee. Some critics of this
huge congressional bureaucracy suggest that its sheer massive-
ness does more to create problems for congressional decision
making than it does to aid legislators in those decisions. "Everybody is working for the staff, staff, staff; driving you nutty. In
fact, they have hearings for me all of this week," complained one
senator. A colleague of his agreed:

If we would fire half the Senate employees we have, fire half
the staff and not permit a paper to be read on the floor of the
U.S. Senate, we would complete our business and adjourn by
July 4th. When you get more staff and more clerks they spend
most of their time thinking up bills, resolutions, amendments.
They write speeches for senators, and they come in here on the

*floor with senators. Unanimous consents are obtained for so-
and-so to sit. He is there prodding, telling the senator how to
spend more money.*[6]

Other students of the legislative process, however, suggest that
the expanded size of congressional staffs has greatly improved
the ability of Congress to function in an increasingly complex
world. Two political scientists who conducted an extensive
study of congressional staffs had this to say about the importance
of staff to the congressional process:

> *Our contention is that staffs perform much of the congressional
> work: They perform almost exclusively the constituent-service
> function; do most of the preliminary legislative research; help
> generate policy ideas; set up hearings, meetings, and confer-
> ences; carry out oversight activities—program evaluations, in-
> vestigations, etc.; draft bills; and meet and talk with executive,
> interest, and constituent groups on substantive matters.*[7]

Whatever their positions on the matter, all students of Congress can agree on the fact that there has been a tremendous
growth in the size of this fifth estate. This fact is sharply brought
home to the thousands of college students who volunteer to work
in congressional offices (for free) during school vacations. The
students are told that there is no room for them because the paid
staff and limited numbers of interns occupy every inch of office
space available. Experienced civil servants and political scientists who take part in fellowship programs that provide free labor
to congressional offices and committee staffs are similarly
shocked to discover that their long experience and impressive
resumés do not automatically lead to a welcome with open arms.
Simply no office space is available for them, and for the most
part, the regular staff adequately covers all policy areas of interest to the legislator or committee member.[8]

Table 7–1 provides a graphic summary of the growth in congressional staff from 1930 to 1980. To put those numbers into
perspective, the cost of managing Congress increased 2,614 percent between 1946 and 1983, or six times the rate of inflation as
measured by the consumer price index (an increase of 410
percent).[9] The Gramm-Rudman Act required Congress to cut its
own fiscal 1986 budget by 4.3 percent, and the legislative appropriations for fiscal 1987 showed a similar reversal of the long-

TABLE 7–1 Congressional Staff: Selected Years, 1935–1985

	House		Senate		
Year	Personal	Committee	Personal	Committee	Total
1935	870	122	424	172	1588
1947	1140	167	590	232	2129
1957	2441	375	1115	558	4489
1967	4055	589	1749	621	7014
1977	6942	1776	3554	1028	13300
1985	7528	2146	4097	1178	14949

Source: Compiled by author from data in Harrison W. Fox, Jr., and Susan Webb Hammond, *Congressional Staffs* (New York: The Free Press, 1977), p. 171, and Norman J. Ornstein, et al., *Vital Statistics in Congress 1986–1987* (Washington, D.C.: American Enterprise Institute, forthcoming).

term trend seen in Table 7–1. While the explosive growth in congressional staff over the past few decades appears to be over, with congressional spending even entering a contractionary period, the congressional bureaucracy created by that earlier growth continues to be a key player in the politics of Congress today. The question is: What do all of those people do?

ROLE OF CONGRESSIONAL STAFF

Some critics of congressional staff suggest that too much staff time is directed toward campaigning and reelection efforts and that public money is really being spent in shoring up the advantages of incumbents in their reelection efforts. In Chapter 3, we considered some of the campaign advantages that incumbents gain through staff allowances, free mailing, and district offices. In response to criticism about incumbents using staff and mailing allowances for reelection purposes, however, Congress voted in 1977 to ban the use of free mailings during the sixty days preceding a primary or general election. An immediate effect of this was that the House folding room, which distributes newsletters and other mass mailings for incumbents, had to add more staff members to handle the big rush in mailings before the sixty-day deadline in the election year 1978.[10] While incumbents, challengers, and critics of Congress decry the use of staff, public funds, and other resources for what seem to be campaign purposes, defenders of the system point out that what others call campaigning is really a part of the legislator's job as representative and handler of constituent problems. One measure of the district orientation and representative function of congressional staffs is the increasing percentage of the total staff that is located in the home district, rather than in Washington, a change that can be seen in Table 7–2.

The patterns in Table 7–2 suggest a couple of points. First, the increasing importance of the legislator as ombudsman, a trend discussed in Chapter 1, is reflected in the increasing proportion of staff that is allocated to district and state offices. For it is these offices, rather than the Washington offices, that are responsible for the bulk of the casework handled by most members' offices. Secondly, many would agree with the congressional staffer who sees this outflow of staff from Washington to the district as directed more toward the reelection campaign than toward the objective handling of casework: "Everyone who's running has guys in his state office working on politics during his campaign—and not just during the campaign, but all year round, every year, all the time, for crying out loud."[11] The expanded allowances for district and state offices and for staff

TABLE 7–2 Congressional Staff in District and State Offices Selected Years 1972–1985

	House		Senate	
Year	Number of Employees	Percentage of Total Personal Staff in District Offices	Number of Employees	Percentage of Total Personal Staff in State Offices
1972	1189	22.5	303	12.5
1978	2317	33.4	816	25.0
1979	2445	34.6	879	24.3
1981	2702	36.1	937	25.8
1983	2785	36.6	1132	27.9
1984	2872	38.9	1140	28.9
1985	2871	38.1	1180	28.8

Source: Norman J. Orstein et al., *Vital Statistics on Congress, 1986–1987* (Washington, D.C.: American Enterprise Institute, forthcoming).

clearly provide one answer to the question of what this growing number of congressional staff members do—they help to reelect incumbents.

Directing our attention to the Washington based staff, we can once again ask: What do they do? Even with this Washington focus, one is struck by how much of the congressional staff activity is oriented toward constituency casework or legislative solutions to problems that arise from the requests or demands of individual constituents. One reason given for the great increase in congressional staffs is the fact that more and more citizens are calling on their representatives in Congress for solutions to their own problems stemming from current government policy. A number of studies of congressional staffs have measured the relative importance of staff activities directed toward lawmaking and of those concerned with representation and constituent casework. In the Eighty-ninth Congress (1965–1966), it was found that about 41 percent of the average staff workweek was devoted to answering the mail, 25 percent to constituent service, and 14 percent to legislative activities.[12] Ten years later, the House Commission on Administrative Review found a similar pattern of emphasis on constituent service. The average House office in the Ninety-fourth Congress (1975–1976) had just under sixteen employees. Of these, four were caseworkers, three were clerical workers, two were office supervisers, two were legislative researchers, one a legislative correspondent, one a communications specialist, and one a personal secretary.[13] Another study done about the same time found that professional staff members in Senate offices, most of whom were hired to perform legislative duties, also devoted much of their time to constituency service such as federal projects and casework.[14] Taken together, these studies suggest that the bulk of the work done by congressional staffs in members' offices deals more with assisting the representative or senator perform representational duties than it does with assisting a member in lawmaking activities.

The fact that so much of the work of congressional staffs is constituency oriented should not lead us to ignore the legislative or lawmaking functions, which staff members also perform. As Table 7–1 indicates, the growth in committee staff accounts for a great deal of the overall increase in congressional staffs shown in the table. The work of committee staff members—doing legislative research, scheduling hearings, and assisting members in drafting legislation—is obviously directed to assisting members perform their lawmaking function. In addition, when we look closely at the increase in staff positions on members' personal staffs, we find the greatest increase has come in the number of aides performing legislative work or who at least have a job title such as legislative assistant or legislative aide.[15]

On the basis of this increase in legislative aides, we would expect to find that legislators depend a great deal on staff members for information relevant to lawmaking. However, a study by Donald Matthews and James Stimson found that legislators relied on their individual staff only occasionally for legislative cues. Close to 30 percent of those interviewed said they never relied on staff for legislative research tasks. The authors cite as typical the remarks of one congressman:

> We have a staff meeting and at that time my legislative assistant will report on the legislation that is coming up in the week, and will give a brief description of it. In all candor I must say that this does not often influence my thinking on the bill.
>
> If it hasn't come up at our [state party delegation] breakfast, I'll run to a guy on the floor just about the time the bill is being considered and say, "Hey, what is this all about and what does it do?" And frequently we'll check with the doorkeeper—who has a pipeline into the leadership and into those committee members who are responsible for it.
>
> I'd much rather be able to answer that my staff thoroughly briefs me on pros and cons in the quiet of my office, and that's how I make up my mind, but that is not true. I think that is really natural. A staff member is reading the cold lifeless reports. They have not been exposed to the various pressure groups or the "gut" arguments for or against something. I think the congressman himself involved in that area, who's been on the firing line, can give you a much better capsule than the more isolated staff man.[16]

A more recent study of House members gives us quite a different picture. During the Ninety-fourth Congress (1975–1976), the Commission on Administrative Review surveyed 151 House members and asked the questions:

1. Where do you turn to get what you need to know to handle your committee work—who do you really rely on for this kind of information?

2. Where do you turn to get what you need to know to vote on the floor on bills which don't come through one of the committees on which you sit?

3. Where do you turn to get what you need to know to be knowledgeable about public issues and policies about which you, as a public person, are expected to be knowledgeable?

Members' responses covered a wide range of information sources—personal and committee staff, executive agencies, party groups, colleagues, congressional support agencies (such as the Congressional Research Service and the Congressional Budget Office), interest groups and lobbyists, sources in the district, personal reading and study, and universities and private research groups. The information source most frequently listed by members, however, was the congressional staff. Sixty percent of the members mentioned personal staff, and 61 percent mentioned committee staff in response to the first question (committee work); 57 percent of the members mentioned personal office staff in response to the second question (bills from other committees); and 49 percent of the members mentioned personal staff in response to the third question (public issues).[17] For all of these issue areas, then, the congressional staffs were found to be the single most important source of information relevant to legislators' performing their lawmaking duties.

While recognizing that a great part of the work done by the expanded congressional bureaucracy is geared toward district and constituency problems, we should not lose sight of the important legislative support role played by committee and personal staffs. We should also recognize that it is difficult to draw a clear cut line between a legislative support activity and a constituency service or a correspondence function. For example, letters of complaint about the same problem are routinely answered by the staff. In answering those letters, staff members are going to dig into the problem and convey to the member the fact that many letters have been coming in concerning it. Most likely, the staff will be in a position to offer some advice as to possible legislative action to correct the problem. The bulk of time spent in such a case might quite naturally be regarded as constituency service or correspondence, yet there is a certain legislative offshoot—staff members have acquired some knowledge about a particular problem that might be useful at a later time to the member, and the legislator has been alerted that a problem area exists that might be subject to legislative solution. The point here is that much of the legislative staff activity does have an overall effect on the lawmaking capabilities of members of Congress.

HIERARCHY OF STAFF

We have been discussing legislative staffs in this section by focusing primarily on the role of personal staffs of House members. This focus has been at least partially a result of the focus of existing studies on congressional staffs. Within the general category of legislative staffs, there is a great deal of variety. Committee staffs in both the House and the Senate tend to be more professional and to have a longer tenure than do personal staffs of individual members. The same sort of differences in longevity of staff exists between personal House staffs and personal Senate staffs. There is a changeable but fairly clear hierarchy among committee, subcommittee, and personal member staffs both within and between the two chambers.

Differences between staffs of the two chambers were summed up in the following comment by a Senate staff member:

> Staff on the Senate side are more pompous than those on the House side. You have a system of layers here—the senators only talk to senators, the administrative assistants to administrative assistants, the legislative assistants to legislative assistants, etc. On the House side, you find out what was going on in forty-five minutes by going from group to group in the cafeteria. Over here, I go down to the cafeteria and eat alone.[18]

Within each chamber there is a similar hierarchy, or systems of layers, extending down from full committee staffs to subcommittee staffs to individual staffs.

Perhaps the best way to understand this hierarchy among different staff levels and to close in on the answer to the question of what congressional staffs do is to conceptualize the legislative system as a communications network. We did this earlier in looking at the party cue within this network. Contrary to popular notions about the limited or inferior information systems available to Congress (especially when compared with those available to executive agencies), both legislative committees and individual members of Congress are continually bombarded with information. Constituents, interest groups, executive agencies, legislative colleagues, congressional committees, the news media, and legislative support systems such as the Congressional Research Service, the General Accounting Office, and special legislative committees or commissions provide a constant source of information on every legislative topic.

The problem faced by individual legislators is generally not one of obtaining enough information but rather one of filtering out information not relevant to the immediate decision and reconstituting information so that it can most efficiently be employed by the decisionmaker. The real impact of congressional staffs on the legislative process is probably best understood within these terms of the communications and information networks of Congress.

Michael Malbin has discussed the impact of congressional staff growth on the information network of the legislature in a book on congressional staffs. He identified four goals or objectives underlying the staff increases over the years:

1. To decrease congressional dependence on the executive branch and outside interest groups for information;
2. To give members of Congress more of an impact on national issues;
3. To provide members with the resources for putting new issues on the legislative agenda;
4. To gain control over the constantly increasing workload of members of Congress.[19]

Malbin has pointed out that staff increases of the past decade have gone a long way toward helping Congress achieve the first three objectives, but that the increase in staff has actually exacerbated the workload problem identified in objective number four. The reason for this is the entrepreneurial role played by many of these congressional staff members. Staff members in this role act as legislative merchants by seeking out products in the form of legislative ideas, which they then sell to their bosses in the form of proposed legislation. The staff system provides incentives for the committee and legislative aides to search for new ideas and legislative proposals that they can bring to their bosses for approval and further action.

The immediate effect of staff members playing this entrepreneurial role is to greatly increase the workload of individual members of Congress. They are continually bombarded with information and new proposals for legislation. One measure of this increased workload is the amount of time that a member of Congress has for legislative research and reading—time that is essential if the member is going to be informed on legislative issues. A survey done in 1965 found that House members spent about one full day a week on legislative research and reading. A similar survey in 1977 found that legislative research and reading time had declined to about one hour a week.[20] Instead of permitting members to gain control over their workload and to have more time for their own research and reading, the increase in staff and emphasis on finding new issues has caused members to lose even more control over their own workloads.

In addition to clogging the information network of Congress, the growing dependence of members on a large congressional staff has another effect noted by Malbin. More and more legislative activity consists of negotiations among staff members rather than deliberation by the legislators themselves. Malbin's book contains a number of case studies in which it is the staff rather than the members of Congress who are engaged in the legislative bargaining and final resolution of bills. "It gets to a point where they're a minus, they compete with each other," said one congressman about staff negotiations in a conference committee. "Sometimes you find that it's the staff member, not the senator, who is holding out."[21] When staff members assume a legislative role we have a Congress filled with many people who are, in effect, what Malbin calls "unelected representatives."

Support Agencies

A Maryland student who was writing a term paper on the foreign policy of the Soviet Union asked her history teacher where to look for information. He suggested that she write Congress. So the student sent letters to Maryland Sen. Charles McC. Mathias, Jr., and to Senate Foreign Relations Committee Chairman Richard G. Lugar. The student asked a number of questions such as: "Do the Soviets expect specific goods and acts in return for giving foreign aid or is it given more to promote their economic and political system?" Senators Mathias and Lugar responded to the student's letter by sending her a number of pamphlets and copies of newspaper and magazine articles on Soviet foreign policy. "The responses were great," said the student. While the information that she received from Congress helped her to write a better paper and to receive a higher grade, it was also clear that using Congress in this way did not give her an exclusive edge over other students: "Lots of teachers say that if you can't find information you should write to your Congressman, because that's what they're there for."[22]

Senators Mathias and Lugar would certainly suggest that helping students to write term papers is pretty low on the list of activities that they are responsible for. But neither the two senators themselves nor their staff had direct involvement in supplying information for the student's paper. However, those staff aides did send the letter to the Congressional Research Service (CRS) in the Library of Congress, and people there put together the information that was sent to the student in Maryland. At the time of the student's letter, there were more than 500 research specialists in the CRS, working with a budget of over $37 million, standing ready to assist legislators who needed information. Although the primary function of the CRS is to provide data and analyses that will help members of Congress and their staffs to make laws, the agency also helps legislators to perform representational tasks by responding to constituents' requests for information. The flavor of those transactions is suggested by the comments of a legislative aide to Rep. Sander Levin (D-MI):

> A whole elementary school class wrote in, asking for information on all 50 states. Their letters said, "I am doing a paper on Nebraska and cannot get to the school library; please send me all the information you can."

> We figure the teacher wrote the letter on the board and told the students to copy it. We referred the requests to CRS, a few at a time.[23]

There is general agreement among legislators, congressional staff, and CRS employees that the CRS should not be devoting much time or effort to that sort of constituent request. The 1986 cuts in the agency's budget (a loss of $3 million from the previous year) underscored a need for CRS to focus more on legislative support and less on helping voters and voters' children find information that is available elsewhere. To that end, CRS has prepared a series of "Info-paks" on the most commonly requested topics like abortion and arms control. The information folders can be sent to constituents with a minimum of staff effort. In addition, CRS now requires student interns working in congressional offices to present requests for information in person to the CRS rather than over the phone, hoping in that way to cut down on a long standing and highly valued tradition of students' receiving termpaper assistance as one of the "perks" of a Capitol Hill internship.

The CRS policy that its function is primarily one of legislative support, however, is one easier to state than to implement. As long as congressional offices forward requests for information to CRS, the agency must respond to those requests. That means, says a CRS spokesperson: "the question is not whether or not we think the requests are appropriate, but whether or not the Congress thinks so."[24] The Congressional Research Service is one of four major support agencies that have been created to give Congress help. The General Accounting Office (GAO), the Office of Technology Assessment (OTA), and the Congressional Budget Office (CBO) also provide information and analysis designed to help members of Congress to meet their lawmaking responsibilities. Just as the Congress determines how the CRS will function, the members and committees of Congress decide what kind of help they want from these other support agencies. Thus, representational concerns come to influence agencies whose very reason for being is to provide support for lawmaking.

CONGRESSIONAL RESEARCH SERVICE

A reference librarian in a Senate basement office of the Congressional Research Service had this to say about her work: "We have to know something about anything that might come up. And preferably know it yesterday, not later today. A senator's staffers are always in a crisis situation."[25] The Congressional Research Service has responsibility for providing information and answering questions on any topic for any member of Congress, committee or subcommittee, and congressional staff. The Legislative Reorganization Act of 1970 transformed the reference service of the Library of Congress into the more comprehensive research service that it is today. Because more than 500 of the total 850 CRS employees in recent years have been research specialists with expertise in particular areas, the agency is often likened to an academic or research institution. That side of CRS is reflected in the professional staff's long-term and ongoing policy analyses in education, energy, and other major policy areas. But the agency is also expected to provide quick responses to more than 400,000 congressional requests for information or analysis that it receives annually. That side of the CRS is reflected in the Info-paks on currently popular subjects and the newsroom-deadline atmosphere found throughout agency offices. One side is like a fine restaurant providing dishes long in preparation, while the other is more like a fast food chain dispensing information rather than burgers.

There is a standing joke on Capitol Hill that a request to the Congressional Research Service for information on toxic waste will come back with a list of the ten good points and the ten bad points about toxic waste. In order to survive in an environment where 535 members and their staff who disagree on most issues must be served, the CRS maintains a neutral position—supplying objective information and analysis to anyone who requests it. For the same reasons, the CRS does not provide any member with another member's voting record, biographical material, or any other information that could be used by a campaign opponent. The CRS also seeks to hold members' support by maintaining an agency-client confidentiality. In most cases, however, when legislators and their staffs make requests of CRS, they want information and analyses that will buttress their own positions on issues rather than objective data that will require further evaluation. A congressional staff member describes the effect such requests can have on CRS objectivity:

> CRS can produce statistics for anybody. I can call CRS and ask for an estimate of how much each barrel of additional oil produced by decontrol will cost, and I'll get my figures: $300 a barrel. Then someone who advocates decontrol can call and ask them how many more barrels of oil it will produce, and he'll get the figures he wants.[26]

The nature of its work makes the Congressional Research Service a reactive organization. While CRS researchers and analysts must always be updating reports and anticipating issues that will appear in any session, Congress sets the agenda for the agency and its researchers. For that reason, CRS employees find themselves dealing with constituents' term papers and members' demands for instant information on district-related matters as well as providing the policy analysis that members and committees need for lawmaking.

GENERAL ACCOUNTING OFFICE

If the CRS role is one of helping members of Congress to learn about almost anything, the role of the General Accounting Office (GAO) is one of helping members to learn more about the government. The CRS focus is more toward library research, whereas the GAO looks more to field investigations and program evaluations.

The GAO provides members with information on the costs and effects of government programs, and in so doing greatly contributes to the legislature's ability to carry on its oversight function. The agency serves as a government auditor reporting to Congress. Those auditors, sometimes referred to as the GAO's "fiscal gumshoes," gained some notoriety in the 1980s for uncovering wildly expensive ashtrays, screwdrivers, and toilet seats hidden away in Defense Department contracts. That record of uncovering government waste led the authors of a book sharply critical of Congress to conclude that "the GAO is a relatively bright spot in Congress's general prospect."[27]

The General Accounting Office is the oldest and the largest of the four support agencies under consideration. It was created in 1921 to serve as Congress's watchdog over federal programs. Since then Congress has continually added to the agency's routine auditing and accounting functions and has called on the GAO's staff of over 5,000 employees for special surveys and reports on particular programs. Recent GAO reports have been on diverse subjects—programs for removing asbestos from schools, government employees entitled to free transportation from home to work, the salaries paid male and female federal employees doing the same work, political refugees from El Salvador who now live in the United States, Medicare abuse, and the military retirement system.

Although the GAO is similar to the CRS in its responsiveness to requests from committee leaders and individual legislators, three out of every four of its studies are initiated by the agency itself. Since the 1970s, the GAO has become increasingly involved in policy studies. Some feel this trend has weakened the agency's primary role of government auditor. Any GAO involvement in creating or recommending a program is likely to create a favorable bias toward the program that can make it difficult for the agency to objectively evaluate that program's operations in the future. And the agency-client relationship between the GAO and individual legislators has once again led some to question how objective the agency really is. His dealings with one division of the GAO led one former Senate staff member to complain:

> *They write controversial reports for colorful congressmen who want to get into Jack Anderson's column. They write the press release before the study, and then bring out this big goddamned study the day the vote takes place on the floor. Their studies are frequently timed to come after the useful debate, and dropped like a bombshell at the last minute.*[28]

When senators or representatives use the GAO in this way, it illustrates once again that congressional support agencies are what members want them to be. The 1,000 or so reports that the GAO produces every year certainly help Congress to oversee the operations of the executive branch and to gain information needed for revising existing programs and creating new ones. In addition, the GAO is another resource that members can use for reasons that have more to do with representation than they do with lawmaking.

OFFICE OF TECHNOLOGY ASSESSMENT

The need for legislators to understand complex scientific problems and the technology behind proposed solutions in areas such as energy and the environment led Congress to create the Office of Technology Assessment (OTA) in 1972. Like the other support agencies, OTA is charged with providing objective information necessary for lawmaking. In contrast to the two previous agencies, however, the Office of Technology Assessment provides information and reports to congressional committees, but it does not respond to requests from individual legislators. This centralized lawmaking focus is heightened even more by a Technology Assessment Board consisting of six senators and six representatives, which establishes priorities for OTA and decides which studies will be undertaken.

Most OTA studies take six months to two years to complete and are aimed at the long range effects of particular technologies and policies. A 1984 OTA report on air pollution, for example, was based on a four-year study of the effects of energy use and air pollution controls for the next fifty years. The air pollution report was also typical of OTA studies in that it provided an overview of scientific knowledge on the subject and an analysis of proposed solutions to the problem but made no specific policy recommendations. Instead, the 318-page report was characterized by the project supervisor as "a handbook for policymakers." The difficulty of separating technical considerations from policy considerations was also made clear in the OTA report's discussion of acid rain—an issue that pits the economic concerns of the Midwest against the environmental concerns of the Northeast. The net effect of the report's acid rain discussion, it was suggested, was one that "confirmed the arguments that have been made by both sides: Yes, pollutants are endangering resources and possibly public health and, yes, it will cost a good deal to control them."[29]

In an essay on the strengths and weaknesses of legislatures, Anthony King has written:

> The question of the price at which oil can be extracted from shale is a technical question; the question of whether oil should be extracted at that price, of the associated costs and benefits for society at large, is a political question.[30]

The Office of Technology Assistance can provide Congress with analysis of and answers to the first question, but it cannot answer the second one. That is why the OTA report on air pollution, based as it was on four years of study, advised Congress that additional research on the subject would still not resolve the underlying policy choices facing Congress. The Office of Technology Assessment can help legislators to better understand the policy options available to them, but congressional decisions on those options will always be based on political as well as technical considerations.

CONGRESSIONAL BUDGET OFFICE

A high ranking official in the Congressional Budget Office (CBO) once compared that agency to a loose cannon:

> We upset a lot of people, no question about it. Some committees won't request analysis from us for that reason, because we're an uncontrolled cannon—they've told us so.

Sometimes a staff will ask, "If we request a study from you, how are you going to come out?" We answer, "We'll come out with a study and we won't change it."[31]

If those sound like fighting words, they accurately portray what has been the usual status of the Congressional Budget Office since its creation in 1974. In addition to the sort of conflicts with standing committees just described, the CBO has often been at the center of controversies between Congress and the president and between Democrats and Republicans in Congress. During its first year of existence, the Congressional Budget Office was criticized for having too many liberal economists, for being too agressive in pushing alternatives to the Republican Administration's budget, and for proposing lower spending in some areas than that sought by labor groups.[32] According to the first director of the Congressional Budget Office, the House and the Senate had two different notions of what the CBO's chief functions should be. The house wanted basically a "numbers shop"—a central place where legislators could get details on federal spending. The Senate saw the Congressional Budget Office as a major source of economic policy alternatives.[33] During the Reagan administration, the President and other executive officials have exchanged charges with CBO officials and congressional leaders about distorting economic data and projections in order to bolster their own policy goals—what is known in Washington as "cooking the numbers." Although the Congressional Budget Office, like other congressional support systems, is expected to provide objective data and to maintain a neutral position in policy debates, the importance of budget politics to both the president and Congress and to Republicans and Democrats inevitably brings the CBO into the middle of budget battles.

The Congressional Budget Office, with a staff of more than 200 economists, M.B.A.s, accountants, and other budget specialists, serves committees rather than individual members of Congress. The priority among those committees is the House and Senate Budget Committees first, the appropriations committees second, tax committees third, and then all other committees. The 1974 Budget Act gave the Congressional Budget Office three major functions:

1. To assist the House and the Senate (especially their budget committees) by providing them with information on the fed-

eral budget and on the economic impact of spending and tax legislation;

2. To provide periodic scorekeeping reports that track all congressional spending decisions to date and relate them to the budgetary targets and levels established by Congress;

3. To furnish the two budget committees with a report on fiscal policy alternatives and national budget priorities.

Whatever the CBO does in carrying out these tasks, particularly the first and third, is likely to be challenged by executive officials and by many members of Congress. It illustrates once again that the objective information provided by the support agencies of Congress quickly loses any semblance of neutrality when it enters the congressional arena.

Caucuses

In recent years, members of Congress have been called on to deal with an Iran-Contra crisis, an energy crisis, a farm crisis, a drug crisis, a Social Security crisis, and a long-standing budget deficit crisis. Yet one representative suggested that the major problem facing the House of Representatives in the 1980s was what he called the "insect crisis." At the time, three House groups had enough members to provide the key votes on major issues. The groups were: the Boll Weevils (forty-six conservative southern Democrats); the Gypsy Moths (twenty-six moderate northern Republicans); and the Yellow Jackets (sixty-four conservative Reagan Republicans). Using insects as a reference group began when Time magazine first applied the Boll Weevil moniker to southern Democrats in the 1960s. Those three splinter groups are part of a broader phenomenon in the modern House of Representatives, the formation of a wide range of informal, ad hoc groups known as caucuses. To deal with the "insect crisis" brought on by the presence of Boll Weevils, Gypsy Moths, and Yellow Jackets, the representative facetiously suggested creating a new caucus: "We ought to have a Praying Mantis caucus so we can eat all the other insects. We've had too much entomological trouble up here."[34]

Informal groups have always played a part in the politics of

Congress, from the boarding house groups of the first congresses to the Northeast–Midwest Coalition, which today has a membership of almost 200 and a staff of twenty. Although two of the close to ninety congressional caucuses in existence today (the Democratic Study Group and Members of Congress for Peace Through Law) were formed in 1959, the greatest growth in caucuses has taken place in recent years. One study found that of the eighty-eight congressional caucuses that came into existence between 1959 and 1982, sixty-seven were created after 1977. Earlier caucuses also tended to be party-oriented groups, while most of the caucuses formed after 1977 were based on shared concerns having to do with constituencies and particular industries and economic interests.[35] Congressional caucuses have been primarily a House phenomenon and can be officially certified as Legislative Service Organizations (LSOs) by the House Administration Committee. Since 1983, LSOs have been prohibited from receiving outside funding, but certification does enable members to use office allowance and clerk-hire funds to support the organization. The Senate does not have a comparable certification process and caucuses have been slower to develop in that chamber. However, more and more Senate and bicameral caucuses have been created in recent years.

All congressional caucuses are voluntary groups of members who have joined together on the basis of a shared characteristic or concern in order to influence lawmaking and to assure that the interests of the group are represented. Some caucuses are primarily party organizations. These include the insect groups discussed earlier (with the Boll Weevils now going under the more dignified name of Conservative Democratic Forum), the Democratic Study Group, the Republican Study Committee, the House and Senate Wednesday Groups (Republican), the Congressional Populist Caucus (Democrat), the Conservative Opportunity Society (Republican), and class clubs or new members caucuses that are organized by party. Another type of congressional caucus is that growing out of members' personal interests in particular issues or areas, for example, the Congressional Arts Caucus; the Renewable Energy Congressional Staff Group; Members of Congress for Peace Through Law; the Congressional Caucus for Science and Technology; the Pro-Life Caucus; and the Military Reform Caucus.

Most other caucuses are constituency-related groups. A caucus may be formed to represent a particular national constituency: the Congressional Black Caucus, the Congressional Hispanic Caucus, and the Congressional Caucus for Women's Issues. Senators and representatives from a particular region form another basis for constituency caucuses and have organized such groups as the Northeast–Midwest Congressional Coalition, the Conference of Great Lakes Congressmen, the Congressional Sunbelt Council, the New England Congressional Caucus, the Border Caucus, and the Washington Metropolitan Area Caucus. A rural caucus and a suburban caucus represent types of districts. Caucuses organized around the major industries or economic interests in members' districts have accounted for much of the recent increase in the number of congressional caucuses. Examples of this type include: the Congressional Automotive Caucus, the Congressional Coal Group, the Congressional Mushroom Caucus, the Jewelry Manufacturing Coalition, and the Congressional Steel Caucus.

Senators and representatives organize and join congressional caucuses so that they can get together with like-minded colleagues to exchange information and to influence policy. There are obvious "strength-in-numbers," coalition-building reasons for legislators to join caucuses. In order to achieve those policy ends, however, most caucuses provide informational and legislative support services that are similar in many ways to those of congressional staff and support agencies. Caucuses draw information from executive agencies, interest groups, constituency organizations, staff research, and members themselves. It is the informational role of caucuses that members seem to value most highly. Listen to the way that Texas Rep. and Conservative Democratic Forum Chairman Charles Stenholm explained what the former Boll Weevils were up to in the Ninety-ninth Congress (1985–1986): "We're not here to build coalitions. All we do is provide a forum and information so members of our group can cast their votes with as much knowledge of the issue as they possibly can get."[36] A first-term Republican in the House saw a similar value to the weekly meetings of a House GOP caucus, the Chowder and Marching Society: "I learn more on Wednesday afternoon about what goes on here than I do the rest of the week."[37] The need to supplement formal congressional structures was recognized by a member of the Senate Rail Caucus when he pointed out that "there is no rail committee or rail subcommittee in the Senate."

> There were a lot of us all over the country who found that rail issues began to dominate our agendas because they were so important to our states. Different people came at it from different perspectives. Some had large rail companies who were experiencing financial difficulties headquartered in their states. Some states are tremendously rail dependent and rail issues recurred over and over again.
>
> It occurred to all of us that if we were going to handle these issues properly, we had to acquire a much deeper knowledge of the intricacies of rail operation, how the operation of a rail company related to shippers' needs, related to employees' needs.[38]

The Conservative Democratic Forum, the Chowder and Marching Society, and the Senate Rail Caucus all provide members with information that is valuable for purposes of both lawmaking and representation. Although senators and representatives could in most cases obtain the same or comparable information through their staff or through legislative support agencies, these congressional caucuses provide that information as a matter of course and in a context that makes it easily accessible.

Legislators know that the information they obtain through any congressional caucus will be slanted toward the interests of that caucus. After all, no one expects the Senate Rail Caucus to find or distribute information favorable to shipping by truck or traveling by air. Caucuses present information in a form closer to a legal brief than to an objective scholarly treatise on the subject. Rather than detracting from the value of this information, however, this bias can actually increase its worth to legislators. For as Stephen Frantzich has pointed out: "Members of Congress do not want objective analyses, they require evaluations that take their own values into account."[39] Information that members obtain through congressional caucuses will reflect the shared values of caucus members and will therefore be of immediate value to them.

Despite their value to members, the future of congressional caucuses was clouded somewhat by the cuts in office accounts and staff budgets initiated in 1986 under the Gramm-Rudman Act. To illustrate, Vermont Rep. James Jeffords found that he could save $8,400 by dropping his membership in seven caucuses. "I didn't want to do it because I find them very valuable," said Jeffords. "But it was a choice between that and closing one of the district offices or relieving more people on the staff." Since money available through members' office accounts provides the funding for most caucuses, future budget cuts might force other members to make the choice that Jeffords did. That is what the staff director of the Congressional Sun Belt Council seems to have had in mind when he admitted: "I'm not sure what the future holds for this kind of group. I guess we're an endangered species."[40]

Conclusion

In the two decades that followed a management consulting firm's conclusion that "Congress needs help," Congress has taken a number of steps to see that it got that help. A greatly expanded congressional staff, a number of new and streamlined support agencies, and a wide array of congressional caucuses now flood Capitol Hill with information. Differences in the form of information and in the values and motives of the purveyors and consumers of information, however, make for wide variations in the effects of this information explosion on Congress. That variety leaves individual members with a wide range of choices on how to use the information resources that are available to them, a freedom of choice that is most evident when members use legislative support systems for purposes of representation and when they draw on representative caucuses for information to use in lawmaking.

Endnotes

1. Representative Ames, quoted in Philip Donham and Robert J. Fahey, *Congress Needs Help* (New York: Random House, 1966), p. 11.

2. Congressional Management Project, Burdett A. Loomis, Director, *Setting Course: A Congressional Management Guide* (Washington, D.C.: The American University, 1984), p. 151.

3. Rep. Al Swift (D-WA), quoted in Stephen E. Frantzich, *Computers in Congress: The Politics of Information* (Beverly Hills, Calif.: Sage, 1982), p. 11.

4. Tom Braden, "The Hidden Fifth Estate," *Washington Post*, March 20, 1976, p. A15.

5. Ibid.

6. Sens. Ernest Hollings and Herman Talmadge, respectively, both quoted in Harrison W. Fox, Jr., and Susan Webb Hammond, *Congressional Staffs: The Invisible Force in American Lawmaking* (New York: Free Press, 1977), pp. 4–5.

7. Ibid., p. 143.

8. See U.S. Congress, House, *Administrative Reorganization and Legislative Management*, Commission on Administrative Review, Ninety-fifth Congress, first session, September 28, 1977, vol. 2, pp. 126ff, for a discussion of office space limitations. The average work area available to a staff member in Congress was found to be 36–40 square feet. In the executive branch and in private industry, the average space per employee considered minimal for effective functioning was 120–150 square feet.

9. Norman J. Ornstein, et al., *Vital Statistics on Congress, 1984–1985 Edition* (Washington, D.C.: American Enterprise Institute, 1984), p. 118.

10. Ann Cooper, "Elections Plus Reforms Equals More House Employees," *Congressional Quarterly Weekly Report*, April 29, 1978, p. 1044.

11. Spencer Rich, "Staff Election Role Troubles Hill," *Washington Post*, January 25, 1976, p. A2.

12. John Saloma, *Congress and the New Politics* (New York: Little, Brown, 1969), p. 185.

13. The figures do not add up to sixteen because of rounding. For the precise figures, see Thomas E. Cavanagh, "The Two Arenas of Congress: Electoral and Institutional Incentives for Performance," a paper prepared for delivery at the 1978 Annual Meeting of the American Political Science Association, New York, N.Y., August 31 to September 3, 1978, pp. 30–31.

14. Fox and Hammond, *Congressional Staffs*, pp. 92–99.

15. Ibid., p. 25.

16. Matthews and Stimson, *Yeas and Nays: Normal Decision-Making in the U.S. House of Representatives*, pp. 23–24. Copyright © 1975 John Wiley and Sons, Inc., reprinted by permission.

17. *Administrative Reorganization and Legislative Management*, pp. 56–57.

18. Harrison W. Fox, Jr., and Susan Webb Hammond, "The Growth of Congressional Staffs," in Harvey C. Mansfield, *Congress Against the President*. Proceedings of the Academy of Political Science, 1975, vol. 32, p. 122.

19. Michael J. Malbin, *Unelected Representatives: Congressional Staff and the Future of Representative Government* (New York: Basic Books, 1980), p. 6.

20. Ibid., p. 243.

21. Steven V. Roberts, "Conferences Are Site of Legislative Showdowns," *New York Times*, November 20, 1981, p. A28.

22. Maryland student, quoted in "How Your Tax Dollars Help Do Term Papers," *New York Times*, May 28, 1986, p. B6.

23. Bill Aseltyne, quoted in ibid.

24. Nancy Davenport, quoted in ibid.

25. Lynne Kennedy, quoted in Francis X. Clines, "The Answer People of Capitol Hill," *New York Times*, October 1, 1985, p. A24.

26. Unidentified staff member, quoted in James Everett Katz, *Congress and National Energy Policy* (New Brunswick, N.J.: Transaction Books, 1984), p. 233.

27. Mark Green, *Who Runs Congress?* (New York: Dell, 1984), p. 196.

28. Unidentified former staff member, quoted in Katz, *Congress and National Energy Policy*, p. 234.

29. Dianne Dumanoski, "Study Says Acid Rain Answer Not in More Research," *Boston Globe*, June 21, 1984, p. 5.

30. Anthony King, "How to Strengthen Legislatures—Assuming That We Want to," in Norman J. Ornstein, ed., *The Role of the Legislature in Western Democracies* (Washington, D.C.: American Enterprise Institute, 1981), p. 85.

31. Dr. Raymond Scheppach, director of Natural Resources and Commerce Division, Congressional Budget Office, quoted in Katz, *Congress and National Energy Policy*, pp. 236–37.

32. Donald Smith, "CBO Director Alice Rivlin: No 'Hidden Agenda' for Congressional Action on Economic Recovery," *Congressional Quarterly Weekly Report*, September 6, 1975, pp. 1924–25.

33. Alice M. Rivlin, former director, Congressional Budget Office, talk before the American Political Science Association Congressional Fellows, The Brookings Institution, Washington, D.C., November 21, 1975.

34. Unidentified representative, quoted in Paul Light, *Artful Work: The Politics of Social Security Reform* (New York: Random House, 1985), p. 16.

35. Susan Webb Hammond, Arthur G. Stevens, Jr., and Daniel P. Mulhollan, "Congressional Caucuses: Legislators as Lobbyists," in Allan J. Cigler and Burdett A. Loomis, eds., *Interest Group Politics* (Washington, D.C.: Congressional Quarterly, 1983), pp. 276–80.

36. Representative Stenholm, quoted in Jacqueline Calmes, " 'Boll Weevils' Now Welcome in House Democratic Fold," *Congressional Quarterly Weekly Report*, April 26, 1986, p. 909.

37. Unidentified representative, quoted in Congressional Management Project, *Setting Course*, p. 45.

38. Unidentified senator, quoted in Hammond, "Congressional Caucuses," p. 290.

39. Frantzich, *Computers in Congress*, p. 43.

40. William A. Connelly, executive director, Congressional Sun Belt Council, quoted in Janet Hook, "Budget Cuts Force Reductions in Every Corner of the Capitol," *Congressional Quarterly Weekly Report*, April 19, 1986, p. 859.

8

Policies and Budgets

The lawmaking process depicted in a chart of "how a bill becomes a law" is an orderly progression; bills move from step to step in the legislative process like checkers across the board. But just about the time a student of Congress has learned the steps in that routine process, he or she is likely to come across legislation like the deficit reduction bill that Congress approved on March 20, 1986. Final House action on that measure began that evening when Budget Committee Chairman William Gray took the House floor to offer an amendment. Gray informed his colleagues that his proposal was an amendment to "the Senate amendment to the House amendment to the Senate amendment to the House amendment to the Senate amendment."[1] That might seem like parliamentary doubletalk, but it was a correct description of the measure before the House. Instead of following an orderly progression through the lawmaking process, the deficit reduction bill had been bouncing back and forth between the two chambers for three months. The House initiated that process when it rejected both the conference committee bill and a Senate amendment to the conference bill on December 19, 1984. New amendments kept the bill moving between the two chambers nine times until the House voted on March 20 to accept the most recent Senate amendment. The normal process of policymaking in Congress lies somewhere in between the order and serenity suggested in charts of the lawmaking process and the turbulent path followed by the deficit reduction bill.

British novelist and one-time Parliamentary candidate Anthony Trollope had this to say about one of his fictional legislators: "No man was more warmly attached to parliamentary government than Sir Timothy Beeswax; but I do not think that he ever cared much for legislation."[2] More than a century later, Oklahoma Senator and former political science professor David Boren offered the following observation about legislative policymaking: "One of the first rules of politics is that just because something is illogical doesn't mean it won't pass Congress."[3] In the first session of the Ninety-ninth Congress (1985–1986), a total of 7,777 bills and resolutions were introduced in Congress and 240 of those passed both chambers and were signed into law by the president.

Congressional policymaking is the process through which a large number of proposals introduced as bills are narrowed down to the relatively few that become laws. Two important characteristics of legislative policymaking that were suggested at earlier points in this book, and in the words of Trollope and Boren, are (1) that legislators have interests in addition to that of legislating and (2) that bills are often so changed by the process itself that they bear little resemblance to the original proposal. Those are two of the many reasons why a particular bill will move through the legislature in a way that is quite different from that suggested in a chart of "how a bill becomes a law."

Budget issues and the congressional budget process have come to dominate the legislative process in the 1980s. The new budget procedures established in 1974 and the changes in that process effected by the 1981 reconciliation bill and the 1985 Gramm-Rudman Act have served to focus more and more congressional attention on the budgetary impact of any bill that is under consideration. "We spend all our time on the budget," explained one representative, because "that is, in fact, where the action is today."[4] Two other legislators provided this assessment: "The Budget has become the pied piper of Congress. Its schedule dictates when Congress convenes and when it recesses, what happens on the floor and what is stalled on the calendar."[5] Because of the central role of the budget process in Congress and the way in which budgetary issues influence all areas of policymaking, the first section of the chapter outlines the congressional budget process. The second and third sections will consider the general stages involved in all policymaking and how Congress has different ways of handling different types of policies.

The Budget Process

The deficit reduction bill mentioned at the beginning of this chapter was also known as the fiscal 1986 reconciliation bill because it was a mixture of revenue increases and spending cuts designed to "reconcile" the overall costs of programs with the deficit targets that Congress had set in an earlier budget resolution. Toward that end, the 310-page reconciliation bill increased cigarette taxes and customs fees and cut more than $12 billion from government programs in the areas of highways, student loans, small businesses, housing, veterans' benefits, and Medicare.

Five years earlier, when the Reagan administration had used a reconciliation bill as the vehicle for the largest domestic spending cuts in U.S. history, a Washington columnist had written: "Reconciliation is a revolution in our government." A nationally recognized expert on Congress was quoted as saying that he knew "of no measure in the long history of Congress with the scope of this year's reconciliation. The process is truly unprecedented in the range of legislative issues it encompasses."[6] House Speaker Tip O'Neill, after losing a key procedural vote on the Reagan budget cuts contained in the reconciliation bill, told members of Congress, "I've never seen anything like this in all my life, to be perfectly truthful."[7] The chairman of the House Committee on Education and Labor complained:

> In all my years in Congress I have never witnessed an action more ill advised, more insensitive or more threatening to the rightful operation of the legislative process than these so-called reconciliation instructions.[8]

A midwestern senator agreed with that assessment when he stated his belief that

> congressional procedures were greatly abused, in spite of the innovative nature of the original reconciliation idea," and warned that "unless we stop short, take stock and revise some of the procedures, the budget reform act itself may die, or worse may destroy the Senate as a deliberative body.[9]

The object of all this attention and criticism was a congressional budget procedure known as reconciliation. That procedure was one of the ways that the Budget and Impoundment Control Act of 1974 sought to give Congress greater control over the federal budget. In addition to establishing budget committees in the House and Senate, the 1974 Act calls for Congress as a whole to vote on overall spending targets for a fiscal year that are guidelines for the standing committees to follow in authorizing programs and appropriating funds for them. Under the original 1974 act, the second budget resolution sets spending ceilings, which are not simply guidelines for total spending in particular areas, but are mandatory limits on federal spending in those areas.

The reconciliation process was included in the 1974 act as a way to enforce the second budget resolution while still recognizing the authority of standing committees to make spending decisions within the limits established by the second budget resolution. If committees with jurisdiction over programs in a particular area have exceeded the spending ceilings, the second budget resolution orders them to "reconcile" spending in that area with the limits provided in the budget resolution. Responsibility for making all of these changes in accord with the second budget resolution rests with the standing committees of Congress. The committees responsible for raising revenue, authorizing programs, and appropriating funds make the changes and bring them to the budget committees, and the budget committees bring all these changes to the floor in the form of one reconciliation measure.

Despite the fact that reconciliation had been on the books since 1974, it was not used as a part of the budget process until 1980. Before that time, Congress would regularly pass the second budget resolution so near to the start of the new fiscal year that there was no time for committees to change earlier decisions in order to comply with a reconciliation bill before the fiscal year began. The spending decisions made by standing committees were also generally upheld by adjusting the second budget resolution upward to reflect actual spending levels embodied in these committee decisions. An expert on the subject described the pre-1980 budget process this way:

> The separate tax, appropriations, and authorizations committees retained legislative power over money; the Budget committees were given the power to coordinate, but not to legislate. In this way, Congress hoped to have the best of both worlds: inte-

grated budgeting and a dispersion of legislative power. Although it specified the basic rules of the budget process, the Budget Act did not establish the relationship between the coordinators and the legislators. During the first five years of the budget process (1975–1979), the legislative committees generally had the upper hand.[10]

Reconciliation was first used in the last year of the Carter administration when, in the spring of 1980, congressional and administration leaders sought to achieve a balanced budget for fiscal 1981. The vehicle for achieving this balance was a reconciliation order attached to the first budget resolution for that year. Under the resolution, the appropriations committees in both chambers and ten Senate and eight House authorizing committees were ordered to make cuts in spending programs and the Ways and Means and Senate Finance Committees were ordered to raise over $4 billion in new tax revenues. The successful use of reconciliation in the 1981 budget produced an overall savings of $8.2 billion for that year.

The precedent established by use of reconciliation in the fiscal 1981 budget process was more important than the savings for any particular year. The Reagan administration later used that precedent as the basis for achieving its program of massive cuts in the federal budget. Knowing that members of Congress are reluctant to cut funding in particular programs, the Reagan administration adopted the strategy of combining all of the individual program cuts into one reconciliation bill, which would force members of Congress to vote yes or no on the general issue of cutting government spending. In July 1981, Congress approved a reconciliation bill ordering fourteen Senate committees and fifteen House committees to cut or change existing programs in order to achieve a savings of about $36 billion. This reconciliation bill produced the largest cut in government spending in United States history and affected 250 different government programs.[11] Although Congress agreed on the need to cut government spending and voted to pass the Reagan budget, there was a great deal of disagreement about the priorities reflected in the cuts, and some members were concerned that Congress was being called on to support a presidential program when it did not know the particulars of that program.

The use of reconciliation to achieve the massive budget cuts proposed by the Reagan administration was a dramatic event that changed not only immediate policy outcomes but the legislative process itself. Throughout the 1980s, Congress has used reconciliation bills to enact its major budget decisions. That procedure has increased the power of the budget committees at the expense of other standing committees, particularly the appropriations committees.

The Gramm-Rudman Act brought further changes in the budgetary process that moved in the same centralizing direction as did the earlier use of reconciliation instructions with the first budget resolution. As we saw in Chapter 1, the Gramm-Rudman Act not only mandated budget cuts through the sequestion process but also changed the congressional budget timetable so that the budget process became even more of a "fast track" than it had been before.

All of these changes can be said to have improved the lawmaking capacity of Congress, but there is much debate about whether the costs in terms of representation have been too high. In order to understand and to evaluate the congressional budget process of the 1980s, it is helpful to look at what that process was like before and after the Budget and Impoundment Control Act of 1974.

The Congressional Budget Act

In 1946, Congress adopted a major budgetary reform provision as part of the Legislative Reorganization Act. Members of both House and Senate tax committees and appropriations committees were required each February to determine the "maximum amount to be appropriated for expenditures" for the following fiscal year. In other words, they would set a spending ceiling for the coming fiscal year. It didn't work.

> The first year, 1947, the two houses could not agree on a ceiling. The second year, having agreed on one, they failed to abide by it. The third year, without even bothering to amend the reorganization act, they gave up trying.[12]

Congress waited almost thirty years before another attempt was made. The Budget and Impoundment Control Act of 1974 was a response to many of the same forces that led to the abortive attempt at congressional budgetary reform in 1946. These forces included a galloping rate of inflation, a tremendous increase in the level of federal government spending, a resultant increase in the national debt, and a general feeling that control over spending levels and the national economy in general was slipping away from Congress and into the hands of the president.

Specific criticisms of congressional performance on the key budgetary matters of appropriations and taxing all focused on the fragmentation and decentralized nature of congressional decision making and on the delay resulting from this process.

An expert on congressional and presidential spending and on budgetary processes, Louis Fisher, has pinpointed the major deficiencies of the old budgetary process that led to the reforms of 1974:[13]

1. *Late appropriations.* Under the old system a fiscal year ran from July to July. Congress was often unable to pass the necessary appropriations for federal agencies before the fiscal year had expired. This led to dependence on a disoriented, crisis-motivated, pattern of appropriations. Federal agencies had to look toward an unreliable system of funding based on congressional continuing resolutions, which covered only a part of the fiscal year.

2. *The size of the budget deficit.* In 1969, the federal deficit was $5.5 billion. In 1970, it was $13.1 billion. In 1971 and 1972, it was $29 billion, and in 1973 it was $34 billion. About one-fourth of the total national debt had accumulated during this short period of time. While there were sharp differences among economists about the relative value of a balanced budget and the countercyclical policies of the federal government pump priming a national economy during private sector economic downturns, most economists agreed that Congress needed to begin paying closer attention to the overall economic impact of its spending and taxing policies.

3. *Uncontrollable expenditures.* More than seventy-five cents of every dollar spent by the federal government during this period came under the heading of uncontrollable expenditures. These expenditures were not dependent on, or subject to, congressional action for their being paid. The bulk of expenditures were accounted for by entitlement programs (those that establish a government expenditure or benefit for persons fitting a particular category, such as retired federal employees, those whose income is below the poverty level, and the unemployed), and by the fact that such program expenditures were generally "in-

dexed" (i.e., the level of benefits is tied in to the rate of inflation as measured by the cost-of-living index). By passing such programs, Congress made a lot of people happy and met their economic needs, but it also lost control over a large part of its power of the purse and its ability to devise a cohesive fiscal policy.

4. *Backdoor spending.* This general term referred to any of the processes Congress used to provide funds for agencies and programs without going through the normal channel of congressional appropriations. It encompassed the following.

- *Contract authority.* This permitted executive agencies to enter into contracts with private firms (consulting agencies), paying certain fees for services received. Congressional approval of appropriations to pay such contract fees had generally been automatic.

- *Borrowing authority.* This was a process by which agencies spent funds by borrowing directly on agency debt receipts or by tapping more general Treasury Department debt receipts. In both cases, an agency was able to rely on leftover funds rather than on congressional appropriations committees.

- *Entitlement programs.* The level of expenditures here was indirectly fixed by congressional action, which established who was entitled to benefits guaranteed by the particular program. Because the economic factors determining the level of benefits were beyond congressional control, the level of expenditures on such programs was also beyond congressional control.

The overall impact of backdoor spending was indicated in its accounting for more than half of all federal government spending about the time the Budget Act took effect.[14]

5. *Impoundment of funds by the executive.* This was perhaps the most blatant form of executive control over national economic issues. The impoundment of funds appropriated by Congress meant simply that the president and the executive branch refused to spend funds allocated for certain programs by Congress. It was another way the executive branch had come to exercise greater budgetary control than the Congress. As of September 30, 1973, $7.4 billion had been impounded by the executive branch. By February 1974, that total had leaped to $11.8 billion in federal funds appropriated by Congress that the executive branch selectively failed to spend.[15]

The Congressional Budget and Impoundment Control Act of 1974 was an attempt by Congress to deal with the problems listed before. The act gave Congress the machinery for providing overall coordination between spending and revenue programs and for determining budget priorities.

Another reason for passage of this legislation was a political reason. The Democrats who controlled Congress wanted to show that it was not the reckless spendthrift institution that President Nixon had identified as the primary cause of the nation's inflation. By passing this legislation, Congress showed that it too was concerned with growing budget deficits and the rate of inflation. But some had doubts about the degree of congressional commitment from the very beginning, a cynicism that was expressed by a House staff member who sniffed:

> There are a lot of guys who voted for this thing [budget reform] who don't really believe in it. They feel that the substantive programs that they are interested in—for instance on health programs, they act on the premise that the more dollars they put in, the quicker they'll find a cure for cancer—that that's more important than the orderly management of fiscal affairs.[16]

The 1974 act was a comprehensive piece of legislation that did all of the following:

1. Established new budget committees in both chambers;
2. Established a Congressional Budget Office to provide economic information and analysis;
3. Set up new congressional budget procedures and a detailed timetable for action on the budget;
4. Created a new fiscal year, beginning in October, that gave Congress more time to react to the president's budget (introduced in January) than did the old fiscal year;
5. Required the use of nineteen functional budget categories so that information and action would be coordinated with the Office of Management and Budget and with the Treasury Department;
6. Prohibited presidential impoundment of funds through recessions unless both houses of Congress approved the action within forty-five days of an impoundment proposal.

The two budget committees established by the Congressional Budget and Impoundment Control Act differ in size and composition. In 1981, the House increased the size of its Budget Committee from the twenty-five members provided in the 1974 act to thirty (eighteen Democrats and twelve Republicans), and in 1984, to thirty-three (twenty Democrats and thirteen Republicans). Membership on the House committee is designed to be representative of the chamber as a whole by requiring a rotating membership of limited terms and by designating slots on the Budget Committee to be held by members of the Appropriations and Ways and Means Committees and by leaders from both parties. The importance of the House committee has been demonstrated over the years by the Democratic majority's insisting on party ratios that assure majority control of the committee, by attempts of members to stay beyond the six-year limit, and by the high number of representatives seeking assignment to the Budget Committee. The Senate Budget Committee has remained stable at twenty-two members (twelve Republicans and ten Democrats in the Ninety-ninth Congress). In contrast to the House practice, membership on the Senate committee is not restricted by the term limitation and mandatory committee representation.

Despite these differences in size and composition, the House and Senate budget committees perform essentially the same functions. The two committees gather and disseminate information on the fiscal impact of legislation, oversee the operations of the Congressional Budget Office, keep track of all spending and revenue bills in the chamber, and draft the concurrent resolutions on the budget that serve to guide all congressional spending and revenue activities for that fiscal year.

The Congressional Budget Office (CBO), one of the support agencies discussed in Chapter 7, is the professional research and information agency created by the 1974 act. It is headed by a director who is appointed, for a term of four years, by the presiding officers of the House and the Senate, although they follow the recommendations of the budget committees. Either house may remove the director. A Democrat and Brookings Institution economist, Alice Rivlin, served two four-year terms as the first CBO director. In 1983, a Republican economist from the American Enterprise Institute, Rudolph Penner, was named to the post after Rivlin resigned.

As the discussion in Chapter 7 indicated, the Congressional

Budget Office provides economic information and professional analysis to the two budget committees. This is routinely done through CBO reports on baseline budget projections (what existing programs would cost in the coming five years if no changes were made), analyses of the president's budget, a general forecast of economic conditions, and analyses of alternative proposals for reducing the deficit. In addition, the CBO acts as congressional scorekeeper of spending during that year, and provides information and analyses upon request to the two budget committees and to other standing committees.

The Budget Act of 1974 moved the start of a fiscal year from July to October and established a number of action-forcing deadlines in the budget process. The two key points in the budget timetable established by the 1974 legislation were (1) a May 15 deadline for congressional adoption of the first budget resolution and (2) a September 15 deadline for the second budget resolution. In order to meet those requirements, the 1974 act also established reporting deadlines for congressional committees to make recommendations to the budget committees (March 15), for the Congressional Budget Office to report on alternative budget strategies (April 1), and for the two budget committees to report the first budget resolution (April 15).

An important modification in the congressional budget process took place in 1980 when the status of the first budget resolution was changed from advisory to mandatory by the reconciliation measure described at the beginning of this chapter. The Gramm-Rudman Act of 1985 continued this trend toward creating a legislative "fast track" for budgets by replacing the two-resolution process with one that called instead for one annual budget resolution. Figure 8–1 shows the streamlined congressional budget process that resulted from the 1985 changes.

Five years after Congress had established the new congressional budget process, the director of the Congressional Budget Office, Alice Rivlin, pointed out that whether or not members thought that it was working depended on what their expectations for the process had been.

> Conservatives wanted the budget process to put a ceiling on expenditures. They saw the purpose as being to hold down expenditures. Liberals, on the other hand, saw it as a way of weighing priorities. They wanted a priorities debate.[17]

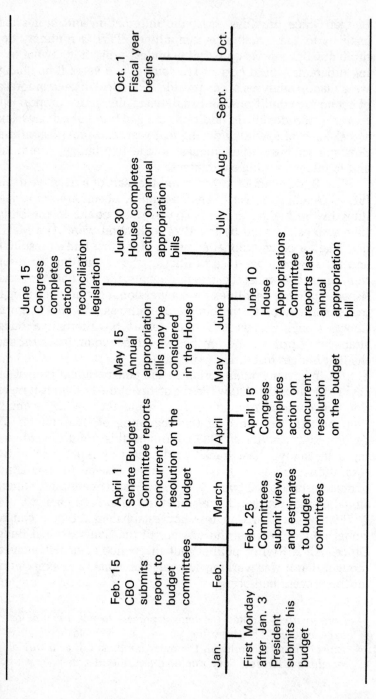

FIGURE 8–1 Congressional Budget Timetable Under Gramm-Rudman-Hollings

Neither group, said Rivlin, had seen its expectations fully met. Conservatives continued to complain that the budget committees were the allies of the "big spenders," while liberals often felt that priorities had not been addressed.

Complicating any assessment about the effectiveness of Congress in making fiscal policy is wide disagreement about what the effects of any fiscal policy will be. While some would argue that a tax cut, for instance, creates greater consumer demand and thus fuels inflation, others would argue that a tax cut leads to greater investment, greater production, and a reduction in prices. There is similar disagreement about both the policy and procedural effects of the 1974 Budget Act.

An assessment offered by a member of the House Budget Committee five years after Congress established the new budget procedure made the following observations: (1) Authorizing committees now plan ahead in a more comprehensive and coordinated way; (2) Congress, under the new system, has been enacting appropriations bills before the end of the fiscal year, thus making planning for the future easier for state and local governments; (3) Congress is paying attention to spending programs that it previously overlooked because of the nature of the appropriations process; and (4) creation of the Congressional Budget Office has greatly increased the amount of information available to members about the economic impact of legislation that they are considering.[18]

Another positive effect often cited at the time was that the new budget process, by providing long-term cost estimates (as well as short-term estimates), makes members of Congress more aware of the uncontrollable aspects of the federal budget, such as spending provided by entitlement programs. This awareness makes them think in a longer time frame than simply annual authorizations. On the other hand, a political scientist who had served as special assistant to the first CBO director suggested that while the Budget Act had enabled Congress to regain the power of the purse, the legislation's "other three goals—meeting budget deadlines, managing internal conflict, and curbing the growth of spending, taxes, and deficits—were not achieved." Despite the deadlines imposed by the 1974 legislation, Congress spent an average of 102 days after the start of the fiscal year to enact its major appropriations bills during the period, 1976–1983. Before those deadlines were established (1968–1975), the average was 101 days. The growth rate of federal spending and the size of the deficit also proved to be higher in the period after the Budget Act than it had been before the legislation. And rather than experiencing reduced conflict, Congress has seen an increase in the degree of partisanship and conflict over budgets and appropriations bills since 1974.[19]

Because missed deadlines have often meant that the fiscal year has started before Congress has completed action on the thirteen regular appropriations bills for that fiscal year, Congress regularly depends on "continuing resolutions" (in Capitol Hill parlance, "CRs"), which temporarily maintain spending levels until Congress passes the full appropriations bills. One provision of the Gramm-Rudman Act moved the House appropriations deadline in the budget timetable from September to June of the preceding fiscal year, and sought to enforce it by requiring the House to stay in session during its traditional July 4th recess if the appropriations bills had not been passed. On June 19, 1986, the first year under the new budget timetable, the House of Representatives voted to waive that particular provision because Congress at that point had not even completed action on the budget resolution, which was due back in April. Whether the continued inability of Congress to meet budget deadlines was simply a difficulty associated with the transition to a new schedule, or whether it was an indication that the schedule itself was unrealistic, was something that members of Congress could ponder as they headed back to the district for the July recess.

One reason for the limited success, or at least survival, of the budget process during its first five years of operation was the fact that the budget reform act did not attempt a complete centralization of budget decision making. The budget timetable and new budget committees did not disturb the existing centers of fiscal authority of the appropriations and tax committees. Congressional budget decisions during this period recognized the power of standing committees by passing final budget resolutions that reflected the taxing and spending decisions made by the standing committees. Even the supposedly binding second resolutions were routinely changed by third budget resolutions that adapted budget ceilings to fit committee decisions.[20] The budget process was being used to coordinate the decision making of the standing committees, but the major spending and taxing decisions were still being made in the committees.

The use of reconciliation orders in the first budget resolutions for fiscal 1981 and 1982 changed the budget process from one of coordination to one requiring committee compliance. Instead of setting spending guidelines or targets, the first resolution now established fixed limits on committee spending levels. Allen Schick, a budget expert who helped to write the 1974 legislation has pointed out:

> *Reconciliation transformed the budget resolutions from 'sense of the Congress' statements into triggers of legislative activity. Reconciliation forced committees to conform existing law to current budget decisions, and it thereby transferred power from the legislative committees to the budget committees.*[21]

Under the budget process established in 1974, says John Ellwood, another scholar with first-hand experience working with the Budget Act, information provided by committees and subcommittees provided the direction needed for budget decision making. But Ellwood suggests that applying reconciliation to the first resolution in 1980 "shifted the budget process from one in which information would provide control to one in which central direction in the form of reconciliation instructions would control the committees and subcommittees."[22]

The Budget and Impoundment Control Act of 1974 and the Gramm-Rudman Act of 1985 are two of the strongest attempts ever made by Congress to overcome the decentralization inherent in the representational and committee systems of Congress. As we have seen, the reconciliation procedure provided in that act served as a vehicle for Congress to enact the largest budget cuts in United States history. Debate over the policies that have been achieved through the new congressional budget process will certainly continue to be a feature of U.S. politics in the foreseeable future. But the impact of the procedural changes is already clear. The reconciliation process provided by the 1974 Budget Act and the action-forcing mechanisms created by the Gramm-Rudman Act have moved Congress to the center of fiscal policymaking and affected all areas of congressional policymaking.

The Policymaking Process

"There is no more important work for anyone interested in public policy than the U.S. Senate," one member of that institution has suggested. "But anyone who is achievement-oriented and likes instant gratification better not come down here."[23] A representative offered a similar assessment of congressional policy-making. "It's good to be in the middle of things, and Congress clearly is a place of action," he said. But twenty years in the House also led him to describe it as "a frustrating place for people who want to push a button and make things happen."[24] Those views seem to be a common theme whenever members of Congress talk about their jobs and the institution. Most of them like the action but have doubts about the final product. Another representative declared:

> There is a frustration level. For example, I've spent a good portion of the last year working on one bill, as chairman of the subcommittee, and we've busted our rears. We got an authorization bill through our committee. I spent a whole weekend in meetings hammering out the agreement on this, and our authorization bill is clearly not going to come to the floor this year. . . . That's frustrating. We kill ourselves and the bill will never see the light of day as best as anybody can determine at this point.[25]

The reference to Anthony Trollope's character, Sir Timothy Beeswax, earlier in this chapter illustrated a point about legislators and policymaking that is often overlooked—lawmaking is just one of the many things that legislators do. One member of Congress, calling the institution "a giant smorgasbord," had this to say about his experience as a legislator:

> If you measure the job satisfaction in terms of having this fantastic variety of things you can do if you want to, issues you can get involved in, or styles of operation on the floor, in committee, or with constituents, then the opportunities are endless.
>
> If, on the other hand, you measure it in terms of the extent to which the process produces the ultimate result you think it ought to produce . . . then it can be terribly frustrating.[26]

Why is it that legislators so often express feelings of frustration with congressional policymaking even when they are satisfied with other aspects of their job? One answer might be that representation can be an individual activity while lawmaking requires coordinated action by a majority in each chamber, a minimum of 218 representatives and 51 senators. Another might be that representation in the form of entering a statement in the

Congressional Record, introducing a symbolic amendment, answering the mail, visiting the district, or intervening with the bureaucracy on behalf of a constituent is something that can be done by pushing a button and making things happen. A representative or senator may not be able to achieve instant gratification through such activities, but the rewards are likely to be quicker in coming than those of successfully shepherding a bill through Congress.

Congressional policymaking is a process rather than a single act. There is a saying in baseball that a game is never over until it's over. In Congress, it's never over. Even when a bill eventually does become a law, often other bills on the same subject are already on deck, and proposals for changing the new legislation will be introduced in the next session. A chart depicting the lawmaking process might properly be entitled: "How a bill becomes a law, which generates new bills, some of which might become laws." It is more a circular process than it is a straight line with a clearly delineated beginning and end.

The budget process outlined in the previous section is a sequential one in which certain actions must be taken by certain committees, agencies, and other bodies before further action can be taken by others. While policymaking in other areas does not have the deadlines and rigid structuring found in budget policymaking, it does have a sequence of activities. The chart of the lawmaking process shows the normal sequence in each chamber:

- Introduction of a bill and assignment to committee,
- Referral to subcommittee,
- Hearings and subcommittee markup,
- Referral back to the full committee for additional action and a report on the bill,
- Rules Committee consideration in the House,
- Debate and amendment on the chamber floor,
- Conference committee action to resolve differences in the House and Senate bills,
- Debate and approval of the conference bill in each chamber.

While this course is taken by most bills that make it through Congress, some of the most important legislation of recent Congresses has not followed that sequence. For example, the crucial decisions regarding the 1983 Social Security reforms—a $170 billion combination of benefit cuts and tax increases—were made outside of the normal legislative process by an ad hoc group of legislative and executive officials and then ratified by the appropriate House and Senate committees.[27] The far reaching Balanced Budget and Emergency Deficit Control Act of 1985— the Gramm-Rudman Act discussed earlier—was passed without benefit of any congressional hearings, without committee consideration in either chamber, and without any direct debate on the substance of the bill on the House floor.[28]

Not all laws, then, go through each stage of the legislative process depicted in charts. Yet there is a sequence to the different activities associated with policymaking, even when it is not a congressional committee or subcommittee that is engaged in that activity. There are different ways for a bill to become a law, but they all seem to involve three types of activities. And the normal sequence of those activities permits us to identify three key stages in congressional policymaking—agenda setting, formulation, and legitimation.[29]

AGENDA SETTING

There are two steps to this initial stage of the policymaking process. The first is the perception and definition of problems regarded as appropriate for government solutions. And as is the case with all political activity, some people have more influence than others. "At any given point in time," Barbara Sinclair points out, "the agenda consists of the problems considered important by those with enough political clout to persuade a considerable number of decisionmakers to share their concerns."[30] The second step is establishing priorities among those problems. Because there are always more problems than there are solutions, and because there is a limit to the number of programs that Congress can consider and the government undertake, the political agenda is always a selective list.

Much of the discussion about agenda setting focuses on who has the most influence over determining the priority of issues. Active presidents often shape the political agenda, as was the case in 1981–1982, when President Reagan's program of budget cuts and tax reductions dominated the congressional schedule. Congress appeared to regain the agenda-setting initiative in 1985, a year characterized by Congress scholar Norman Ornstein as one in which "the whole agenda was set by Congress."[31] Washington columnist Robert Healy's review of 1986 Senate action on the defense budget, judicial nominations, sanctions against South Africa, and aid to the "contras" of Nicaragua led him to conclude that "the Republican-controlled Senate has been a major factor in setting the agenda in the Reagan administration." Healy suggested that President Reagan's heavy schedule of campaigning for Republican senatorial candidates in 1986 was best explained in the same terms. "If the Democrats take the Senate, they will set the agenda for Reagan's last two years, so Reagan has nothing to lose by putting himself on the line."[32]

Competition over agenda setting takes place between the two chambers and among senators and representatives as well as between the executive and the legislature. Outside events such as a foreign policy crisis or economic downturn often determine what the main course on the congressional plate will be at any time, but there is always room for arguing over the side dishes. To a degree, party leaders and the committee system shape the congressional agenda. However, as congressional policymaking has become more of a collegial activity in which all members fully participate, the influence of congressional leaders has diminished. In his analysis of this new pattern of decision making in Congress, Steven Smith has written:

> Setting the agenda is likely to be a more difficult task in the collegial pattern as members with a variety of interests seek meaningful participation. As a result, predicting which issues and political divisions will surface is more difficult.[33]

The expansion of the professional staffs in Congress and the development of the "entrepreneurial" staff style that was discussed in Chapter 7 have also affected agenda setting in Congress. Staff members generate new agenda items through their own research and through their interaction with issue specialists from both interest groups and the executive branch. In addition, members become aware of problems that call for government attention when they engage in oversight of executive agencies and in casework for constituents. Much of that activity is a part of representation, but the normal tension between the two values is also present. The value of representation is best served by a congressional agenda that is open and highly accessible, while lawmaking requires a limited agenda with clearly established priorities. A legislator describes what happens when representational considerations override lawmaking ones in agenda setting: "I think we get ourselves involved in too many things—we see there is some need, and we try to address the need rather than not having anybody address it, especially when it's in the committee you're on. Consequently, you dissipate yourself."[34]

FORMULATION

At a time when filibuster threats by Democratic opponents had stalled action on the Gramm-Rudman bill, Senate Majority Leader Robert Dole complained that "the longer something hangs around here, the staler it gets." "People start reading it," he added.[35] That particular bill, as we noted earlier, did not follow the normal course of congressional policymaking. Neither chamber, for example, had conducted committee hearings on the legislation. And it is congressional hearings that represent the most visible part of the formulation stage of congressional policymaking. The formulation stage is one where members take the following course:

1. Review data and analyze policy options in a particular areas.
2. Evaluate those options,
3. Select among alternative policies, and in most cases,
4. Issue a committee report that summarizes the process and supports a recommendation on the bill.

When these steps are skipped, members of Congress have to find other and usually less efficient ways of learning about a bill, such as reading it.

In most cases, the processing of technical and political information that characterizes policy formulation will result in members' knowing something about legislative proposals before they come to the floor for a vote. Congressional committees, their staffs, and legislative support agencies play an important part in the formulation stage of policymaking. Policy specialists and technical experts from those staffs and agencies provide extensive quantitative data that have been generated from what seems to be objective research and analysis.

At this stage of the policymaking process, members and staff often will use these data to play a numbers game. For example, what is the percentage increase that is needed in the defense budget to maintain an adequate deterrent against the Soviet Union or what will be the net gain for individuals earning $50,000 a year under a proposed tax reform? Because quantitative data serve to focus the policy debate and to give one side a tactical advantage, legislators want to have numbers at this stage even if the validity of those numbers is questionable.

Former Congressional Budget Director Alice Rivlin, whose agency is one of the most important sources of numbers used in economic decision making, described their importance: "If somebody says, 'Did you know that there are 27 percent more of something than last year?' he dominates the discussion, even though he's probably wrong." If the numbers being cited by a legislator are questionable, those figures must still be shown to be wrong by opponents before they can get others to accept their own. The member with the best numbers, said a veteran House staff member, will always be, at least temporarily, "King of the Hill."[36]

While agreeing that "a person who has control of numbers, whether accurate or not, will carry the day," one scholar also suggested that there is what he called "a fallacy of misplaced concreteness" in the search for quantitative data by members of Congress. To illustrate, he recalled a case in which:

> A Cabinet Secretary, asked to estimate the cost of a proposed change in Social Security put the figure at $600 million to $700 million. The committee chairman asked for a more specific figure, and the witness promised to return with one the next day.
>
> The Secretary left the hearing room, had lunch, saw a movie, enjoyed dinner, watched television and came in the next morning with a precise figure: $627.3 million. The chairman was pleased.[37]

The value of the precise figure in this case has little to do with its accuracy. Rather, it provided the chairman with an authoritative number that he could use to support his position in the ongoing Social Security debate.

Indiana Rep. Lee Hamilton has also described the subjective way that members draw on the quantitative data that they receive: "We use the numbers when they serve our purpose and discard them when they don't." And even though "the members of this institution are skillful at using numbers," Hamilton said, "they recognize how slippery most of them are." "I don't think we are fooled by the numbers. We use them as tools to buttress our views."[38]

The formulation stage is one that generates a great deal of information on Capitol Hill. Members expect their staff and support agencies to provide them with numbers that they can use to support their policy positions and to counter those advanced by opponents in the policy debate. The subjective use of that information and the adversary manner in which it is employed does not diminish the importance of information to policy formulation. Members become aware of the policy alternatives before them and the reasons for selecting one over the others. That information also plays a role in the next stage of the policy process.

LEGITIMATION

The building of a legislative majority shapes all of the specific activities of this stage, which include the identification of key interests in a policy proposal, communication among those interests, and bargaining in order to produce a compromise policy. Legitimation takes place both in committee and on the floor of each chamber. The need to satisfy a wide range of interests in order to build a majority can result in major changes to policy proposals that come out of the formulation stage. For example, the Immigration Reform Bill that the House Judiciary Committee approved in June 1986 sought to meet the interests of western growers by giving foreign farm workers the legal status of permanent residents—a section of the bill that a number of the bill's original sponsors felt worked against the bill's primary goals of controlling immigration. One of those sponsors, Rep. Dan Lungren (R-CA) likened what the committee had done to "drawing a racehorse and coming up with a camel."[39]

Information likely to produce major changes in policy proposals at the legitimation stage is likely to be of a political rather than technical nature. Although members such as those advancing the cause of western growers in the immigration reform case will disseminate economic and demographic data that support their position, the type of information that is most important at this stage is political information. How many votes are there for the bill in committee and on the floor with and without the farm worker provision? What compromises need to be made to gain the support of western legislators without losing the original support of those from other geographic areas?

The members' cue system that was described in Chapter 4 is the primary information network at this stage of policymaking. This is so because members require not only objective information at this stage but also information on the values underlying the choices before them. Committee leaders with expertise in an area, the initial cue givers of Chapter 4, provide other members with both types of information, while colleagues from the same state party delegation and other intermediary cuegivers provide information that is evaluative and political. Legislators engaged in coalition building are more concerned with how other legislators *feel* about policy proposals than they are with what staff members *know* about them.

For a number of reasons members look to their colleagues for the information they need at the legitimation stage. One reason is that fellow senators and representatives have all been elected to their positions rather than appointed, and that fact alone demonstrates a certain degree of political skill and ability to make political judgments. Another reason is that all legislators share membership in a collegial and nonhierarchical organization, in which an individual's influence depends on the support of his or her peers. That makes members accountable to one another and enhances the reliability of information they receive from other members. And lastly, members look to colleagues for information that is simply not available elsewhere.

The members' cue network can provide legislators with information about constituency opinion in districts other than their own, about the intensity of other members' commitments to particular policy proposals, and about the chances of putting together various compromises in that area. All of that is information that can generally be provided only by one's fellow legislators and congressional leaders and not by even the most competent and well-informed staff.

Once again, the representative character of Congress provides a basis for the institution's lawmaking role of legitimation. And many of the characteristics that are said to make congressional policymaking a lengthy and inefficient process—the constituency focus of members, the decentralized committee system, and bicameralism—contribute to legitimation. This stage of the policy process helps to produce the frustration of members that was expressed at the beginning of this section, but without it Congress would cease to exist as a lawmaking institution.

Policies

There are several points in every session of Congress when senators and representatives find themselves face-to-face with a situation that some refer to as "the term paper syndrome." In the Ninety-ninth Congress (1985–1986), such a time came one Monday in August, when members looked at the issues up for decision in the coming week—tax reform, a required increase in the debt ceiling, changes in the Gramm-Rudman Act, aid to the "contras" of Nicaragua, sanctions against South Africa, reorganization of the Pentagon, political action committee (PAC) reform, an important defense bill, antidrug legislation, and appropriations bills for just about all major federal programs. "That's like sitting there at midnight with 500 notecards and a history class at 9 in the morning," was a description offered by one close observer of the scene that Monday.[40] And just as any writer of term papers needs a scheme for ordering those notecards and making sense out of all that information, legislators also need a way to order the hundreds of important bills before them.

Some of the bills will be considered routine legislation, and others major policy proposals. Some will be perceived as having no direct effect on a particular legislator's constituents, whereas others will be seen as having a profound impact on the lifestyle or economic situation of every person in the state or district. All legislators, in short, develop some scheme for classifying policies and allocating their time and efforts in line with that classification. Students of the congressional process must do the same thing. One could not possibly consider all of the proposed bills introduced in each Congress and make any sense out of the legislative process. However, by classifying these bills according to policy types, one can compare different patterns of congressional behavior and better understand the politics of Congress.

Two assumptions underlie the common description of the legislative process found in charts of "how a bill becomes a law." One is that the process is relatively stable and remains pretty much the same for almost all legislation. The other is that policy is the dependent variable, that the reason for describing the process is to explain why the bill came out the way that it did.

If we reverse this formulation and consider policies as independent variables, we uncover new ground for understanding the politics of Congress. This new way of thinking permits us to see that certain types of policies produce corresponding types of congressional politics and that different legislative processes are used for handling different types of policies. Discussions earlier in this chapter and throughout the book have provided evidence of that in the form of the 1985 Gramm-Rudman Act and the 1986 Deficit Reduction Bill, neither of which followed the normal progression found in charts of "how a bill becomes a law." On the other hand, that chart does describe the steps that the same Congress followed in passing tax reform legislation and indeed most bills that became law in the Ninety-ninth Congress. What accounts for these differences in how Congress deals with policies?

A classification scheme that would provide some guidance in answering that question must be one that is based on the perceptions that policymakers themselves have of the policies before them. For it is how lawmakers see issues that determines how they will behave, not how others see them. Political scientist Theodore Lowi has developed a policy classification that does this by ordering policies on the basis of the relative impact that decisionmakers see those policies having on the larger society.

Three types of policies were identified by Lowi—distributive, regulatory, and redistributive. Distributive policies directly affect few people in society, whereas redistributive policies have a broad impact on the entire society. An essential point of the Lowi formulation is that "these areas of policy or government activity constitute real arenas of power. Each arena tends to develop its own characteristic political structure, political process, elites, and group relations."[41]

Samuel Huntington and other scholars have classified foreign and defense policies in a manner similar to Lowi's classification of domestic policies.[42] The three types of foreign and defense policies are structural, strategic, and crisis. Structural policies are decisions about the development, organization, and deployment of resources in support of the nation's defense and foreign policy goals. They are similar to distributive policies on the domestic scene. Strategic policies are the more fundamental decisions about what the nation's defense and foreign policy goals will be and how to achieve them. Strategic policies include decisions about foreign aid and arms sales to particular countries, the mix of weapons and forces in the nation's military, and treaties and executive agreements with other nations. Strategic decisions have to do with the ends or goals of foreign and defense policy, while structural decisions have to do with the means for attaining those goals. Crisis policies are immediate responses to specific military or foreign policy threats and include events such as the 1962 Cuban Missile Crisis and numerous and recent cases of hostage-taking and state-sponsored terrorism.

The politics of the 1980s, an era of budget deficits and talk about the limits of government, has generated a type of policy that is different enough from distributive, regulatory, and redistributive policies to be classified as a separate policy type. To illustrate, the Social Security Amendments of 1983 fit into a category of policies that reduces government deficits by simultaneously raising taxes and cutting benefits. Paul Light studied the legislative history of that bill and concluded: "Long before Reagan's tax cuts, government was facing a serious budget crisis. It was no longer possible to do everything. Congress began to face more and more *dedistributive* policy issues."[43] And a representative who played a key role in the congressional action on Social Security suggested: "We in Congress are very good at giving people relative advantages but incredibly inept at assigning relative disadvantages. In Social Security, we've run out of goodies to pass out, and we have no choice but to ask some part of all the people involved to lower their expectations."[44] Instead of taking from some and giving to others, as redistributive policies do, dedistributive policies, in effect, take from all. The focus of dedistributive policymaking thus becomes one of determining who will be deprived of what, and of the relative deprivations of different groups in society rather than the relative benefits to those groups.

Table 8–1 provides a summary of the major characteristics of each of these policy types and of the nature of political activity associated with each type. You should keep in mind that these different policy types are not distinct and mutually exclusive, but rather points on a continuum reflecting the impact of policies on society. It is not easy to fit all laws passed by Congress into one or another of these categories. Some exhibit characteristics of more than one type. Tax legislation, for instance, is distributive in its granting loopholes and exemptions to certain groups (for example, the transition rules discussed in Chapter 5), regulatory in its providing general rules to be applied to individual decisions (tax rates for different income groups), and redistributive in its underlying principle of a graduated federal income tax. The emergence of dedistributive policies in the 1980s also points to the fact that policies change over time. That was the case with Social Security legislation, and Lowi found it also to be true of trade policies, which were distributive in an earlier part of this century, became more regulatory after World War II, and completely regulatory by the time of the Trade Expansion Act of 1962.

The classification scheme depicted in Table 8–1 should not be regarded as a deterministic one; it does not suggest that something in the inanimate nature of a tax bill causes legislators to behave certain ways. Rather, it is based on a belief that the perceptions of legislators about the potential impact of a proposed policy on society will shape their behavior in regard to that legislation. Representatives' and senators' perceptions about societal impact will vary over time for different policy areas, and different legislators might have quite different perceptions about the impact of a particular bill. But the framework rests on the notion that underlying a variety in perceptions is a tendency for legislators to share perceptions about the potential impact of certain types of legislation. It is this pattern of shared perceptions that forms the basis of the policy classifications.

Conclusion

The congressional budget process and the now regular use of reconciliation under that process have sometimes been credited with forcing an institution that favors distributive policymaking to think in redistributive terms.[45] Along those lines, Congressional Budget Office Director Rudolph Penner has suggested:

> The most important function of the budget process is to constrain—though not always successfully—politicians from simultaneously supporting new programs and opposing higher taxes or higher deficits.[46]

The budget process, in other words, puts lawmaking restrictions on what members can do as representatives. Legislators must now determine who will pay for increasing or even continuing

TABLE 8–1 Policies and Their Politics

Policy Type	Primary Actors	Relationship among Actors	Visibility of Decisions	Most Influential Actors	
				Executive	*Legislative*
Distributive	Congressional subcommittees and committees; executive bureaus, small interest groups	Logrolling (everyone gains)	Low	Bureaus	Subcommittees
Regulatory	Congress: subunits and full chamber; executive agencies; trade associations	Bargaining; compromise	Moderate	Centralized bureaucracy	Whole chamber
Redistributive	President and his appointees; committees and/or Congress; largest interest groups (peak associations); "liberals, conservatives"	Ideological; and class conflict	High	President and centralized bureaucracy	Whole chamber

Dedistributive	Small group of executive & legislative actors	Bargaining	Low	Equal actors	
Structural	Congressional subcommittees and committees; executive bureaus; small bureaus; small interest groups	Logrolling (everyone gains)	Low	Bureaus	Subcommittees
Strategic	Executive agencies; President	Bargaining; compromise	Low until publicized then low to high	President and centralized bureaucracy	Whole chamber
Crisis	President and advisers	Cooperation	Low until publicized then generally high	President	Little congressional influence

Source: Adapted from Randall B. Ripley and Grace A. Franklin, *Congress, the Bureaucracy and Public Policy* (Homewood, Ill.: Dorsey Press, 1987) pp. 22–23.

government programs. The dedistributive policymaking that is becoming common in the 1980s makes matters even more difficult for elected decisionmakers; they must also determine the extent of different groups' losses in a policy that has no winners.

On the other hand, the shift toward redistributive policies and lawmaking has not completely transformed Congress. The value of representation continues to be important to the institution and its members. Keep in mind, too, that legislators do not make policy in isolation or by themselves. They get a lot of help from interest groups and from the executive. A full consideration of congressional policymaking must include those two outside influences on the legislative product. Chapter 9 will provide a look at the role of those outside actors in the different arenas of congressional policymaking.

Endnotes

1. Stephen Gettinger, "Deficit-Reduction Bill's Tortuous Journey Ends," *Congressional Quarterly Weekly Report*, April 5, 1986, p. 751.

2. Anthony Trollope, *The Duke's Children* (1880; reprint, London: Oxford University Press, 1963), p. 199.

3. Senator Boren, quoted in David Rosenbaum, "The Senate Seems to Be Going Along to Get Along," *New York Times*, February 2, 1986, p. E4.

4. Unidentified representative, quoted in John F. Bibby, *Congress Off the Record* (Washington, D.C.: American Enterprise Institute, 1983), p. 19.

5. Reps. David R. Obey (D-WI) and Richard A. Gephardt (D-MO), quoted in Roger H. Davidson, "The Congressional Budget: How Much Change? How Much Reform?" in Thomas Wander, F. Ted Hebert, and Gary W. Copeland, eds., *Congressional Budgeting* (Baltimore: Johns Hopkins, 1984), p. 167. John Ellwood has cited figures that support Obey's and Gephardt's general point: "During the 1960s less than 20 percent of floor votes in the House and the Senate were on money and revenue bills (appropriations, tax bills, debt ceiling resolutions, budget resolutions, and reconciliation bills). By the 1980s, these matters account for about half of the floor votes in the Senate and more than 30 percent of the roll calls in the House." John W. Ellwood, "The Great Exception: The Congressional Budget Process in an Age of Decentralization," in Lawrence C. Dodd and Bruce I. Oppenheimer, eds., *Congress Reconsidered* (Washington, D.C.: Congressional Quarterly Press, 1985), p. 342.

6. Robert Healy, "There's a New Power Sweeping Capitol Hill," *Boston Globe*, May 22, 1981, p. 15.

7. Former Speaker O'Neill, quoted in Dale Tate and Andy Plattner, "House Ratifies Savings Plan in Stunning Reagan Victory," *Congressional Quarterly Weekly Report*, June 27, 1981, p. 1128.

8. Rep. Carl Perkins, quoted in Dale Tate, "Reconciliation Changes Still Face Tough Hill Battles," *Congressional Quarterly Weekly Report*, June 13, 1981, p. 1029.

9. Sen. William Proxmire, quoted in Dale Tate, "Reconciliation's Long-Term Consequences in Question as Reagan Signs Massive Bill," *Congressional Quarterly Weekly Report*, August 15, 1981, p. 1463.

10. Allen Schick, "In Congress Reassembled: Reconciliation and the Legislative Process," *PS*, vol. XIV, no. 4 (Fall, 1981), p. 748.

11. For a description of the budget process of 1981, see Jean Peters, "Reconciliation 1982: What Happened?" *PS*, vol. XIV, no. 4 (Fall, 1981), pp. 732–36.

12. Peter Milius, "Minding Money on the Hill: Is Change Real?" *Washington Post*, January 18, 1976, p. F1.

13. Louis Fisher, "Budget Reform and Impoundment Control," (The Library of Congress, Congressional Research Service, Issue Brief Number IB 74079, updated February 23, 1976), pp. 1–3.

14. George Gross, *The Congressional Budget and Impoundment Control Act of 1974: A General Explanation*, U.S. House of Representatives, Committee on the Budget, October, 1975, p. 2.

15. *Congressional Quarterly Weekly Report*, March 2, 1974, pp. 569–70. For a thorough discussion of the process of impounding funds, see Louis Fisher, *Presidential Spending Power* (Princeton, N.J.: Princeton University Press, 1975), Chapters 7 and 8.

16. *Congressional Quarterly Weekly Report*, September 7, 1974, p. 2418.

17. *Congressional Quarterly Weekly Report*, January 6, 1979, p. 11.

18. Ibid., p. 12.

19. Ellwood, "The Great Exception," p. 328.

20. Edward Cowan, "Battered Budget Act Limps into 1982," *New York Times*, December 31, 1981, p. A10.

21. Schick, "In Congress Reassembled," p. 749.

22. Ellwood, "The Great Exception," p. 331.

23. Sen. Warren Rudman (R-NH), quoted in Martin Tolchin, "Senators Assail Anarchy in New Chamber of Equals," *New York Times*, November 25, 1984, p. 40.

24. Former Rep. Barber Conable (R-NY), quoted in Paul Light, *Artful Work* (New York: Random House, 1985), p. 13.

25. Unidentified representative, quoted in Bibby, *Congress Off the Record*, p. 19.

26. Ibid., p. 50.

27. For more on the 1983 Social Security reforms, see Light's *Artful Work*.

28. John Hoadley, "Easy Riders: Gramm-Rudman-Hollings and the Legislative Fast Track," *PS*, vol XIX, no. 1 (Winter, 1986), p. 31.

29. Charles O. Jones, *An Introduction to the Study of Public Policy* (North Scituate, Mass.: Duxbury Press, 1977); Charles O. Jones, *The United States Congress: People, Place, Policy* (Homewood, Ill.: Dorsey, 1982), pp. 354–78; and David Price, *Who Makes the Laws?* (Cambridge, Mass.: Schenkman, 1972), pp. 4–5.

30. Barbara Sinclair, "Agenda, Policy, and Alignment Change From Coolidge to Reagan," in Dodd and Oppenheimer, *Congress Reconsidered*, p. 312.

31. Norman Ornstein, quoted in Diane Granat, "On Balance, a Year of Taking the Initiative," *Congressional Quarterly Weekly Report*, December 28, 1985, p. 2727.

32. Robert Healy, "Is Reagan's Gamble to Retain the Senate Worth the Time and Effort?" *Boston Globe*, September 5, 1986, p. 19.

33. Steven S. Smith, "New Patterns of Decisionmaking in Congress," John E. Chubb and Paul E. Peterson, eds., *The New Directions in American Politics* (Washington, D.C.: The Brookings Institution, 1985), p. 219.

34. Unidentified representative, quoted in Bibby, *Congress Off the Record*, p. 48.

35. Senator Dole, quoted in Helen Dewar, "Balanced-Budget Move Stalls Despite President's Plea," *Washington Post*, October 5, 1985, p. A6.

36. Alice Rivlin and Kirk O'Donnell, former counsel to the Speaker of the House, quoted in Martin Tolchin, "Pick a Number, Any Politically Powerful Number," *New York Times*, June 5, 1984, p. A24.

37. Herbert Kaufman, quoted in ibid.

38. Rep. Lee Hamilton (D-IN), quoted in ibid.

39. Rep. Dan Lungren, quoted in Nadine Cohodas, "House Panel Breaks Deadlock, Send Immigration Bill to Floor," *Congressional Quarterly Weekly Report*, June 28, 1986, p. 1480.

40. Susan Trausch, "Burning the Midnight Oil," *Boston Globe*, August 11, 1986, p. 2.

41. Theodore Lowi, "American Business, Public Policy, Case Studies, and Political Theory," *World Politics*, vol. 16, no. 4 (July, 1964), pp. 689–690. For a refinement and expansion of Lowi's framework, see Randall B. Ripley and Grace A. Franklin, *Congress, the Bureaucracy, and Public Policy* (Homewood, Ill., 1980), pp. 20–28.

42. Samuel P. Huntington, *The Common Defense* (New York: Columbia University Press, 1961).

43. Light, *Artful Work*, p. 15.

44. Former Rep. Barber Conable (R-NY), quoted in ibid., p. 15.

45. Allen Schick, *Reconciliation and the Congressional Budget Process* (Washington, D.C.: American Enterprise Institute, 1981), p. 34.; and Carl E. Van Horn, "Fear and Loathing on Capitol Hill: The 99th Congress and Economic Policy," *PS*, vol. XIX, no. 1 (Winter, 1986), p. 23.

46. Rudolph G. Penner, "An Appraisal of the Congressional Budget Process," in Allen Schick, *Crisis in the Budget Process* (Washington, D.C.: American Enterprise Institute, 1986), p. 67.

9

Representation
and Lawmaking
Interests and Presidents

Sen. Bill Bradley (D-NJ), a longtime advocate of tax reform and one of the key players in that area in Congress, once attributed his interest in tax policy to something that happened when he was a player of a different sort. For ten years, Bradley had played forward for the New York Knicks. One day he learned that the Knick's were gaining tax benefits by listing him as a depreciable asset. "I found it surprising," Bradley said. "Now I find it humorous. They could write me off like a piece of equipment." Then, referring to the 1986 tax bill in conference committee at the time, the senator pointed out that "under tax reform, I think they still could do that."[1] A different economic matter came to the attention of all senators in the Ninety-ninth Congress (1985–1986) through a letter to Senate Majority Leader Robert Dole from Deputy Treasury Secretary Richard Darman. In an effort to get quick congressional action to raise the debt ceiling, Darman wrote:

> As of this morning, we estimated that cash balances may be zero or negative tomorrow and will certainly be negative by Wednesday.
>
> When we formally determine that the next day's balance is to be negative, we will need to notify the Federal Reserve. It is my

understanding that, upon such notification, the Federal Reserve will then have to notify the banking system not to honor any government checks or electronic fund transfers.

Accordingly, all those with federal payment claims—whether Social Security recipients or defense contractors or holders of government securities with interest payments due—would then be unable to have those claims honored.[2]

Another issue before Congress at the same time was one that legislators often treated in a lighter vein than they could the need for raising the debt ceiling to $2.078 trillion. Both the House and the Senate passed legislation in the Ninety-ninth Congress to extend daylight saving time. The extension bill had the strong support of the Barbecue Industry Association (which predicted an increase of $56 million annually in charcoal sales), the National Golf Foundation (which said the bill would add almost $35 million and $12 million respectively to the sale of golf balls and golf clubs), and the American Amateur Baseball Congress (which said the number of games played would increase by 15 percent). The RP Foundation, speaking in behalf of the 400,000 sufferers of retinitis pigmentosa, a disease that causes night blindness, also lobbied hard for the daylight saving extension. A spokesperson for the American Association of Nurserymen said that passage of the bill would mean that "people will step right back into the spring and buy more plants, trees, and shrubs." The executive director of an organization representing fast-food establishments reported a study showing that "while an extra hour of darkness would not affect breakfast sales, an extra hour of daylight in the evening would increase sales $800 a week per store." But the proposal also had opponents. One was the American Farm Bureau Federation, which issued this statement on the effect of the extension of farmers:

They'll lose some time waiting for the dew to clear, waiting for the sun to come up. Then they'll lose out on the other end because they have to work until the sun goes down. It cuts out their normal church and social activities. It may sound trivial, but that's the stuff of basic rural life.[3]

Whenever members of Congress consider legislation, whether it has to do with tax reform, the debt ceiling, or daylight saving time, the representative nature of the institution insures that they will not make that decision in isolation or alone. Legislators bring to those decisions their own experiences off of Capitol Hill, and they hear from those who live and work beyond the marble corridors of Congress. And even though the facetious description of Washington, D.C. as a city of six hundred thousand people bordered on four sides by reality might at times seem accurate, representatives and senators constantly seek ways of connecting what they do in Washington to life beyond those borders. "Congress does not act in a vacuum," congressional scholar Phillip Brenner has written. "It is very much a part of the world around it." And further, says Brenner:

> The world to which the Congress relates is a messy place. It is neither static nor orderly, and that presents members of Congress with a daily problem. The problem is to figure out how to make some order of the confusion, how to get a handle on the constant changes so that they can be directed toward ends that the members of Congress seek.[4]

The politics of Congress are linked to the outside world in many ways. Earlier chapters have discussed the part that elections and political parties play in the linkage process. The information provided by staff and support agencies is directed at a similar goal of fitting congressional action to the broad social, economic, and technological context. In this chapter, we will look at two of the more important outside forces affecting congressional behavior—interests groups and the executive. The classification of policies found in Chapter 8 provides a useful organizational focus for looking at the role of interests and the executive in the congressional policymaking process. Confronted with some studies that find interest groups and lobbyists to have a great deal of influence over legislative policies and other studies that suggest they play only a minimal role, we can try to answer the question: Who is right? The answer might be that they all are. Some types of policies are decided in a way that gives special interest groups a lot of influence in determining the eventual outcome, while others are decided in a manner that minimizes their influence. Similarly, we might find that the executive has a great deal of influence in some areas of congressional policymaking, while in others the executive plays a minor role.

Interest Representation in Congress

The tax benefits that a professional basketball team can gain by depreciating star players like Bill Bradley are just one of many spelled out in federal tax law. Senator Bradley and his colleagues on the 1986 conference committee who worked on rewriting that law devoted a great deal of time to the 130 depreciation schedules that Congress would establish in the new legislation. In fact, Senate and House disagreement on depreciation accounted for most of the more than $20 billion difference in revenue under the two chambers' bills. Should railroad cars be depreciated over thirteen years, as the House bill said, or the five years provided in the Senate bill? What about the fifteen separate depreciation schedules affecting the telephone industry? One point of dispute in conference, what Capitol Hill staffers dubbed a "black and white issue," arose over the depreciation schedule for tuxedos. House and Senate conferees debated whether the useful life of a tuxedo was three years or five, and tuxedo manufacturing interests were upset when the head of the Senate Finance Committee advocated a nine-year depreciation schedule. "We understand he feels that way because he has a 17-year-old tuxedo in his closet and thinks they last long," an industry spokesperson suggested.[5] Major corporations in oil, railroads, timber, and other industries had a great deal at stake in these conference committee decisions. For example, an executive from one railroad, Union Pacific, said that a special depreciation schedule in effect from 1981 to 1985 had permitted the company to save $1 billion over that period. Those representing the paper industry claimed the industry could lose $6 billion under the timber-related depreciation rates in the House bill.[6] Those are some of the reasons why the hall outside the conference committee meeting room in which legislators worked on the tax bill was filled with lobbyists and why, in the words of one lobbyist, "If you're not up here when they're making decisions, you're a dead duck."[7]

In April 1790, when the First Congress was barely a year old, a group of Philadelphia mustard manufacturers petitioned Congress to impose "an additional duty on imported mustard." About the same time, domestic manufacturers of cotton cloth, rope, and paint sought similar protection from foreign competition. A wide range of groups seeking special legislation petitioned Congress in its early years:

Quakers demanding an end to slavery; German immigrants wanting government documents printed in their own language; Revolutionary War veterans requesting compensation for their wounds; printers looking for government contracts; an inventor seeking a patent for a new way to make candles out of whale oil; relatives of seamen held hostage by Barbary pirates asking for ransom money.[8]

Just as the representation of interests in Congress is something that has been around from the institution's beginnings, so too has the debate over the effects of that representation on congressional policymaking. On one side of that debate are those who would agree with a recent assessment that Congress follows a "Golden Rule of Politics": whoever has the gold rules.[9] The view that Congress is dominated by special interests is one that has a rich tradition: In his 1906 book, *Treason of the Senate*, David Graham Phillips accused twenty-one senators of serving the special interests of large corporations in return for money and favors; about seventy years later, an agent for the government of South Korea reported distributing almost $1 million to buy foreign aid votes from thirty representatives; and a more recent study by Common Cause concluded that "special interest money pouring into political campaigns is contributing to legislative paralysis and interest group domination of Congress."[10] Mark Green's analysis in *Who Runs Congress* provides a contemporary example of this view:

In its broadest sense "lobbying" is anything but sinister. A lobbyist is, by definition, anyone who works to influence decisions by public officials—including a concerned citizen who writes his congressman urging a vote for stricter air pollution laws. This right to "petition the Government for a redress of grievances" is firmly grounded in the Constitution's First Amendment.

But the way the armies of special-interest agents have dominated this process has made "lobbyist" synonymous with corruption and improper influence.[11]

That view of interest representation in Congress is one that is often found in current discussions of political action committees (PACs), whose role in funding congressional campaigns was analyzed in Chapter 3. While not everyone shares that view, of course, enough people do that a professional lobbyist once admitted: "When I say I'm a lobbyist, it's about the same as saying I'm a pimp."[12]

What one person sees as influence peddling is democratic representation to another. There are strong disagreements among members of Congress and the general public about the effects of lobbying on Congress. What is not subject to dispute, however, is the presence of a large and growing force of lobbyists on Capitol Hill. There were more than 9,000 active lobbyists registered with the House of Representatives in the first quarter of 1986, and they reported spending almost $14 million to influence Congress during that period—about three times the number of lobbyists and levels of spending that were reported ten years earlier.[13] The presence of highly paid lobbyists in Congress has become a part of Capitol Hill folklore and its jargon. When the walls outside the Senate Finance Committee meeting room had to be repainted after a particularly long session, Senator Dole laid the blame on the expensive soft leather loafers favored by many lobbyists. The painters, said Dole, had to be called in to clean up the scuff marks on the walls left by all those milling lobbyists "with their Guccis." The term, "Gucci," quickly became Capitol Hill short-hand for any of the prosperous, well-heeled lobbyists found on the Hill. Senators and representatives on the 1986 tax reform conference complained about having to run a "Gucci gauntlet" to get to meetings; a heavily lobbied committee session would be described as "wall-to-wall Guccis"; and any popular gathering place for lobbyists would soon become known as "Gucci Gulch." If a lobbyist seemed to be asking for the impossible, legislators and their staffs might suggest that the lobbyist "doesn't have a Gucci to stand on."[14]

A representative has pointed out that even though Washington lobbyists receive the most attention, "the most effective lobbyists are the ones back home." The legislator pointed to the example of a recently defeated hospital cost containment bill, which

> got beat not by anybody here in Washington lobbying heavily. It got beat by people who were on the boards of directors of various community hospitals back home who personally wrote you a letter or called you on the phone or stopped by to see you.[15]

This form of direct mail and grass-roots lobbying has developed into one of Washington's most successful growth industries over the last decade. "The only lobbyists that I'll let into my office are those who come in with constituents," said Massachusetts Rep. Gerry Studds. "But that's the approach that more and more of them are using." Rep. Brian Donnelly (D-MA) saw the same trend:

> It's part of a lobbyist's handbook now—make the case as local as possible. The problem we face sometime is identifying who is really behind the blitz of local interest that we get deluged by.[16]

Whether one regards a grass-roots campaign as manipulation or the genuine expression of public opinion depends on whether one agrees with the legislative goals of a particular lobbying effort. But no one denies that grass-roots lobbying has an effect. For as one of the most successful practitioners of this technique has suggested:

> If an official tells you he got 40,000 pieces of mail from his district on a particular issue and he's going to ignore them, you know one of two things. He's lying to you, or he's not going to be around very long.[17]

The effectiveness of grass-roots lobbying stems from its constituency base, which makes it a form of representation. Interest representation and lobbying can also serve to support the lawmaking activities of Congress. This connection between lobbying and the functions of representation and lawmaking helps to explain the favorable view of lobbying that is often found among members of Congress and in the scholarly literature on the subject. In contrast to the muckracking descriptions of payoffs and the popular notion of legislators giving in to pressure, a number of studies portray a network of accommodation and mutual assistance between lobbyists and legislators.[18]

> According to one representative: What congressmen appreciate in a lobbyist, is knowing he's a professional and will be back— that he values your good will and won't push you in the wrong direction, that he gives you information you can rely on, that he won't get you in the funny papers.[19]

The positive role of lobbyists in congressional policymaking is also evident in the comments of two other members:[20]

A professional lobbyist becomes part of the woodwork here. He becomes a source of information. A lot of people talk about "the invidious special interests," but we shouldn't engage in legislation without knowing who's affected by it, and usually the people who are affected by it are the best sources of information.

There are a few guys up here who vote a certain way because they're bought, but most of us don't like to deal with people who have only a short range interest in us.

Congressmen, almost by definition, have to be generalists, but we also have to deal with very technical issues requiring the skills of specialists. We often have to turn to lobbyists for information. The trick, though, is to use lobbyists rather than have the lobbyists use you—and to get the perspective of lobbyists who differ with each other.

The supportive nature of lobbying that provides lawmakers with information is also reflected in lobbying that is directed toward reinforcing the opinions of legislators who are already in basic agreement with the group position. Instead of attempting to convert legislators, lobbyists are often trying to hold supporters in line or to activate those who agree with the group position but who might not vote unless convinced of the importance of that vote. This focus on sympathetic legislators can be a result of lobbyists' belief that most votes on a particular bill have been decided long before the actual vote, and that the outcome will depend more on mobilizing supporters than it will on converting opponents.

Another reason for the generally benign descriptions of interest representation and lobbying so often found on Capitol Hill has to do with the system of cue networks discussed in earlier chapters. You will recall that constituents, lobbyists, staff, and party leaders all serve as cue sources for legislators on different issues. But the most consistent source of cues for legislative voting is other senators and representatives. Lobbyists sometimes use congressional staff as a way of tapping into that cue network, an indirect approach that one observer has described this way:

The key point of contact is usually between a highly specialized lobbyist and the specialized staff people of a standing committee. Intimate friendships spring up there—it's the rivet point.[21]

A Senate staff member describes how lobbyists can also use members' personal staff as a way of getting information into the internal cue network:

> *My boss demands a speech and a statement for the Congressional Record for every bill we introduce or cosponsor—and we have a lot of bills. I just can't do it all myself. The better lobbyists, when they have a proposal they are pushing, bring it to me along with a couple of speeches, a Record insert, and a fact sheet. They know their clout is tripled that way.*[22]

Because legislators often use staff to assist them with representation, a point that was discussed in Chapter 7, the lawmaking support that lobbyists provide can be valuable. A professional lobbyist comments: "The conventional wisdom today is that members are overstaffed. What so many people overlook is that members of Congress have become ombudsmen—they spend most of their time taking care of their constituents' problems with the government—so it becomes difficult to do good legislative work. So to an extent we become an extension of the staff."[23]

The importance of the internal cue network in Congress is reflected in the fact that the most effective lobbyists are senators and representatives themselves. Inside lobbying by legislators is generally viewed as a form of legitimate representation by members of Congress. Whether a legislator's ties to a particular group stem from his or her own occupational background or whether the group is an important part of his or her constituency, the legislator is expected to try to convince colleagues to support the group's legislative goals. "Lobbying by other congressmen is the most difficult for me to resist," is the way one legislator put it.[24] Years of covering Congress for the *Washington Post* led T. R. Reid to conclude that

> *despite all the high-powered lobbyists, the constituent mail, and the briefs, brochures, and broadsides that might engulf Capitol Hill over a particularly controversial issue, the most important influence on an undecided Senator is usually the personal appeal of another Senator.*[25]

A representative has described a similar pattern of internal influence in the House of Representatives:

> Congressmen tend to have a high regard for one another, and if
> someone had a pet bill, you tend to make efforts to accommo-
> date him if it is at all possible. When Congressman ―――――
> had his cranberry bill, everybody said, "let's do something for
> good old Nick," and so they passed the bill. It wasn't a very
> good bill and probably shouldn't have passed; but the "good
> old Nick" slogan was enough to do it. No lobby could have
> pushed that bill through. It was just a personal hand for a
> member.[26]

The members' caucuses that were discussed in Chapter 7 are
institutionalized forms of legislator-to-legislator lobbying in the
modern Congress. Congressional committees also serve to structure internal lobbying. The nature of congressional bargaining
and the norms of reciprocity and specialization make committee
members sensitive to the interests being advanced by their fellow
representatives and senators. The debate and decisions on transition rules and depreciation schedules in the 1986 tax reform bill
illustrate the general pattern described by tax policy specialist,
Stanley Surrey:

> The desire—sometimes the need—of a congressman to be use-
> ful often places a congressman who sits on one of the tax com-
> mittees, the House Committee on Ways and Means or the Sen-
> ate Committee on Finance, in a difficult position. A fellow
> congressman who sits on the Public Works Committee, for ex-
> ample, can respond to constituency pressure by approving the
> project involved; a member of the Appropriations Committee
> can respond by a favorable vote on a specific appropriation.
> But a congressman on a tax committee can respond only by
> pushing through a special tax provision.

> His legislative stock in trade, so to speak, is special tax treat-
> ment. This difficulty is especially acute in the case of those
> congressmen who come to sit on a tax committee only after
> they have been members of other committees and have become
> so accustomed to using their committee powers in helpful ways
> that the habit persists.[27]

Legislative bargaining is predicated on the ability of committee
members to deliver tangible benefits, an aspect of policymaking
on the 1986 tax bill that Ways and Means Chairman Dan Rostenkowski referred to as "moving the dollars around in the special
interest vineyards."[28] And while the internal nature of much in-

terest representation makes it seem to be more a matter of legislative politics than lobbying by interest groups, the results in terms of policy payoffs for particular groups are much the same.

Organized interests are able to get tangible benefits written into legislation, not by bribing legislators, but rather by using the advantages that the politics of Congress give them. By providing information that reinforces the position of legislative supporters, by relying on inside lobbyists, by invoking legislative norms and political values that strengthen their position, and by working in conjunction with other political elites for shared benefits, these groups are able to benefit from policies coming out of Congress.

As even a brief review of interest representation makes clear, there is disagreement as to the effects of lobbying on legislators' behavior and the content of legislative policies. Sometimes those who emphasize the great influence of pressure groups seem to be right. At other times those who downplay their importance seem more nearly correct. A full appreciation of the relative nature of interest representation in Congress must begin with a point made in Chapter 8—Different types of policies are handled in different ways by Congress. The classification of policy types shown in Table 8–1 provides a structure for this consideration of interest representation in Congress. By employing this framework, we can resolve some of the seeming contradictions about the importance of lobbyists in Congress or at least more fully understand them.

DISTRIBUTIVE AND STRUCTURAL POLICYMAKING

Distributive domestic policies and structural military and foreign policies involve the awarding of material benefits to some narrow segment of the general population. Awarding federal funds for the development of a harbor or building a bridge, granting special tax benefits for certain industries or occupations, keeping price supports at a certain level for particular crops, or awarding defense contracts or military bases to a particular congressional district are all examples of these types of policies. They are generally characterized by the government's giving something to somebody. The politics of distributive and structural policies focus more on "Who gets what?" than on "Who pays?"

Accounts of lobbying in Congress that stress the influence of groups on policy outcomes most often deal with distributive issues. An example of this can be seen in *Who Runs Congress?*, where Mark Green and his associates describe the oil lobby, the military armaments lobby, the tobacco lobby, the automobile lobby, and the National Rifle Association among others. Their picture of lobbying is perhaps best illustrated in this characterization of the oil lobby:

> *When fully mobilized, oil can send into action lawyers from the most respectable law firms, public relations consultants, numerous ex-government officials, newsmen who serve as "advisors," company executives, corporate legal departments, government officials in several of the executive departments, trade association representatives, and—though only a small fraction of the total—men who actually register as lobbyists.*

> *Whenever legislation affecting oil is on the docket, the oilers can easily afford to have a corporate vice-president or similarly impressive official assigned to persuade every member of every relevant committee. If reinforcements should be needed, the industry can call on a vast reserve of sales agents, filling station operators, and other small businessmen. In other words, they are different from you and me.[29]*

Common Cause, a well-known national public interest group, provided a similar description of lobbying in a pamphlet entitled, *How Money Talks in Congress.* Here is how that group described the lobbying on a cargo preference bill (which would have required that 30 percent, rather than 4 percent, of all oil imported to the United States be carried in U.S. flagships):

> *The lobbying campaign conducted by the maritime interests for their legislation was massive. A million dollar public relations/ advertising effort was undertaken. It was financed primarily by maritime companies. . . .*

> *The lobbying campaign included television commercials, full page ads in major newspapers, and efforts to stimulate grassroots lobbying. In addition, the stage had been set for victory by the more than $1 million in maritime contributions made to 1976 congressional candidates.[30]*

In this particular instance, the intense lobbying effort was not successful: The House of Representatives defeated the cargo preference bill. The point here is not whether such lobbying is always successful but rather that these types of characterizations of intense lobbying efforts generally are associated with policies that affect particular economic interests, be they the oil industry and tax provisions, the maritime industry and unions and a cargo preference bill, the American Medical Association and a hospital cost containment bill, or trial lawyers and insurance companies and no-fault automobile insurance legislation.

Other examples of lobbyists directly influencing legislators tend to come from similarly distributive policy fields. One is the case of a former senator from Maryland who was found guilty of accepting an unlawful gratuity from a Washington lobbyist to influence his vote on postal rate legislation. The lobbyist represented a Chicago mail business that would have had to pay $1 million a year for every one-penny increase in third class postal rates. During the trial the senator's former chief assistant described his legislative office as

> one where lobbyists wrote speeches, where a Federal job was purchased for cash, where money flowed into his and the Senator's pockets and where the Senator's signature was so widely copied by staff members that they even signed it to (the Senator's) final divorce decree.[31]

Another Senate staff member's description of decision making on tax policy presents a similar picture: "It's like there's a bushel basket in the middle of the table. Everybody is trying to throw as many of their things into the barrel as they can."[32]

The paradoxical nature of interest representation in this type of policymaking is evident in descriptions that emphasize the influence of lobbyists on legislation and those offered by legislators who claim that they are not subjected to much pressure to vote one way or another. The nature of interest group activity in distributive policymaking is such that the close link between concerned economic interests and members of relevant committees or subcommittees and the narrow scope of the issue mean only a limited number of lawmakers need be directly involved. The close links support conclusions about lobbyists' influence and the narrow scope helps to account for the low visibility of lobbying activity. Interest representation in this policy arena is characterized by a large number of small, intensely organized interests based on narrow economic grounds. These groups pursue their interests in a low-conflict political process that stresses the norm of mutual noninterference. Policy coalitions will be made up of unlike interests brought together through a logrolling process; and the primary focus is on the subcommittee or committee that has jurisdiction over that policy area.

REGULATORY POLICYMAKING

Those who study Congress often use the distributive model of lobbying in their research. As Lewis Anthony Dexter notes, " 'pressure' and 'pressure politics' are regarded by most 'sophisticated' people today as 'explaining' a great deal that happens."[33] There is the expectation that affected interests will marshal their forces to influence legislators directly on the matter and that the level of lobbying activity will be related to the economic stakes those interests have in the issue. Raymond Bauer, Ithiel de Sola Pool, and Lewis Anthony Dexter, authors of a prize-winning book on trade policy, point out that they "started with the notion that public officials would see themselves as under almost constant pressure from those who have a stake in the decisions they make."[34]

Sometimes these scholars find much less lobbying (in the distributive sense) than they expected. This happened with the study of trade policy and with a study of the 1970 Political Broadcast Act limiting campaign spending. In the latter, the authors observed:

> Probably the most striking aspect of pressure group activity in this case was the lack of it. Considering the importance of the measure and the potential impact of the various versions of the bill upon the broadcasting industry, it is somewhat surprising that more intense lobbying did not occur.[35]

Lowi suggests that the reason Bauer, Pool, and Dexter found little pressure group activity in their study of postwar trade policies is because trade policy, which had long been regarded as distributive policy, was becoming *regulatory*. Instead of being conceived as domestic policy that was designed to serve the interests of a vast array of unrelated native industries, trade policy came to be regarded as an instrument of foreign policy that required cohesion and the application of a general rule to all trade decisions.

In regulatory policymaking, interest groups are based on shared attitudes rather than just narrow economic interests. Coalitions of groups are formed through a bargaining process of conflict and compromise over goals rather than a logrolling process that produces mutual noninterference in each group's seeking its own goals. These coalitions change with different issues, but all groups in a coalition seek to build a majority on the issue by compromising with other groups in the coalition. Lastly, these groups focus their activity on the whole chamber and not just the concerned committees.

Some examples of regulatory policies are trade policies enacted since the 1960s, federal aid to education, campaign finance regulations, and Medicare. By drawing on case studies dealing with these types of policies, we can provide some general observations about the nature of pressure group activity in regulatory policymaking.

One characteristic of interest group activity in the regulatory arena seems to be that groups seek broad social goals rather than just their own economic gain. This can be seen in the case of Medicare, which Congress passed in 1965. The battle over Medicare produced coalitions of interest groups that were concerned with more than just the immediate del··ery of benefits from the government. On one side was a coalition made up of the AFL–CIO, the National Council of Senior Citizens, and members of the Democratic political coalition and administration. The coalition of opposition included the American Medical Association (which reported spending several millions of dollars), the American Dental Association, the American Hospital Association, and the American Nursing Homes Association. The fact that Medicare was passed supports the general conclusion of one study that "labor has been stymied on many strict labor issues, where the unions find themselves without allies, but has had some striking successes as part of coalitions working on broader social issues."[36] The essence of these interest group coalitions that form around regulatory policies seems to be the fact that they are based on a shared attitude toward some broad policy issue and not just collections of people who agree to stay out of each other's affairs.

When we consider regulatory policies and lobbying, another characteristic comes to mind that might help to explain the fact that there is seldom a feeling among members of Congress that they are being pressured to vote in a particular way. That is, that coalitions of interests on regulatory policies tend to form long before a bill on the issue is subject to vote. A case study of the Elementary and Secondary Education Act of 1965 reports "the private groups that had represented the varieties of opinion on federal aid legislation began their realignment a full year before the Eighty-ninth Congress convened."[37] Similarly, labor group activity in behalf of Medicare began nine years before the legislation was passed.

This early formation of coalitions on regulatory policies is related to the need to develop compromise positions among members of the coalition and to the fact that these interest groups must deal with bills when they reach the chamber floor and not just in their committee or subcommittee stage. Reaching a compromise position among different elements in a coalition obviously takes longer than mobilizing interests with the same economic base. There is bound to be some disagreement about political attitudes on broad policy, while all members of the same economic interest group can readily agree on their shared interests. Effective lobbying on regulatory policies also involves the mobilization of public opinion and the building of a broader base of support than does lobbying for distributive issues.[38] Both processes take more time than those associated with distributive policies, where interest groups need only make sure that they have the standing commitment of subcommittee and committee decisionmakers.

REDISTRIBUTIVE AND DEDISTRIBUTIVE POLICYMAKING

Unlike the other policies just discussed, redistributive and dedistributive policies occur less often and are put forth to meet some kind of crisis. The atypical nature of policymaking in this area is reflected in Paul Light's description of the Social Security Amendments of 1983: "This was no longer an issue for the normal legislative process." And at the end of his extensive case study of the bill, Light concluded that "most of the crucial decisions came *outside* the normal process."[39] Redistributive and dedistributive policies always involve a crisis of some sort— widespread unemployment and economic stagnation, patterns of racial discrimination, extensive poverty in a seemingly wealthy society, or the possibility of a bankrupt Social Security system.

Briefly, we can say this about legislative politics surrounding redistributive and dedistributive policies: The group conflict involves large coalitions made up of peak associations (such as the National Association of Manufacturers, the Chamber of Commerce, the AFL-CIO) that share a broad consensus on goals to be achieved; both sides of the conflict advance ideological, rather than self-interest, arguments; much of the discussion revolves around the possible long-term effects of the proposed policies; and the president generally plays an active role in the legislative process.

The scope of the coalitions of interests is illustrated by the number of liberal and labor groups that made up the "Lib-Lab Lobby," which was instrumental in the passage of one of the major redistributive policies of this century, the Employment Act of 1946. The most active lobbyists for the bill were the Union for Democratic Action, the CIO Political Action Committee, the American Federation of Labor, and an ad hoc collection of interests known as the Continuations Group. A simple listing of the organizations represented in this Continuations Group shows the breadth of this coalition. Included were—the American Federation of Labor; Americans United for World Organization; the Brotherhood of Maintenance of Way Employees; the Brotherhood of Railway Trainmen; Business of America, Inc.; the Congress of Industrial Organizations; the Council for Social Action of the Congregational Christian Churches; the Independent Citizens Committee of the Arts, Sciences, and Professions; the National Association for the Advancement of Colored People; the Young Women's Christian Association; the National Catholic Welfare Conference; the National Conference of Jewish Women; the National Farmers Union; the National Women's Trade Union League of America; the Railway Labor Executive Association; the Union for Democratic Action; and the National League of Women Shoppers. In addition, support for the bill came from a variety of other groups such as university professors; religious, racial, and educational groups; veterans; welfare workers; the National Lawyers Guild; and independent businessmen. Opposition to the bill also drew on a broad coalition of interests including the National Association of Manufacturers, Chambers of Commerce, the Committee for Constitutional Government, and the American Farm Bureau Federation.[40]

Pressure group activity for the 1964 Civil Rights Act, the antipoverty programs of the Economic Opportunity Act of 1964, and the Social Security Amendments of 1983 displayed a pattern similar to that of the Employment Act. The most active lobby for civil rights legislation was the Leadership Conference on Civil Rights, which was a broad coalition of labor, liberal, race, and church groups. By 1963, a total of seventy-nine organizations were represented in the Leadership Conference. The House subcommittee hearings on the Economic Opportunity Act of 1964 brought out a similarly broad coalition of groups, described in one study as "an impressive range of civic, welfare, and religious groups." "AFL-CIO President George Meany and the National Urban League's executive director, Whitney Young, Jr., led off, followed by representatives of such groups as the National Council of Churches, the National Catholic Welfare Council, the National Education Association, the American Public Welfare Association, the National Farmers Union, the National Grange, the American Friends Service Committee, and the General Federation of Women's Clubs."[41] In 1983, much of the lobbying activity on the social security bill was carried on by what Paul Light has described as "temporary coalitions of organizations," which "come together on a specific issue, fall apart after victory or defeat, and come back together the next time the issue arises." Light describes the advantages of these coalitions:

> In this way, single-issue groups can survive as organizations while generating much greater influence than they could ever build on their own. Mid-sized organizations such as the National Council of Senior Citizens and the National Federation of Independent Business can also benefit. By joining with other groups, they supplement their lobbying strength, improve their reputations in the Washington community, and compete against even larger groups.[42]

The discussion in the preceding sections showed that pressure group activity for regulatory policies differed from that of distributive policies. With distributive issues, outside interests trying to influence Congress generally represent a single economic interest or industry that is seeking only to maximize the benefits it receives from government. There is little concern for what others are doing. Any coalitions that do form are based on an agreement not to interfere with each other's interests. Regulatory policies, however, saw some broadening of group goals and a tendency for groups to share some common social policy, to compromise their differences, and to jointly seek legislative action. The group activity in redistributive and dedistributive policymaking is a continuation of this expansion of the scope of the conflict and the breadth of the coalitions involved.

Arguments advanced on both sides of a redistributive or dedistributive issue are much broader and more ideological than those put forward in debates over distributive policies ("this is in the interest of cotton growers, the construction industry, etc.") or regulatory policies ("this is in the interest of certain broad segments of the population such as school children or the elderly"). The participants in redistributive and dedistributive policymaking invoke broad values such as free enterprise, the right to work, and political freedom. In opposing the Employment Act, for example, the Committee for Constitutional Government said that the bill might "turn America permanently from constitutional private enterprise toward a system of collective statism," and the National Association of Manufacturers talked about "state socialism" in their literature against the bill.[43] In a similar vein, debate on the civil rights bill often centered on the question of the freedom of elections and debate on Social Security reform raised questions of whether the program should be a voluntary pension program rather than one that is mandated by the government.

SUMMARY

At the beginning of this section on interest representation in Congress, we looked at some different and often contradictory statements about interest groups and congressional policymaking. They ranged from descriptions of benign lobbyists helping the members of Congress do a better job, to conspiratorial rumblings about boodlers, bagmen, and sellouts to the highest bidder. By recognizing that different types of policies are handled in different ways, we have perhaps made a small step toward understanding the contradictory reports about lobbyists and legislators. Organized interest groups certainly do have an influence on congressional policymaking, but the character and effectiveness of that influence will vary with the type of policy that is before Congress.

Lawmaking and the Executive Branch

The constitutional principles of separation of powers and checks and balances guarantee a rivalry between presidents and Congresses to match any found in college or professional sports. The way in which the Constitution grants and divides legislative and executive powers creates, in effect, "an invitation to struggle."[44] And just as it is in any sporting event, the question most often raised is "Who's winning?" or "Who won?" After reviewing the relationship with Congress of recent presidents, for example, Mark Green concludes:

> It is misleading to discuss the legislative and executive branches so as to suggest that an equal struggle is on between two sides, and that whichever side is stronger on an issue will prevail.

> A battle does go on—and Congress has indeed recently won several important skirmishes—but the field of play exists far from the executive goal line.

> No matter how hard the Congress may struggle on one issue, it is frequently overwhelmed by the vastly greater forces and focus of the presidency.[45]

That description of the president's winning the battle with Congress appeared during the Reagan administration, and before that administration's Iran-contra activities had been revealed, but the same words were used by Green in earlier editions of the book published during the Nixon, Ford, and Carter presidencies. The long history of conflicts between presidents and Congress, a "Battle of the Potomac," that has raged since the earliest presidencies, suggests that the struggle is one that is inherent to the two institutions.

Writing before the Constitution was adopted, James Madison warned:

> The legislative department is everywhere extending the sphere of its activity, and drawing all power into its impetuous vortex, [and that] In republican government the legislative authority necessarily predominates.[46]

Thomas Jefferson expressed a similar concern about congressional dominance when he wrote:

> The tyranny of the legislature is really the danger most to be feared and will continue to be so for so many years to come. The tyranny of the executive power will come in its turn, but at a more distant period.[47]

Particular actions by strong presidents inevitably provoke suggestions that Jefferson's "more distant period" has arrived. To illustrate, President Reagan's insistence in his first year in office that Congress pass his budget without change or delay, led one House veteran to characterize the president's action as "incipient tyranny." "A popular President," he warned his colleagues, "is attempting to tyrannize a whole Congress, a whole people."[48]

Answers to the question of who is winning the struggle between the president and Congress can lead to comparisons of the influence over Congress exercised by different presidents. The presidencies of Jimmy Carter and Ronald Reagan provide such a contrast. Carter's reluctance to lobby members of Congress led his own press secretary to remark that Carter "went all over the country for two years asking everybody he saw to vote for him for president, but he doesn't like to call up a Congressman and ask for his support on a bill."[49] President Reagan, on the other hand, issued a standing order to his legislative assistants: "Tell me who you want me to call and I'll do it," a contrast that led some House members to comment that they had seen more of Reagan in four months than they had of Carter in four years.[50] The later years of the Carter administration saw an improvement in the president's lobbying effort and influence in Congress, and the second term of the Reagan administration led to discussions of diminishing presidential influence, but the contrast between the two presidents as legislative leaders continues to be sharp.

The problem of ascertaining executive impact on congressional policymaking is made even more difficult by the fact that we hear conflicting reports within the same administration and the same time period. When personal lobbying by the president turned around an earlier House vote on the issue of tax reform in December 1985, Steven Pressman of *Congressional Quarterly* wrote that "Reagan once again demonstrated the almost mystical powers of political persuasion that have been his hallmark as president."[51] Yet an assessment of the 1985 session by *Congressional Quarterly's* Diane Granat, which appeared one week later, suggested: "Congress seized the legislative initiative from the White House in 1985 and dominated the Capitol Hill agenda to a degree unmatched since President Reagan took office almost five years ago." "Congress called the shots in 1985," Granat said, and "that was in stark contrast to the opening year of Reagan's first term, when he clearly ran the show."[52] A column that same week by Washington correspondent David Nyhan echoed Granat's assessment in even stronger terms:

> Power has passed from President Reagan's hands to Congress in the last month of his fifth year in office.
>
> The Gipper's popularity waxed as his influence over Capitol Hill waned. We didn't realize it at the time, but congressional dominance over the Reagan second-term agenda began when he was forced to impose economic sanctions against South Africa. Since then, every important legislative initiative has been pressed on a defensive, yielding president by a resurgent Congress. The Great Communicator became the Great Re-Actor.[53]

Assessments of executive influence on legislation show a similarity to assessments of interest representation presented earlier in this chapter. Some observers, looking at particular instances, find that the president and the executive bureaucracy wield great power. Others, focusing on different issues or different periods of time, find that the impact of these outside actors on legislation is not very great. We hear warnings about the president becoming an absolute monarch who can completely ignore Congress and make policies by executive fiat, about an emerging dictatorship of the bureaucrats that would relegate both the president and Congress to minor roles in the policymaking process, and about a powerful but unresponsive Congress that fails to tailor policies to meet pressing social needs and prevents the president from doing so.

Discussions of presidential power relative to Congress are more valuable when a distinction is made among different types of policies. We find, for instance, that people who stress the president's growing dominance of the policy process often point to foreign policy or strategic defense issues to support their assertions. The use of executive agreements rather than treaties and the minor congressional role in making decisions about the war in Vietnam are excellent cases to support the suggestion that Congress has little say in the policy process. "The United States has one President, but it has two presidencies," says Aaron Wildavsky.

> One presidency is for domestic affairs, and the other is concerned with defense and foreign policy. Since World War II, Presidents have had much greater success in controlling the

nation's defense and foreign policies than in dominating its domestic policies.[54]

More recent studies of the same subject indicate that institutional, legislative, and public opinion changes during the post-Vietnam era have increased the congressional role in foreign policymaking. As a result, the domestic-foreign distinction of Wildavsky is less clear now than it was in the period covered in his study.[55] Differences between structural and strategic defense policies also help to explain some of the other conclusions about the relative influence of Congress and the president. As noted earlier, strategic policies deal with questions about the strength of military forces, their makeup, and their ability to be deployed, choices about the development of certain weapons, and matters having to do with the development of military forces. Structural policies have to do with the amount of money to be spent to maintain overall levels of men and material and how these force levels should be organized. Congress plays a major role in deciding structural issues, but the focus of decision making on strategic matters lies within the executive branch. Samuel Huntington's study of defense policymaking led him to conclude: "Structural issues of military policy are usually handled through what might be termed the domestic legislative process," while strategic issues fit more correctly into the foreign policy category.[56]

Distinguishing between foreign and domestic policies and between strategic and structural defense policies occurs when talking about the relative influence of the executive and legislative branches on policy. This distinction helps us to move away from overly general statements that Congress has lost all influence over policies to the executive, or that the legislative branch is the primary policymaker on all issues. Three major participants need to be considered in any discussion of executive-legislative influence on policy:

1. The president and top administration officials, all of whom depend on the political power of the president;
2. The executive bureaucracy, whose source of power is an expertise in a specialized field;
3. The legislature, whose members combine expertise in particular areas with a political base that is often different from that of the president.

In short, we have a political world that is much more complicated than popular images of an ideologically committed president versus a recalcitrant Congress or an arrogant president being
held in line by the wisdom of a thoughtful Congress. The battles
about who should determine policies are likely to involve many
people in both the executive and legislative branches, not just
the president and Congress.

Distributive domestic policies and structural defense and
foreign policies are determined chiefly by subgovernments made
up of congressional subcommittees and representatives of executive bureaus, with little direct intervention by the president.
Regulatory policies are more likely to involve political participants in the president's administration, with the president often
playing a direct role in the legislative process, and are decided
by the whole Congress rather than by committees or subcommittees. Redistributive and dedistributive domestic policies, strategic and crisis defense, and foreign policies are settled in a
process that comes closest to being one of executive dominance.
The executive's near monopoly on information in this policy
category often leaves Congress with a minor role of legitimizing
decisions made elsewhere. Not all cases fit so neatly into that
overall framework, of course, but organizing the discussion in
this way does underscore the general point that the influence of
the executive on legislative policies will vary with the types of
policies under consideration.

DISTRIBUTIVE POLICIES AND
SUBGOVERNMENTS

The water resources bills that passed both the House and the
Senate in 1986 were examples of distributive policies. The
House bill provided $20 billion in funding for 360 projects all
over the country, while the Senate bill funded 180 major projects
to the tune of $12 billion. This type of omnibus bill authorizing a
large number of what are sometimes called "pork-barrel" projects distributed across a wide range of congressional districts has
long represented a classic example of a distributive policy.

The overall policy is such that it can be separated into component parts and dealt with in piecemeal fashion. Only certain
segments of the general population are concerned with the policy outcome. The policy is a low-visibility one that carries no
great political implications for the president or for most legisla-

tors. The normal legislative process for dealing with such policies is that of logrolling, or gaining support from unconcerned
interests in return for support on other issues important to them.
Because the details of the policy are of no great importance for
the president or for most legislators, influence over distributive
policies goes, by default, to bureaucrats, those legislators whose
districts will benefit, and interest groups who do have a stake in
the policy outcome.

Distributive policymaking is fashioned in low-visibility units
variously called subsystems, subgovernments, and whirlpools by
political analysts. Grant McConnell has identified the key elements of any subgovernment as:

> (1) a federal administrative agency within the executive
> branch; (2) a heavily committed group of congressmen, usually
> members of a particular committee or subcommittee; (3) a pri-
> vate (or quasi-private) association representing the agency cli-
> entele; (4) a quite homogeneous constituency usually com-
> posed of local elites.[57]

These subgovernments are relatively stable entities, which fashion policies that provide government benefits in the form of
price supports for particular farm crops, highway projects, veterans' assistance, airport construction, sewage treatment plants,
scientific research, and similar industry-specific programs.

Distributive policymaking is not one of those areas that reflect
a growing dominance of the president. For the most part, he stays
out. Rather, it is the bureaucracy of both the executive and legislative branches that exerts the most influence in this area. The currency of distributive policymaking is technical information and
expertise. That is clear in the following description by a member
of the legislative bureaucracy of how he and other Senate aides
depend on the executive component of a subgovernment:

> It's not bad enough that the Senators rely so totally on us. We
> rely on the executive branch's bureaucracy downtown. I can't
> tell you if we need a bill for V.A. benefits until I check with the
> Veterans Administration. We make hundreds of calls a day to
> the agencies. All these bills are so complex that we can't un-
> derstand them without help from the bureaucrats.[58]

Executive influence in distributive policymaking does not
take the form of a strong president wielding power over Con-

gress. Rather, it is a process in which experts from executive agencies, congressional committees and subcommittees, and concerned interest groups come together to determine who gets what from the government. Those who talk about a decline in congressional policymaking power relative to that of the president's are not, in most cases, referring to distributive policymaking. On the other hand, those who talk about the increasing power of the executive bureaucracy are probably most accurate when describing distributive policymaking.

The 1986 water resources bills illustrate another point about distributive policies and Congress that has been brought up earlier. The point is changes in the budget process since 1974 have moved Congress away from distributive policymaking and toward regulatory and redistributive policymaking. At one time, water resources bills would pass the legislature in every Congress. But the 1986 measures in the House and Senate represented the first omnibus bills authorizing water resources projects to be passed in a decade. The centralized budget process and the high visibility of budget pressures have made it more difficult to find routine distributive policymaking in Congress.

REGULATORY POLICIES

When we look at the president's role in the policy process dealing with regulatory policies such as Medicare or federal aid to education, we find that the president is more actively involved than with distributive policies. A difference between distributive policies and regulatory policies, which was discussed earlier, is that the former consists of many small decisions affecting only special groups while the latter represents a coordinated, overall policy affecting most or all of the public. The president's role in regulatory policymaking is one of coordinating the demands made by various interests and shaping a compromise legislative program through bargaining.

Executive coordination early in the policymaking process was a key to the success of a major education bill in the Johnson administration, which was said to have come out of the White House with "just enough aid to parochial schools to push away the veto of the Roman Catholic Church but not enough to drive away the support of the National Education Association."[59] The lobbying effort of top Carter administration officials in behalf of a hospital cost containment bill—a campaign which sought to coordinate the activities of a coalition of over twenty-five different organizations to lobby for the bill—is another example of the executive role in regulatory policymaking.[60] The Reagan administration has been even more effective than previous administrations in developing the White House role of coordinator of grass-roots lobbying by organized interest groups. This was illustrated in the administration's first year by the successful grass-roots campaign for budget cuts, in which White House officials coordinated the efforts of the national Chamber of Commerce, the National Association of Manufacturers, the American Medical Association, and a number of other national and local groups. The Office of Public Liaison (OPL), a part of the White House staff, now coordinates the legislative lobbying effort of interest groups. An OPL staff member characterized that office as "a vehicle for organizing many, many groups around their own particular strong priorities."[61]

An area of regulatory policy important to executive influence is that of expenditures for programs approved by Congress. Because they are held accountable for the state of the economy, presidents have often decided not to spend funds that had been allocated for certain programs by Congress. This practice of impounding funds has been common since World War II and represents another facet of the president's power to affect policies. Although executive impoundment of funds is found in both distributive and redistributive areas, the general practice is one that reflects characteristics of regulatory policies. While the effects of impounding funds might be felt in specific and narrow programs that give funds to specialized segments of the population, the guiding principle behind such withholdings is the regulatory one of maintaining fiscal integrity and controlling overall government spending.

During the Nixon administration, presidential impoundment of funds appropriated by Congress rose to new heights. The president was using impoundment as a way not only to control government spending but also to circumvent the goals of Congress in providing funding for programs. In all, President Nixon impounded $18 billion in funds that Congress had appropriated for public housing, water and sewer grants, highways, rural electrification, water pollution control, and education programs. Congress responded by passing the Congressional Budget and Impoundment Control Act of 1974, which required the president to report all impoundments and provided a means for Congress to limit the amount of funds impounded by the president. This act led to a much more limited use of the impoundment power by both the Ford and the Carter administrations.

One of the criticisms made of the presidential impoundment of funds was that it gave the president, in effect, an item veto—that is, the power to accept parts of a law passed by Congress and to reject other parts. This power was specifically denied the president in the Philadelphia Convention of 1787. But Congress has been exercising its own form of an item veto in an attempt to control what it sees as lawmaking by the federal bureaucracy. The legislative veto consists of a requirement that Congress review and/or approve any executive action. Legislative review provisions range from the major requirements of congressional approval written into the War Powers Act of 1973 and the Federal Election Campaign Act to relatively minor requirements that certain executive agencies inform Congress of new regulations. The practice of including legislative veto provisions in laws dates back to 1932, but the vast majority of them were enacted during the 1970s. There are many different forms of legislative veto, but they all represent an attempt by Congress to narrow executive discretion or to check executive power. A driving force behind many legislative veto provisions was a belief on the part of legislators that executive bureaucrats were engaged in lawmaking in their issuing comprehensive regulations. The legislative veto was seen as a way of checking the lawmaking power of presidents and executive officials.

In a 1983 case, *Immigration and Naturalization Service* v. *Chadha*, the Supreme Court declared the most common form of the legislative veto to be unconstitutional. That decision effectively struck down more than 200 separate veto provisions in 126 laws.[62] While the *Chadha* decision has had a dramatic effect on the ability of Congress to check the executive through a legislative veto, it did not outlaw all forms of that veto. Pointing to more than twenty legislative veto provisions passed by Congress after *Chadha*, Joseph Cooper concluded: "Clearly the veto is not going to disappear. Indeed, even in this first post-*Chadha* year it has figured in three of the hottest issues before Congress—Stinger missile sales in the Middle East, the production of MX missiles, and military aid to El Salvador."[63]

Before moving to a consideration of executive influence in the area of redistributive and foreign policymaking, let us first summarize the general characteristics of executive influence over regulatory policies. First, the president plays a more direct and active role in regulatory policymaking than in distributive policies. Sometimes, this role is chiefly a coordinating one—bringing in various interests' demands at the bill-drafting stage and working out a compromise through a bargaining process. At other times, the president plays a more public role and uses that office to build support for a measure pending in Congress. The executive also influences these policies through their implementation. Impoundment, impoundment control, and the legislative veto represent an ongoing contest between the highest levels of the executive branch and the entire Congress to control regulatory policymaking. As we move from distributive to redistributive policies, we find that the president's influence increases. The expended power of the executive that we have seen in the regulatory area becomes even more pronounced when we look at redistributive and foreign policymaking.

REDISTRIBUTIVE, DEDISTRIBUTIVE, AND FOREIGN POLICIES

Most of the domestic policies passed by Congress are incremental in nature. The new policy will often take the form of marginal changes in existing policy, and there is an expectation that further adjustments will be made in the future. But redistributive and dedistributive domestic policies and some foreign policies represent more fundamental changes that often carry with them the sense of being irrevocable. They call for basic decisions that will, in turn, affect other policies for a long time. They are seen as commitments to follow through with basic value decisions involved in that one particular choice. That is why the debate over these policies often focuses more on what they might lead to than it does on immediate effects. There is a sense of importance about redistributive, dedistributive, and some foreign policy issues that greatly surpasses that of distributive or regulatory policies.

These types of policies require that both Congress and the president make some overall commitment to the general direction of policy in that area. There is no room to say "Yes, but . . ." or to accept parts of a policy while delaying decision on others to a future time, in order to reach an immediate compromise. As a result, the normal legislative processes of logrolling and bargaining are less effective in these policy areas than they are in distributive and regulatory policymaking. The overall coherence of redistributive, dedistributive, and foreign policies is further reflected in the ideological nature of the policy debate surrounding them, a point that was discussed earlier in the chapter.

Members of Congress can approach in two ways redistributive, dedistributive, and foreign policymaking: (1) Either they disagree with the basic value premises embodied in a policy proposal and fight it on ideological grounds, or (2) they accept the basic ideological framework and concern themselves with the best means for achieving the accepted end. In either case, legislators are in an inferior position relative to the president. If they choose to fight on ideological grounds, they face an elected official who can claim to represent the general electorate's basic ideological sense of direction, no matter how crudely expressed. If they accept the executive's delineation of goals, they are subjected to the fact that the executive branch can claim superior sources of information on the best means for achieving those ends.

Those who talk about the growing presidential domination of Congress in the policy process are probably closest to the mark in discussing redistributive, dedistributive, and foreign policymaking. For it is in those areas that legislators often play a relatively passive role of ratifying decisions made in the executive branch. That was the case with the redistributive antipoverty program, as is evident in James Donovan's description: "The Congressional role in developing the Economic Opportunity Act was essentially a minor one . . . it was written in the executive branch and subsequently endorsed by Congress."[64] A similar pattern emerged in the dedistributive policy area represented by the Social Security Amendments of 1983; as is clear in the comments of one observer cited in Paul Light's case study:

> Congress is not well adapted for dealing with complex issues that also have high political risks unless the President becomes involved. The Democrats and Republicans can negotiate all they want, but at some point they have to ask "Can you deliver the President?"[65]

And while Congress has seized the initiative from the president on a number of foreign policy issues in the 1980s, the authors of a recent book on the subject suggest a continued presidential dominance in foreign policymaking:

If the House and Senate have now established—and can be expected to maintain—an influential congressional presence in the foreign policy field, how well are they equipped to continue to play this role?

Recent experience indicates that the answer must be: rather poorly and inadequately. To date, in terms of organizational, procedural, and behavioral changes required, few members of Congress have faced up squarely to the necessary implications of their demand for a position of equal partnership with the White House in foreign affairs.[66]

This section of the chapter has described and analyzed patterns of executive influence on congressional policymaking, from the relatively minor influence of the president and control by subgovernments that we found in distributive policy areas, to the far greater influence of the president and the executive branch that we found in redistributive, dedistributive, and foreign policies. And that discussion brings us back to the basic premise stated at the beginning of the chapter: Different policies are handled in different ways by the American political system, and broad statements about Congress being the captive of interest groups or the president in formulating policies are misleading. Sometimes, these outside groups are found to have a great deal of influence over policy, while at other times their impact is minor.

Conclusion

The value of the policy framework discussed in this and the preceding chapter is that it makes us aware of both change and continuity in the politics of Congress. The specific content of policies and the way in which Congress deals with particular policies are always changing. But there is an underlying stability to how legislators perceive the dimensions of change and to the values that guide their behavior. Members of Congress know that it should be a representative institution, and the value of representation supports the claims of interest groups in the policymaking process. In similar fashion, the executive's influence in congressional policymaking is strengthened by legislators' acceptance of the value of lawmaking. As long as both values receive support from members of Congress, we are likely to find that organized interests and the executive can influence congressional policymaking, but that they cannot dominate it. The tension between representation and lawmaking has provided a framework for analyzing the politics of Congress. And that analysis, in turn, has been based on the premise that it is the tension between lawmaking and representation that accounts for both the change and the continuity of congressional behavior.

Endnotes

1. Senator Bradley, quoted in Michael Kranish, "Battle Over Depreciation Benefits," *Boston Globe*, August 10, 1986, p. 83.

2. Deputy Secretary Darman, quoted in Helen Dewar, "White House Pressures Hill to Raise the Debt Ceiling," *Washington Post*, October 8, 1985, p. A5.

3. Information and quotations in this paragraph are from Clyde H. Farnsworth, "To Every Time There Is a Purpose," *New York Times*, April 29, 1985, p. A14; and Dave Kaplan, "Senate Votes Early Start for Daylight Saving," *Congressional Quarterly Weekly Report*, May 24, 1986, p. 1177.

4. Philip Brenner, "An Approach to the Limits and Possibilities of Congress," in Lawrence C. Dodd and Bruce I. Oppenheimer, eds., *Congress Reconsidered* (Washington, D.C.: Congressional Quarterly Press, 1981), p. 373. For a fuller discussion, see Philip Brenner, *The Limits and Possibilities of Congress* (New York: St. Martin's, 1983).

5. Kranish, "Battle Over Depreciation Benefits," p. 83.

6. Ibid.

7. Donald C. Evans, quoted in Robin Toner, "Fear and Shoe Leather Among the Lobbyists," *New York Times*, July 31, 1986, p. A18.

8. Steven V. Roberts, "Of Special Interests Then and Now," *New York Times*, June 6, 1986, p. A14.

9. Mark Green, *Who Runs Congress?* (New York: Dell, 1984), p. 160.

10. *How Money Talks in Congress: A Common Cause Study of the Impact of Money on Congressional Decision-making* (Washington, D.C.: Common Cause, 1979), p. 7.

11. Green, *Who Runs Congress?* p. 59.

12. Carl P. Chelf, *Congress in the American System* (New York: Nelson-Hall, 1977), p. 166.

13. Stephen Kurkjian, "Lobbyists' Ranks Bulge in Congress," *Boston Globe*, May 24, 1986, p. 1; and Associated Press, "Tax-Revision Bill Spurs Big Lobbyist Spending," *Boston Globe*, September 2, 1986, p. 31.

14. Toner, "Fear and Shoe Leather Among the Lobbyists," p. A18.

15. Unidentified representative, quoted in John Bibby, *Congress Off the Record* (Washington, D.C.: American Enterprise Institute, 1983), p. 34.

16. Representatives Studds and Donnelly, quoted in Kurkjian, "Lobbyists' Ranks Bulge in Congress," p. 6.

17. Richard Viguerie, quoted in Bill Keller, "Special-Interest Lobbyists Cultivate the 'Grass Roots' to Influence Capitol Hill," *Congressional Quarterly Weekly Report*, September 12, 1981, p. 1740.

18. Lester Milbraith, *The Washington Lobbyists* (Chicago: Rand McNally, 1963), and Lewis Anthony Dexter, *How Organizations Are Represented in Washington* (Indianapolis: Bobbs-Merrill, 1969).

19. Unidentified representative, quoted in Elizabeth Drew, "Charlie: A Portrait of a Lobbyist," in Allan J. Cigler and Burdett A. Loomis, eds., *Interest Group Politics* (Washington, D.C.: Congressional Quarterly Press, 1983), p. 230.

20. Ibid.; and David Shribman, "Lobbying: Business by Nuance, Feint and Gamble," *New York Times*, November 21, 1981, p. 11.

21. Edwin M. Yoder, "Washington Report," *Harpers*, June 1970, p. 34.

22. Norman J. Ornstein and Shirley Elder, *Interest Groups, Lobbying, and Policymaking* (Washington, D.C.: Congressional Quarterly Press, 1978), p. 85.

23. Drew, "Charlie: Portrait of a Lobbyist," p. 230.

24. Charles Clapp, *The Congressman: His Work as He Sees It* (Washington, D.C.: The Brookings Institution, 1963), p. 180.

25. T. R. Reid, *Congressional Odyssey: The Saga of a Senate Bill* (San Francisco: W. H. Freeman, 1980), p. 60.

26. Clapp, *The Congressman*, p. 181.

27. Stanley Surrey, "The Congress and the Tax Lobbyist—How Special Tax Provisions Get Enacted," *Harvard Law Review*, May 1957, pp. 1155–56.

28. Representative Rostenkowski, quoted in Eileen Shanahan, "Tax Conferees Decide to Tackle Big Issues First," *Congressional Quarterly Weekly Report*, July 26, 1986, p. 1677.

29. Green, *Who Runs Congress?* p. 79.

30. *How Money Talks in Congress*, p. 11.

31. *New York Times*, November 18, 1972, p. 20.

32. The statement is by a former committee staff member, quoted in Mark Green et al., *Who Runs Congress?* (New York: Bantam, 1972 ed.), p. 40.

33. Lewis Anthony Dexter, "The Representative and His District," in Nelson Polsby and Robert Peabody, eds., *New Perspectives on the House of Representatives* (Chicago: Rand McNally, 1969), p. 24.

34. Raymond Bauer, Ithiel de Sola Pool, and Lewis Anthony Dexter, *American Business and Public Policy* (New York: Atherton, 1963), pp. 434–35.

35. Robert Peabody, Jeffrey Berry, William Frasure, and Jerry Goldman, *To Enact a Law* (New York: Praeger, 1972), p. 60.

36. Green et al., *Who Runs Congress?* (1979), p. 36.

37. Eugene Eidenburg and Roy Morey, *An Act of Congress* (New York: W. W. Norton, 1969), p. 60.

38. David Truman discusses these differences between forming an alliance and engaging in logrolling in *The Governmental Process* (New York: Alfred A. Knopf, 1962), pp. 362–68. For an example of this broader base of lobbying on regulatory policies, see Lawrence E. Gladieux and Thomas R. Wolanin, *Congress and Colleges* (Lexington, Mass.: D.C. Heath, 1976), p. 119.

39. Paul Light, *Artful Work: The Politics of Social Security Reform* (New York: Random House, 1985), pp. 127, 233.

40. Stephen Kemp Bailey, *Congress Makes a Law* (New York: Vintage, 1964), pp. 75–76.

41. John Bibby and Roger Davidson, *On Capitol Hill* (New York: Holt, Rinehart & Winston, 1967), pp. 239–40.

42. Light, *Artful Work*, p. 81.

43. Bailey, *Congress Makes a Law*, pp. 145, 134.

44. Edward S. Corwin, *The Presidency: Office and Powers* (New York: New York University Press, 1957), p. 171.

45. Green, *Who Runs Congress?* (1984), p. 164.

46. James Madison, "Federalist Numbers 48 and 51," in Alexander Hamilton, John Jay, and James Madison, *The Federalist Papers* (New York: Washington Square Press, 1976), pp. 112, 123.

47. Thomas Jefferson, quoted in Alexis de Tocqueville, *Democracy in America* (New York: Washington Square Press, 1964), p. 101.

48. Former Rep. Richard Bolling, quoted in Steven V. Roberts, "Rules Chairman Says Reagan Uses Budget as a Method to 'Tyrannize,'" *New York Times*, June 17, 1981, p. 25.

49. Jody Powell, quoted in Barbara Kellerman, *The Political Presidency* (New York: Oxford, 1984), p. 217.

50. Ibid., pp. 249, 250.

51. Steven Pressman, "President's Fabled Power of Persuasion Switches GOP Votes, Resurrects Tax Bill," *Congressional Quarterly Weekly Report*, December 21, 1985, p. 2706.

52. Diane Granat, "On Balance, A Year of Taking the Initiative," *Congressional Quarterly Weekly Report*, December 28, 1985, p. 2727.

53. David Nyhan, "Congress Eclipsing Reagan," *Boston Globe*, December 22, 1985, p. A21.

54. Aaron Wildavsky, "The Two Presidencies," reprinted in his reader, *The Presidency* (Boston: Little, Brown, 1969), p. 230. Presidential dominance in this area is also supported by James Robinson's findings in *Congress and Foreign Policy-Making* (Homewood, Ill.: Dorsey, 1967).

55. George C. Edwards III, *Presidential Influence in Congress* (San Francisco: Freeman, 1980), pp. 15–18.

56. Samuel P. Huntington, *The Common Defense* (New York: Columbia University Press, 1961), p. 124.

57. Grant McConnell, *Private Power and American Democracy* (New York: Vintage, 1966), p. 244. Other descriptions of these subgovernments may be found in Ernest S. Griffith, *The Impasse of Democracy* (Harrison-Hilton Books, 1939), p. 182; Douglass Cater, *Power in Washington* (New York: Random House, 1964), and J. Leiper Freeman, *The Political Process* (New York: Random House, 1965).

58. Robert Sherrill, "Who Runs Congress?" *New York Times Magazine*, November 22, 1970, p. 85.

59. James Sundquist, *Politics and Policy* (Washington, D.C.: The Brookings Institution, 1968). p. 212.

60. Alan Berlow, "Carter Administration Pits Its Lobbying Efforts Against Hospital Industry's on Cost Control Issue," *Congressional Quarterly Weekly Report*, March 17, 1979, p. 474.

61. Unidentified Office of Public Liaison staff member, quoted in Joseph A. Pika, "Interest Groups and the Executive: Presidential Intervention," in Cigler and Loomis, *Interest Group Politics*, p. 320.

62. Joseph Cooper, "The Legislative Veto in the 1980s," in Lawrence C. Dodd and Bruce I Oppenheimer, eds., *Congress Reconsidered* (Washington, D.C.: Congressional Quarterly, 1985), p. 368.

63. Ibid., p. 385.

64. John C. Donovan, *The Politics of Poverty* (New York: Pegasus, 1967), p. 37.

65. Light, *Artful Work*, p. 22.

66. Cecil V. Crabb, Jr., and Pat M. Holt, *Invitation to Struggle: Congress, the President, and Foreign Policy* (Washington, D.C.: Congressional Quarterly Press, 1984), p. 243.

Index